# On the Edge: Women Making Hockey History

# ON THE EDGE

## WOMEN MAKING
## HOCKEY HISTORY

*Elizabeth Etue*
*&*
*Megan K. Williams*

SECOND
STORY
Press

CANADIAN CATALOGUING IN PUBLICATION DATA

Etue, Elizabeth, 1948-
On the edge

Includes bibliographical references and index.
ISBN 0-929005-79-1

1. Hockey for women. 2. Hockey players. 3. Women athletes.
I. Williams, Megan K., 1965-   . II. Title.

GV847.E88 1996    796.962'082    C96-931606-2

Edited by Elizabeth MacLeod
Copyedited by Debbie Viets
Index by Heather L. Ebbs

Cover photograph by F. Scott Grant/Canadian Sport Images
Photo credits appear on page 336

*Second Story Press gratefully acknowledges the assistance of
the Ontario Arts Council and The Canada Council*

Printed and bound in Canada
Second printing September 1997

*Published by*
SECOND STORY PRESS
720 Bathurst Street, Suite 301
Toronto, Canada
M5S 2R4

# Contents

# CONTENTS

# ACKNOWLEDGEMENTS

The women's sports and hockey community is a very generous one. We thank all those who lent their time, attention and encouragement to this book. In particular, thanks to Julia Ashmun, Therese Brisson, Frank Libera, Wendy Long, Bev Mallory, Orchid Mazurkiewicz, Marg McGregor, Kay McQuaid, Glynis Peters, Fran Rider, Julie Stevens, Rhonda Taylor, Nancy Theberge and Lucie Valois. Phyllis Berck, Bruce Kidd, Shannon Miller, Angela James, Cathy Phillips and Gord Renwick have been especially helpful.

Liz MacLeod's patient editing and Second Story Press's confidence in this project have been instrumental in seeing this book to completion.

A special thanks to Sam Freedman from Megan Williams for his superb teaching and unstinting encouragement.

The marathon hours that go into writing a book require the most intimate support. For this, our deepest gratitude to Helen Dryz and Lorenzo Vallecchi.

# INTRODUCTION

*ON THE EDGE* is a testament to the grit and tenacity of the players and leaders who drive women's hockey forward. It also discusses the issues and obstacles that continue to impede the advancement of the game. But the game itself is a work in progress, and this book is just a first step in paying tribute to the women who continue to make hockey history.

Many of the central themes of women's hockey are reflected in the authors' experiences. Elizabeth Etue grew up surrounded by hockey — male hockey, that is. She grew up in a tiny town on Lake Huron, Ontario which was home to the largest Peewee hockey tournament in the country. For years she and her father shared the *Hockey Night in Canada* ritual in their basement rec room. Later, Elizabeth sat in the stands cheering for her boyfriend when he scored. Her sister even married a hockey coach. But it wasn't until she played hockey that she realized what she was missing. She joined the charmed circle of people who play The Game.

Although she was an accomplished athlete in many sports throughout high school and university, Elizabeth never considered playing hockey. It was simply outside the female domain. In her forties she was a late-comer to the game. Captivated by the sport, she also marvelled at the on-ice exploits of her new-found hockey heroes. She was surprised that stories of these trailblazing women and exceptional athletes had not been told. Ultimately, the story-telling urge overtook her. A book idea was born.

Megan Williams's involvement in the book came about through a similar relationship to sports. Like thousands of girls growing up in Canada, Megan's contact with hockey was limited to hanging around rinks on Saturday mornings while her brothers played or practised. For her, hockey consisted of sensations, mainly smells, that represented odours of exclusion: stale popcorn on the cold rink floor, the gamy sweat of her brothers' hockey gear emanating from the basement corner, even the scent of the worn leather pads she and her younger sister occasionally struggled into when the neighbourhood boys needed someone in net.

Because team sports such as hockey so strongly represented an area in which women were not welcome, Megan avoided them for years. She was a competitive athlete in her early teens and later wrote about and was active in promoting women's rights in other sectors of society. Like so many women, however, she was more than happy to leave the inhospitable and often violent world of team sports to men. But in her late twenties something changed: with a small group of friends who felt equally ambivalent about team sports, she rediscovered the joys of chasing a ball across a field and whacking a puck into the net on a frosty winter evening. The sense of freedom and exhilaration that has come with these weekly encounters has dramatically altered her attitude towards team sports. The gifts of confidence, skill and delight that playing with others brings is too important to be abandoned.

Playing hockey can be mystical: it can transform ordinary individuals into winged warriors. In hockey, the metamorphosis begins in the dressing room, where you armour yourself with full-body padding that renders you larger than life, virtually invincible. Next, you step into black leather boots with steel blades. Finally, you secure a helmet and facemask on your head to complete the warrior attire. You then glide onto the frozen water, moving faster than seems humanly possible, flying on ice. For women, the transformation is remarkable: from spectator to competitor, cautious to courageous, defenceless to defender. It is not surprising that women have fought for over one hundred years for the right to play.

Yet only two previous books have been written on women's hockey: one, an anecdotal and pictorial history, the other, an instructional book aimed at young girls. This paucity of information about the women's game accounts in part for the shape of *On the Edge*. In many ways, this book is several books in one — part history, part player profiles, part politics and even part primer on teams heading to the Olympics. *On the Edge* brings together many of the issues that affect women's sports all over the world. For this reason, it will have a wide audience. We hope it will inform hockey and sports buffs, stimulate Women's Studies classes and, most importantly, at last provide young women with inspirational stories of female hockey heroes.

— *Elizabeth Etue and Megan K. Williams*
*Toronto, 1996*

*Chapter One*

# THE GAME OF THEIR LIVES

*Sunday March 25, 1990, 3:00 PM,*
*Ottawa Civic Centre, Ottawa, Canada*

CATHY PHILLIPS STEPPED from the narrow corridor of grey cement walls onto the sudden spread of whiteness. Nothing in her past had prepared her for this moment: almost nine thousand ecstatic fans stood cheering while a sea of turbulent pompoms, banners and flags urged her forward. And the roar. Never before had she or the others been greeted with such a welcoming roar. The ten-thousand-seat arena, the press booth in the rafters, the TV cameras transmitting the players' images to a million and a half viewers, and even the electronic scoreboard echoed the crowd's acknowledgement. At last — the first official women's world championship.

Like most of the others on Team Canada, Phillips had grown up playing shinny alongside her brothers on the backyard rink. She had practised and dreamed hockey without having "somewhere to go," as she would later put it in a speech. "When I was playing we set our own goals," she recalled. "Now we have world championships .... [We] are playing for all the women who never had the opportunity .... They never had the chance because it wasn't their time." [1] Today was their time, and the first female Team Canada was determined to seize it.

For the first time in their lives the women were not paying to play; instead they were provided with equipment, jackets, travel money and hotel rooms. Despite the female sport's almost one-hundred-year history, these elite players received little or no financial support. Even the national selection camp held in January had cost each player a fee of three hundred dollars and a significant chunk of their vacation time from work — expenses their male counterparts were not asked to cover. But now was not the time to consider the obstacles. Now was the time to focus on the game of their lives.

Two posters hung on the dressing room wall. One had the words "Positive, Prepared and Proud" emblazoned across the top; inspiring quotations penned by teammates crowded the space below. The other poster displayed a hand-drawn pyramid of Canada's opponents stacked one on top of the other. The names of Sweden, Japan, West Germany and Finland were no longer discernible, having been buried under the rising pile of red dots that had been stuck over each of these countries' team after a Team Canada victory. Only Team USA, the final hurdle, remained visible at the top.

Including Canada, eight countries had come to play hockey in Ottawa. The cream of Europe included Finland, Norway, Sweden, Switzerland and West Germany. Japan represented Asia, after China had yielded to world pressure following the Tiananmen Square massacre and pulled out of the Asian Cup competition. So far, the results of this world championship were vivid proof of Canada's proficiency on ice. Canada had outscored its opponents 50–1 in the four round-robin games. This gaping difference was a blunt reminder to the other countries, with the exception of Team USA, of just how far they lagged behind Canada in terms of both skill and numbers. Canada surpassed every country with 7,500 women registered with the Canadian Amateur Hockey Association (CAHA) and estimates as high as 15,000 female players in total. Most of its competitors, on the other hand, had selected their players from a pool of fewer than 400 players. Six hundred Swedish women played the game; fewer than 300 had taken to the ice in Finland and Norway each.

Phillips swept down the ice to the net. Her short tousled hair, playful grey eyes and wide-open smile belied the steely control she could command in front of the net. At twenty-nine, she was a goaltender with seventeen years' experience and was considered the best in the world. Phillips was a stand-up goalie who had perfected "quiet feet." For a whole season when she was sixteen, her father, a former goaltender himself, took shot after shot on her, repeating relentlessly, "You're moving again ... you're moving again ... you're moving again ...." His incantation made her dizzy with frustration, but she continued to practise with him, smacking her pads with her stick and mumbling to herself, "Gotta calm down, gotta calm down."[2] The years of practice had paid off. Now during games, she waited at the top of the crease, always letting the shooter move first, refusing to commit. "Watch the goaltender's feet," Phillips would say, "and if she moves before the shot is taken, she can be beaten."[3]

Phillips also honed her game as a girl by studying the NHL goalies on television. She admired Tony Esposito most of all and once wrote him a letter she never mailed suggesting ways in which he could improve his goaltending. When she was eleven, she joined a boys' team in her hometown of Burlington, Ontario, as no girls' teams existed for her age group. She was turned away after the first game because of her sex. Two years later Phillips joined a girls' team. Driving home after games with her mother and father, she would tap her father on the shoulder from the backseat and groan, "O.K., tell me. I can't stand it." Unlike many hockey fathers, Bob was reluctant to criticize his daughter. When he did let her know what had gone wrong in a game, he inevitably mentioned just a few

*Cathy Phillips at the 1983 Canadian national championship.*

ways she could improve. "He would never tell me what I did wrong if I didn't ask," says Phillips of her father. "It would always come from me. And then he'd always put a lot of positive in with the negative."[4]

But here today, at the pinnacle of her career, all that Phillips had worked for was in jeopardy. For almost a year now, she had been plagued by double vision. At first she put it down to a pinched nerve, but by October 1989 her game was seriously off and she had to make a concentrated effort to compensate for what had turned into a real disability. Her peripheral vision was damaged on the left side. In order to see out of that side, she was forced to back into the net to focus on the oncoming puck with her centre vision. Using her left-side vision meant that she saw two pucks coming at her, not just the one. But it wasn't only her game that was affected. Off the ice, exhaustion nagged her. When she lay down, dizzy spells or migraines set in. In January 1990, after what seemed like an endless series of visits to various doctors, Phillips learned she might have multiple sclerosis. She would have to undergo an MRI (magnetic resonance imagery) scan, a procedure similar to a CAT scan; the earliest appointment available was five months away. In the meantime, Phillips kept her illness a secret: deep down she knew this would be her final championship and she did not want the memory of it marred by special treatment, or worse, pity.

Phillips served as an emblem for the others because of both the talent and consistency she had demonstrated over a long career. She was one of the team's veterans, one of the women who provided inspiration and reassurance for younger players. Another veteran was Shirley Cameron; at thirty-seven she was Team Canada's oldest player. Cameron had been with the Edmonton Chimos, a dynasty in women's hockey in Western Canada, through almost twenty years of trailblazing. Thirty-three-year-old team captain Sue Scherer came next in age. She was originally from New Hamburg, Ontario and, like the other Ontario players, was one of the few on the team who had grown up playing hockey with girls. Her godmother had played in the 1920s, and Scherer cherished her as a role model. By the age of ten, Scherer had pulled together a team on which she played the first of many years of organized female hockey. Although she stopped playing to coach for a few years in the mid-1980s, she returned to play in 1989, several years after bodychecking had been banned nationally (although not internationally) in female competition. The ban meant that the game was now safer for Scherer and many others who could not afford to take time off work due to injuries. In Scherer's case, a hockey injury could also put her out of softball, another sport she played at the international level.

Thirty-one-year-old forward France St. Louis also counted as one of the older players. Despite her age, however, St. Louis represented a new breed of players who considered themselves elite athletes. The distinction between the veteran and the new players would rapidly become more pronounced. Women in the past had played for the sheer love of the game and the fun and sense of community that came from belonging to a team. The newer players, however, were less drawn by the social aspect of team play and more by the athletic heights it allowed them to reach. This distinction would emerge fully with future world championships and, eventually, the long-dreamed-of Olympics. The ground was shifting with this championship; the terrain was becoming steeper with competition.

St. Louis had come relatively late to women's hockey. Like many of her teammates, the Québécoise had played shinny in a pair of figure skates with sawed-off picks as a young girl. Until 1978 girls were legally barred from joining boys' teams — the only teams that existed in Quebec — and in her late teens by then, St. Louis had no interest in playing in a male league. She was an exceptionally focussed athlete and when she picked up the game again, at age nineteen, she did so with breathtaking alacrity. St. Louis was an intense player, a two-way forward who handled both ends of the ice with equal mastery. She also possessed an exceptional capacity to anticipate plays. Inevitably when she rounded up a season, her points total consisted of half assists and half goals — testimony to her ability to set up goal-scoring opportunities for both herself and her teammates.

Hockey was the second sport that St. Louis played internationally. Her dedication to lacrosse had led her to be named Quebec's Athlete of the Year in 1986, and later Athlete of the Decade for the period 1980 to 1990. Nineteen eighty-nine had been her fourth and last year on the national lacrosse team; she had given up the sport to devote more time to hockey. In her home town of Brossard, Quebec, St. Louis played for the successful Quebec hockey team Repentigny. She had her first taste of international hockey competition in 1987 as the only Québécoise member of Team Canada in the unofficial women's world hockey tournament.

At 5 ft. 8 in. (172 cm) and 140 lbs. (64 kg), St. Louis' toned, resilient body reflected her dedication as an athlete. She stuck to a strict physical regime that involved going to bed by 9:00 PM and rising to train at 6:00 AM. St. Louis was a natural leader and acted as the link between the anglos and francophones on the team, often translating for members from Quebec who could not speak English. She possessed a stern sense of right and wrong and would admonish fellow players for dressing too casually when they went out together for the evening or for behaving in a manner that she considered unworthy of role models.

Today, however, St. Louis remained silent. During an earlier game against West Germany, a player had jabbed her accidentally below the chin with a stick. She suffered a bruised larynx and spent two days in the hospital struggling to breathe through a swollen throat. But St. Louis had waited too long to play at this calibre and was not going to let a minor injury keep her off the ice. After much coaxing she convinced the team doctor to allow her to join the team for the semifinal against Finland. She emerged from the game with one goal and two assists. Still, she was here today with a strict order from her doctor: don't talk.

Stacy Wilson was the team's only representative from

Atlantic Canada. Born and raised in Salisbury, New Brunswick, a small village near Moncton, Wilson grew up playing on boys' teams, always the only female in the league. When she turned fourteen, she moved up to bantam, a level at which the physical differences between girls and boys come into play. Wilson looked for a girls' team in the area and when she learned that none existed, she had to give up the game. It was a painful sacrifice and for years she avoided hockey rinks. They were an acute reminder of what she had lost and what others — her former male teammates — continued to enjoy.

It was not until 1984 when Wilson was nineteen and attending Acadia University in Nova Scotia that she picked up the game again. Only three other women on her team had ever held a stick before. There were few teams to play against, but the Acadia team improved quickly and eventually represented the province in the national championships. When she returned to Moncton after graduating, Wilson played again in the national championship, this time as part of the New Brunswick team. With the help of her coach, she was selected for the Team Canada tryouts, pulled together the money for the camp, and flew to Mississauga, Ontario.

Although her integrity off ice shone through at the selection camp, her stickhandling and knowledge of the game did not: Wilson was wracked by nerves. She had played against many of the women from Ontario in national championships, but always as part of the underdog team and never in a gold-medal game. Atlantic Canada, like Manitoba, Saskatchewan and British Columbia, lagged far behind Quebec, Ontario and Alberta in terms of development of the women's game. A handful of women's teams existed in the whole Atlantic region, with only one Senior A team in New Brunswick. The camp, therefore, proved to be an intimidating experience for the Easterner. Coaching terminology that Wilson would later take for granted dumbfounded her. For instance, at the start of the camp the players were handed a sheet of questions about terms such as cycling, an offensive team tactic in which all three forwards maintain control of the puck while continually moving. The only cycling Wilson knew of was on a bike.

It was not until the scrimmage on the final evening of the selection camp that Wilson shed her hesitancy and surged forward in her trademark style of unstinting play. At the time, however, the effort seemed to go unnoticed. The next day, when one by one the players met with McMaster to hear whether they had made the team, Wilson was informed that she had had a good week but would not be joining the team in Ottawa. Wilson was crestfallen but understood. An hour later, however, she bumped into McMaster in the corridor of the hotel. He pulled her aside and told her that there was something in the way she played that had caused him to reconsider his decision. There would be another selection camp at which she would be reevaluated, he informed her. A few months later Wilson received a call. The selection had been completed without any more camps and she was now invited to join Team Canada.

Wilson may not have been the most agile stickhandler, but the moment this self-effacing woman stepped on the ice a player of rare tenacity took over. Coaches often said that Wilson brought new meaning to the term "workhorse." Whatever system or strategy a coach laid down Wilson would stick to it unfalteringly. She was the player teammates could count on to block shots, hold up checks and take a hit so others could deliver the puck deep into the offensive zone. Wilson was a player who made opportunities for other players and was never one to retaliate when cross-checked or hooked.

These qualities that pulled the team together on ice acted as an emotional adhesive off ice. Wilson set a tone free of cheap putdowns of the opposition and when she took the floor in the dressing room, she spoke from the heart, subtly and naturally conjuring a feeling of team togetherness.

While Wilson with her quiet virtue had come to represent the heart of the team, teammate Judy Diduck was the stress-buster. The twenty-four-year-old Albertan exuded an endearing goofiness that made even the most anxious player laugh. Earlier today Diduck had flashed a surprise at her delighted teammates. Below her neck, just above her chest protector, "hung" a gold medal that teammate Laura Schuler had drawn with a felt pen. Although Diduck was not one for displays of cockiness, The Sports Network (TSN) had gotten wind of the temporary tattoo and coaxed her into revealing it on air before the game.

Behind Diduck's quirky demeanour, though, stood a quiet leader. On ice her true nature was just as deceiving. Diduck was not a player opponents noticed right away since she rarely took big risks. During key games, however, she treated the competition to a cornucopia of little tricks using her skates and stick. If playing one-on-one in the corner, she would at times get beaten initially. Rather than panic and rush after the puck, Diduck would hold back. When the opportune moment arrived, she would almost imperceptibly tap the shooter's elbow or lift her opponent's stick, causing her to overshoot the puck. In front of the net, Diduck would often hover in the middle of two offensive players, refusing to commit to blocking one. When it was time for the opposition to shoot, however, she displayed an uncanny sense of which of the two players to tie up to prevent a goal.

This was the second world championship in one year for Diduck. In January she had represented Canada in the first ringette world championship. Hockey had been Diduck's greatest love, however. She had tried out for a boys' team at the age of ten but was not permitted to join. She contented herself by playing in net against her brother Gerald, who would go on to the NHL, and the other kids in her Sherwood Park neighbourhood, near Edmonton. Diduck would stand for hours between the two lumps of snow that served as goal posts, using only a baseball glove to stop the shots. She held back tears as pucks pummelled her unprotected shins, refusing to give the boys any excuse to exclude her from the game. The same stead-fastness she showed as a girl shone through today. Diduck had formally taken up the game only five years earlier and had moved from offence to defence less than a year ago. When she was asked to try out for the national hockey team, she held lit-tle hope of making it. Her detachment worked in her favour — she was as relaxed as ever and performed superbly.

While Diduck and Wilson helped sustain the team with their humour and integrity, forward Angela James injected it with raw, powerful energy. James, or simply AJ, was disputably the best — and toughest — female player in the world. She was also a player who had dedicated most of her twenty-six years to the game. The only mixed-race member of the team, James had grown up in a low-income housing area in east Toronto, the child of a white mother and black father. She knew through experience how the interest of a coach or teacher could change the course of a child's life, so she now committed any spare time she had to helping other girls by coaching and refereeing female hockey games. She also knew the value of fighting to be part of something you love. As a girl, every night until the lights went out, she had played shin-ny with the neighbourhood boys in an outdoor arena beside the local school. She honed her resilience there, retaliating against the boys who whacked her over the head with their sticks by wheeling past them with the puck.

Solidly built with thick, powerful legs, AJ carried her body low to the ground. At 5 ft. 6 in. (145 cm) and 160 lbs. (72 kg) she was a forward who thrived on bodychecking and the rush it gave her both to hit and be hit. With her clever dekes and cannonball slapshot, she toyed with players, dominating every league she was part of and invariably breaking scoring records. This week had been "the ultimate"[5] for AJ: she played or practised every day; her mother and older siblings sat in the stands cheering her on during games; and she luxuriated in her own hotel room and could eat all she wanted at the hotel buffet. She had also scored eleven of the fifty goals in the round-robin games, sent a Japanese player to the hospital with a broken leg, and was bruised from head to toe.

Three thousand kilometres west, across long stretches of ice-strewn prairies and lakes rigid with winter, sat eleven-year-old Hayley Wickenheiser in her home in Calgary. Her tiny frame buried under the jersey of her favourite team, the Edmonton Oilers, Hayley perched at the edge of the chestnut leather armchair in the basement rec room, excitedly waiting for the first women's world championship on television.

Hayley had been playing since she was four. Born and raised in Shaunavon, Saskatchewan, Hayley spent every spare moment on the triangular span of ice that her father laid down each winter between their home and two others. There was not a feeling in the world she loved more than flying on her skates at night, the Saskatchewan wind biting into her face, her body on fire, flying, just flying.

Before she could even walk, she would trail around the town's public skating rink on a sleigh behind her mother, Marilyn. When she was two and a half, she wailed when Marilyn bundled her up to go home: the hockey players were going on the ice and she wanted to watch.

Hayley signed up at age five for minor hockey and had since always played with boys. She was lucky: her father, Tom, coached her team, and not only spent hours teaching her to think hockey, but also shielded her from other parents' resistance to her presence. Hayley's dad put her on defence for five years to teach her patience because she rushed too much. She was fiercely aggressive, possessing a natural offensive instinct.

She also had the speed, finesse and toughness to make a remarkable forward. She would need these skills. When she moved up to centre at age ten, she invariably became the target of slashing and hitting. But she never once cried — instead, she took revenge by putting the puck into her opponents' net. She scored the lion's share of goals for her team and won the award for most valuable player (MVP) almost every year.

*Hayley Wickenheiser, age five.*

Until this week, when she had read about the first world hockey championship for women in the paper, her hockey dreams had been nothing more than fantasies. She used to imagine herself playing in the NHL, usually for the Edmonton Oilers. She knew that she would never make the big league — no women ever had at that point — and certainly it seemed unlikely that a woman who did not play in goal ever would. The physical differences between the sexes seemed just too great. But what else could she aspire to? There was no female hockey in the Olympics, no professional women's leagues, and she had never before heard of an international tournament. But now, she thought with a flicker of hope, maybe there would be something else.

Back at the Ottawa Civic Centre the players streamed past the bench where head coach Dave McMaster and assistant coaches Rick Polutnik and Lucie Valois stood. McMaster paced anxiously, pursing his lips in nervous jerks. McMaster was a thirteen-year veteran with the University of Toronto Lady Blues and the winning coach of Team Canada in the 1987 world tournament. He was a soft-spoken man, renowned for his fairness. Earlier in the tournament he had told his players to keep the score down by passing the puck five times before shooting. Today, however, he gave no such advice.

During the two days of pre-tournament training, the women had soaked up the coach's suggestions. They were hungry for any technical training and volleyed question after question at the coaches. Most of the players had encountered mediocre coaching at best and — victorious or not — were determined to leave the championship knowing the most they could about hockey. For Rick Polutnik, who was used to wrestling with the egos of male hockey players, coaching this team was an unexpected challenge. "With guys you have to kick the can and put on a show before they'll react," he explained. "Women aren't like that, and certainly you wouldn't get away with that. [They] want to know the plan, the long-term vision, the criterion to be successful. So as a coach, you have to plan your work more, because they want to know why and how. Guys won't necessarily take that much information."[6]

They would need the training to slip any pucks past enormous American goaltender Kelly Dyer. American coach Don MacLeod and assistant coach Karen Kay had selected a team of strapping players, attempting to make up for what they lacked in depth with brawn and aggression. MacLeod, commentator Howie Meeker pointed out, was notorious for his "one-second play" in which he sent all the bulky players on ice and had the forwards rush the opponents' net on one side. When all else failed, intimidation and confusion often worked. Dyer, a daunting 5 ft. 11 in. (178 cm) and 172 lbs. (78 kg), was the team's centrepiece. When she moved out of her net, she gave the impression of a wall sliding forward. Not only was she a threatening physical presence, but she generated an aura of cockiness that got under the skin of her opponents. Dyer wouldn't hesitate to yell, "Shoot!" to put an approaching forward off guard or to shove a saved puck triumphantly in the face of a failed shooter.

If Dyer provided a formidable target for the Canadians, for her own relatively young team she was a confidence-booster. Cammi Granato was one of the younger players who appreciated Dyer's presence. Granato led the American team's offensive threat. Although not exceptionally quick, she possessed a long reach and a powerful, accurate shot. Granato sprang from a family that had produced four hockey-playing boys, the most famous of whom is her brother Tony, who played for the NHL's Los Angeles Kings. When Granato chose to pursue hockey at the university level, she turned down scholarships and lucrative offers to continue with tennis, volleyball, basketball, handball

*Kelly Dyer makes a save in the first women's world championship.*

and soccer — all sports at which she had excelled in high school. Instead, she opted for a hockey scholarship at Providence College.

Nineteen on the day of the gold medal game, Granato felt

young and inexperienced — and also beat up after four full-contact games in one week. Now here was Canada, the real challenge of the championship, and like the rest of her team-mates, Granato knew next to nothing about its players. A stadium of fans booing Team USA did not help matters. Still, she thought, better nine thousand boos than the usual silence.

From the announcer's booth, Howie Meeker, veteran sportswriter, author and NHL commentator — one of the "voices" of hockey — surveyed the scene. Initially, Meeker had been less than enthusiastic about the assignment of covering women's hockey. After the first few games of the tournament, however, his scepticism had been transformed into infectious delight.

The brand of hockey Team Canada played proved to be a startling reminder of just how far the men's game had slipped away. This, Meeker announced, was how the game was meant to be played: strong skating, crisp passes, clean bodychecks, slapshots low and on the net, few offsides, and plays free of re-taliatory stick work, boarding and fights.

Michael Landsberg from TSN chatted in the stands below with rookie colour commentator and former US college play-er, Canadian Donna-Lynn Rosa. Much of Landsberg's initial commentary focussed on the uniforms. "They say the key to today is pink power," Landsberg's typically inane commentary went. "You see the pink uniforms. They wear the white with the pink numbers and pink socks. Pink is the colour of the day. Everybody's wearing pink pompoms and waving them and wearing pink Canadian flags on their faces. Just that kind of excitement in this building."

And, indeed, Team Canada's jerseys were fuchsia pink and its pants, not the usual black, but silky white. Unconvinced that the tournament itself would attract media attention, the CAHA had selected pink as a way to generate controversy. The arena staff wore pink ties, and the pink flags, banners and pompoms waved by the fans were compliments of the CAHA. Even the Zamboni driver had motored about in a giant pink flamingo costume before the game, ten pink plastic flamingos jutting out from his vehicle. Many of the players resented the inherent sexism of the gimmick, but went along with it knowing that disagreeing openly could spell the end of their national team experience. They were all too aware of the "image problem" that surrounded women's hockey: many parents denounced the game as too rough and masculine, and there were insinuations of lesbianism. Not one of these women hadn't undergone some form of harassment when playing hockey. The players had laughed outright at the white pants, though, musing aloud that they hoped they wouldn't get their period during the game or that their boxer shorts wouldn't show through.

The teams completed their warm-ups and Canada pressed into a tight cluster around its net for one last round of energetic chanting before the face-off. Ken Dryden, former NHL goalie, author of *The Game* and vocal supporter of female hockey, stepped forward to centre ice to drop the official puck. Beside him stood his daughter Sarah, and Fran Rider, director of the Female Council for the CAHA and the driving force behind women's hockey in Ontario.

At last the whistle blew. For the first fifteen minutes, Team USA overpowered the Canadians, who played tentatively, firing a few weak shots and struggling to clear the puck out of their own zone. The US took advantage of the situation, slipping two goals past Phillips. Cindy Curley popped in the first one at 2:25. Shawna Davidson poked in the second at 15:20. On the second goal, Phillips's vision faltered. The puck came from the blue line on her left, hit the boards and bounced in front of the net, where Davidson slipped it in. Unable to see what was happening, Phillips assumed the puck had slid safely around the net.

Sue Scherer, left wing, and France St. Louis, centre, conferred at centre ice. "It's time we do something about this,"

Scherer urged.[7] St. Louis nodded. Her eyes alone said she wanted the game badly. Thirty seconds later, St. Louis fired the Canadian engines with a quick wrist shot past Kelly Dyer. Another goal followed three minutes later when St. Louis passed to Judy Diduck, who swept down from her defensive position on a power play. Diduck flipped a shot high into the left corner after a rookie US defence allowed her to skate up to the doorstep, tying the game just before the end of the first period.

TSN used the intermission to read a telegram from Judy Diduck's brother Gerald of the New York Islanders before it aired a profile of his sister. Rather than focussing on Judy, most of the interview consisted of questions about her brother's role in her success. This typified the approach the media had long taken to the sport, inevitably seeking a link to the male game, rarely confident the female game could stand on its own. It was an angle female players found wearisome.

"I wish they'd [journalists] just take the game as a female hockey game and not compare it to [male] hockey or to boys," summed up Diduck at the end of the interview. "Female hockey is getting a bad rap that way."

The second period was marked by open-ice hits and end-to-end rushes. With the score tied at 2–2, the crowd was hungry for Canada to assert its authority. Team Canada kept the puck in the American zone, leaving little room for the Americans to manoeuvre. With just two minutes left in the period, defence Geraldine Heaney scored what would become known as "The Goal" in hockey circles. Heaney was a daring player from Weston, Ontario, ever poised to attempt the impossible. Her style fused humour and arrogance, a combination that on more than several occasions had paid off well. Today, Heaney broke from her own blue line and flew down centre ice, smelling the upcoming pass from France Montour. Taking the pass, Heaney faked US defender Lauren Apollo, slid the puck between her legs and whipped past her. Goalie Kelly Dyer sprang out of the goal-crease to cut Heaney off — but not quickly enough. Heaney whistled a wrist shot over Dyer's shoulder into the net before swan diving over Dyer into the boards. The crowd broke into a frenzied blur of pink. From the media box, Howie Meeker squealed in delight, "She has the great goaltender playing the net like a beached whale!" The Canadians' confidence soared: not only did they lead the game on the scoreboard, but they now also led it in their minds.

Hayley raced to the phone at the second intermission to call her best friend, Danielle, in Shaunavon.

"Isn't it incredible?"[8] she exclaimed into the phone.

Already they knew each player by name. Susie Yuen was Hayley's favourite because she was so fiery and was the shortest on the team, just like Hayley.

She hated the uniforms, though. Why had they chosen such a girlie colour? she wondered. Why wasn't Team Canada wearing the national red and white? Even the long hair that had slid down from the backs of helmets bothered her. The fans, on the other hand, awed her. She had never seen such a crazed crowd except at NHL games. There just seemed to be tons and tons of them.

The two friends commiserated about the ugly uniforms and guffawed over the size of some of the Americans such as Kelly Dyer and Kelly O'Leary. Those players were so huge and chunky! They admired AJ for her speed and toughness. "Wow, these women are totally trying to kill each other," Hayley laughed. "I totally love it!"[9] They replayed Geraldine Heaney's amazing goal and went over Diduck's as well, which had seemed impossibly difficult to them.

What affected them the most, however, was what was said during and between the games. Hayley had listened closely to the interview with Judy Diduck on TSN. Having played on boys' teams her whole life, Hayley had only known being compared with boys. The idea that there could be a separate, distinct female game seemed strange and novel to her. Howie Meeker's comments about how hard the women played and how men could learn something from watching the women also astounded her. If Howie Meeker said it, she thought, then that really meant something.

With the score 3–2 going into the third period, Canada was in full swing. St. Louis opened up with a slapshot on Dyer; AJ decked an American forward. "Maybe people out there will believe us now that she can hit!" cackled Meeker. In a resplendent display of skills, Dawn McGuire on defence swooped, wove and swung her way between the net before clearing the defensive zone of the puck. Cathy Phillips performed a spectacular skate save on a slapshot by Cammi Granato, kicking off to the right and blocking the puck with the tip of her skate.

Halfway through the period, the youngest line of players on the Canadian team — forwards Vicky Sunohara, Susana Yuen and Laura Schuler, who had been affectionately dubbed the "Kiddie Connection" by the press [10] — showed its colours. Schuler and Sunohara brought the puck down the ice, Sunohara taking an unsuccessful shot on net. Yuen picked up the rebound and scored in a scramble in front of the net. It was a sweet victory for the petite player with lightning-fast feet and bruising resolve. Only 4 ft. 10 in. (145 cm) and 93 lbs. (42 kg), Yuen had been trounced mercilessly by the Americans throughout the game.

With less than six minutes to play, US Coach Don MacLeod put hard-hitting Kelley Owen on ice to inject some force into the team. The strategy backfired: Owen was sent to the penalty box just minutes after surging into play. For the remainder of the game, Canada played cautiously, protecting its lead. Thirty seconds before the game ended, St. Louis stole the puck from the American defence at their blue line and scored on the empty net. The goal clinched a come-from-behind 5–2 victory and dream game for the Canadians.

Team Canada rushed towards Cathy Phillips, forming a squirming nest of arms, helmets, gloves. For the first time in their lives the media swarmed around them. In the stands, a quartet of Canadian flags swayed in unison, pink pompoms fluttering on top. "Na-na na na, na-na na na, hey hey hey, goodbye ...," the crowd chanted.

Shirley Cameron joyously told a reporter, "We sort of felt that women's hockey had been the best-kept secret in the country for one hundred years. Then all of a sudden they unveiled us in one weekend and the Canadian public came to the party."[11]

"It's like all you ever wished and never thought would happen was coming true," exclaimed a beaming Sue Scherer.[12] With these words, Scherer echoed the emotions of the eighty-year-old woman from Smith Falls, Ontario, who had made her way through the crowd earlier in the week to shake hands with Scherer. The woman had insisted her son drive her to the game in Ottawa. Clasping a worn photograph of her own hockey team from the early 1900s, she had told Scherer that her lifelong dream had come true that week: at last she had seen a world hockey championship for women.

It was just outside the dressing room that the most poignant reward took shape for the players. Champagne-soaked and giddy, the team stepped into a corridor packed with family, friends and dozens of young girls and boys clamouring for autographs and used sticks from their new-found heroes. Team Canada had succeeded at what many of its players most desired: it had shown a new generation of girls like Hayley Wickenheiser — who would devote the next years of her life to making this team — that they could claim a place in what was now the game of their lives, too.

*Chapter Two*

# LITTLE SISTERS AND THE NATIONAL GAME

GLYNIS PETERS HUNCHES OVER her desk in a makeshift office at the Teen Ranch Ice Corral in Caledon, Ontario, scanning yet another checklist for this Team Canada selection camp. Hockey bags, video cameras and posters lie amid the boxes that surround her tiny desk. Peters's wavy black hair is peppered lightly with silver, no doubt partly due to her demanding schedule and the diverse responsibilities she must assume as manager of women's hockey at the Canadian Hockey Association (CHA). This week, in her capacity as national team manager, she's overseeing an intensive session that involves fifty-three players from across the country, as well as five coaches from the national team pool and other advisers. It's been a hectic week of interviews, practices and games. Later tonight before the intersquad game, she must squeeze in time for a short talk to parents and kids as part of a Hockey Hall of Fame presentation.

Judging by Peters's schedule, things look good for women's hockey in Canada. The CHA is the only hockey association in the world that employs a manager to oversee the women's game. Registration is burgeoning and Team Canada is expected to win its fourth consecutive gold medal at the 1997 world championship and its first gold medal in the 1998 Olympics.

Furthermore, in 1995, after a long hiatus, the final game of
the national championship returned to television, thanks to a
new sponsor. At a quick glance these changes seem to mark a
new trend in Canada's national pastime: the women's game finally appears to be receiving the money, support and recognition it deserves.

Despite these gains, women's hockey in Canada remains a
second-class citizen within the Canadian Hockey Association
and its branches. The reasons are many. First and foremost, the
CHA operates on what could be called the "little sister principle," a principle that informs the way most male-identified
sports function. Like the legions of girls who have played in goal
for their brothers when an extra player was needed, women in
the game today are more tolerated than respected. Female players are still largely looked upon as the little sisters who don't really belong in hockey. The little sister principle permeates both
national and provincial hockey organizations. The success of
Team Canada, the appearance of female players on television
and the decision to include women's hockey for the first time in
the 1998 Olympics would suggest that women have managed
to counteract this principle in the 1990s. Professional hockey
sets the standards for the game, and its overwhelming influence
underscores the little sister principle. Given the widespread adoration of the NHL, it is not surprising that there is little room for
the amateur female game to thrive. As Canadian Press sports
journalist Alan Adams puts it, "[Women] are tolerated, they are
appeased. Hockey is a male game."[1] The underlying pro hockey mentality only intensifies the benign neglect and patronizing
attitudes that continue to keep women off the ice, away from
sponsors and absent from the media.

In order to appreciate the way in which professional hockey influences amateur hockey, and in turn, women's hockey, it
is essential to understand the Canadian Hockey Association,
the national governing body of the sport in Canada. (The CHA

was known as the Canadian Amateur Hockey Association [CAHA] until 1994.) In the first decade of this century, professional and amateur hockey organizations sprang up across the country. The CAHA was founded in 1914 to establish national rules and standards along with interbranch and international tournaments in the amateur game. By the late 1920s the National Hockey League, founded in 1917, prevailed as the dominant league for professional teams.[2] Some amateur junior and senior teams were closely associated with the NHL, but amateur leagues also enjoyed tremendous popularity in the twenties and thirties, competing for both players and fans with the pro leagues. Afraid of losing more players to the NHL, in 1935 the CAHA signed a contract in which the NHL agreed not to recruit junior players and to pay senior teams for players acquired by NHL teams. But a series of agreements over the next ten years gradually eroded the control the CAHA had over its players and the game. "Indeed, by 1947 the CAHA had become little more than a junior partner of the NHL; it couldn't even determine the eligibility of its own members or change its own playing rules without NHL approval," write sociologists Richard Gruneau and David Whitson in their book, *Hockey Night in Canada*, a cultural critique of hockey.[3]

It wasn't until the 1960s that concern surfaced about professional hockey's domination of the amateur game. This concern stemmed from Canada's lacklustre performance at world competitions throughout the decade. A national task force on sport, with an emphasis on hockey, was soon created to look into this situation. One of the issues that concerned the task force was "the refusal of professional teams to loan promising junior players to the national team as well as the NHL's general antagonism towards the national team concept."[4] As a result of the task force, a separate quasi-professional organization called Hockey Canada was formed in the late 1960s to represent Canada at the international level and to develop a national team. This new organization (whose board of directors included representatives from the NHL and the National Hockey League Players Association) proved to have little influence over the NHL and so the links between amateur hockey and professional hockey remained strong. It wasn't until 1977 that the CAHA reestablished its presence at world competitions with the men's junior national team, and the women's national team in 1990.

Parental concern about the high incidence of injury led several provinces, including the Ontario Ministry of Community and Social Services, to launch inquiries into amateur hockey. The recommendations that resulted from those inquiries focussed on the need to educate coaches and players' parents about the value of participation versus winning at all costs.[5] In the 1980s thousands of boys abandoned the game. From 1983 to 1989 male minor hockey suffered a 17.4 percent drop in registration while registration in the female game — a game without the violence and far from the pro hockey sphere — increased by 68.6 percent.[6] Until the 1990s, when the CAHA launched new programs directed at developing fair play and making hockey more fun, very little changed in male minor hockey. The positive results were evident in 1994–95 when the CHA reported that it had a total of 450,884 male minor hockey players (in all age categories under senior and junior). This represented an increase of almost 30 percent since the 1989–90 season.

Minor hockey is the foundation of amateur hockey in Canada, accounting for more than 90 percent of the CHA's registered players. In 1994–95, 513,207 players were registered with the CHA, 19,050 of whom were female. If coaches, parents and volunteers are added, the total figure balloons to approximately four million.[7] In addition thousands of male and female Canadians play on high school, university or recreational hockey teams which are not registered with the CHA.

The estimated number of girls and women who play on these teams (some belong to male teams) is 20,000.

The CHA's involvement with women's hockey is relatively recent; in fact, it is only a few decades old. However, the first female game was recorded in Ottawa, Ontario, in 1891. Women's hockey flourished at the turn of the century, and according to newspaper reports, pockets of female players were scattered across Canada. Some were as far north as Dawson City, others as far east as the shores of Newfoundland. These female players competed on outdoor rinks lit by lanterns, the boards piled high with snow. In the freewheeling 1920s and 1930s, the national championship for women's hockey meant the top women's teams from the East (including Quebec and Atlantic Canada) and the West vied for the Dominion title. Teams travelled and lived on trains, playing in front of enthusiastic audiences for the Canadian crown. In 1935 the Preston Rivulettes drew six thousand fans to the arena in Galt, Ontario, for the two-game playoff for the national title against Winnipeg.[8] The championships were arranged by women's hockey representatives across the country but fluctuated according to the availability of funds for facilities and travel.

The Rivulettes dominated women's hockey from 1930 to 1939. Their astonishing win–loss record of 348–2 stands unrivalled in the history of Canadian hockey, male or female. In Atlantic Canada and the West several leagues evolved from teams set up by telephone company employees. "Telephone teams" from Sydney and Halifax competed and there was even a "telephone league" in Manitoba. Telephone teams were also members of the Quebec Ladies Amateur Hockey League, with whom they faced off for the Lady Meredith Trophy to claim the provincial title.[9]

While the female game's popularity began to decline in the 1930s, the pro male game's popularity soared. The NHL took over the Stanley Cup in 1926, and in 1931 fans across Canada

listened to the first radio broadcasts of games by Foster Hewitt, who became known as the "voice of hockey." In 1952
television ushered in a new era with the program "Hockey
Night in Canada." Indoor rinks proliferated and a plethora of
men's hockey associations quickly gained control of the prime
ice time in the arenas, effectively edging women off the ice.
Women's hockey had also lost many of its leaders after World
War II, leaders such as Bobbie Rosenfeld, a hockey star, all-
round athlete and sports columnist, and Marie Parkes, the organizer of intercollegiate hockey.[10] Moreover, the conservative
1950s with their "Ozzie and Harriet" family values sent
women back to the kitchen and into more traditional roles.
They were now expected to cheer for television hockey heroes
rather than play their own game.

Helen Lenskyj, a sport sociologist at the Toronto-based
Ontario Institute for Studies in Education, contends that the
widespread input from conservative sectors within education,
the recreation movement and the church led to the demise of
interschool and intercollegiate competition for girls as early as
the 1930s in most of the US and in some parts of Canada.[11] By
the forties and fifties, the distinction between male and female
activities had been concretized. This meant that most of the
state-launched fitness and recreation programs established
during the war maintained the custom of providing team
sports for males and "fitness activities" for females.[12]

Where girls and women were concerned both Canadian and
American athletic organizations emphasized participation rather
than winning in order to avoid the hazards of overly aggressive
play, a win-at-all-cost mentality, and the commercialization associated with boys' and men's sports. But the conservative tone
in community sport had a stifling effect on women, which
lingers even today. Sociologist Mary Keyes writes:

> [This attitude] was exhibited by nineteenth-century
> male sport leaders, notably the French patriot Baron

Pierre de Coubertin, founder of the modern Olympics, which began in 1896. He espoused the view that women's sport was against the 'laws of nature' and therefore reserved the modern Olympic Games for men. This paternalism, emphasizing the biological differences between men and women, also characterized the attitude of doctors, educators and legislators. The rules and regulations for sport perpetuated the view that girls and women were fragile and inferior — physically and psychologically — to their male peers and should be protected from injuries that were bound to result from any exertion in sport.[13]

The effect of this ideology at the university level was especially devastating. In Ontario and Quebec competition among teams from McGill University, Queen's University and the University of Toronto was sporadic during the 1920s and 1930s and the Women's Collegiate Ice Hockey League ceased altogether in 1933.[14] It was not until the 1960s that university women slowly began to reclaim their place in hockey, with Ontario emerging as the leader. Female students successfully lobbied universities in Ontario to reestablish a women's interuniversity hockey league.

The community game also reemerged with events such as the Canadettes Dominion Ladies Tournament held in Brampton, Ontario, in the 1967–68 season. Invitational tournaments for senior players were held in various parts of Ontario, from Haileybury to Ottawa. In the same year, women's hockey boasted two thriving leagues in Montreal, and several clubs travelled as far as Manchester, New Hampshire, to play exhibition games. In the 1960s the Western Shield tournament was also launched, involving the four Western provinces.

In the meantime a new game, ringette, both paralleled and inhibited the development of women's hockey. Ringette's inventor, Sam Jacks, a director of parks and recreation in North

Bay, devised the sport as a female alternative to hockey. In 1963 he created this hybrid game of lacrosse and basketball, which is played on ice with skates; players use a straight stick to shoot a rubber ring. Although his three sons were excellent hockey players, it didn't occur to Jacks that girls should also play hockey, according to his wife, Agnes.[15]

Ringette caught on very quickly. It offered a safe, all-female environment in which girls could compete without fear of harassment. And there were no male standards against which the game could be judged. The majority of parents considered hockey too violent for girls. This gentler sport with its feminine image seemed the ideal solution. A study of ringette players conducted by Aniko Varpalotai in 1991 indicated that many girls had longed to play hockey when they were younger but were "redirected by parents or others to a more suitable sport for girls, usually figure skating. Their participation in ringette frequently evolved from both a dissatisfaction with figure skating and peer influence."[16]

In 1969, six years before the Ontario Women's Hockey Association (OWHA) was formed, ringette enthusiasts founded the first provincial ringette association in Ontario. In the next decade organizers established a national office and launched national championships. The western provinces and Quebec also played a key role in the quick growth of ringette. Eight years later the association created the Ontario Ringette Association Hall of Fame. By 1983, twenty years after the first game, there were more than 14,500 registered ringette players. During the same year — ninety-two years after the first female hockey game — the number of players registered in women's hockey was a mere 5,379, less than 40 percent of ringette's numbers.[17]

Ringette thrived in the seventies and eighties. Its enthusiastic volunteer base swelled thanks to highly organized national training programs. One of ringette's greatest strengths was its ability to attract parents as volunteers. By 1994 there were

12,000 certified coaches, trainers and managers among the volunteers, in addition to 2,600 officials, both unusually high figures, given the 27,200 registered players. Volunteers were instrumental in increasing membership, which climbed rapidly. They also helped the sport's national organization to establish credibility in the larger sports community. Ringette holds national championships for four age groups with the help of a whopping six hundred local associations. This number provides strong evidence of the game's acceptance at the community level. Both women's hockey and ringette were added to the Canada Winter Games in 1991. So far, however, ringette has failed to gain Olympic status, and only four countries competed against the Canadian team in the 1994 world championship.

Ringette has been particularly appealing to young women and girls because of its feminine image. The vast majority of ringette players are eighteen years old and under. In fact, 80 percent of Ontario's 10,000 players during the 1994–95 season fell into this minor category. By comparison, in the 1994–95 season participation in the eighteen-years and under category in female hockey accounted for 61 percent of the total registration. Ringette's appeal to this age category lies in its "girls only" image and the fact that it is supported by parents and communities alike. The names of the various subcategories within this category leave no room for confusion about one's sexual identity. They are: Petites (for nine-year-olds and under), Tweens, Belles, Juniors, and Debs (the latter is short for debutantes and is for twenty-two-year-olds and under). Research has shown that a high percentage of girls drop out of organized sports in their early teens when boys and peer pressure come into play. As sociologist Helen Lenskyj puts it, "the power of compulsory heterosexuality hits them with a bang ... [they feel] they should not be able to run faster than a boy or play tennis better than a boy or do math better than a boy."[18] Indeed, when a survey was conducted of American girls aged seven to eighteen, researchers found that 36 percent of the subjects maintained boys made fun of them when they played sports.[19]

The feminine image of ringette has clearly attracted sponsors, who are undoubtedly aware of the sport's appeal to parents and local communities. Six official sponsors signed on for the 1994–95 season, including Shoppers Drug Mart and the Royal Bank. The Royal Bank also sponsored a full-colour ringette poster, 10,000 of which were distributed by provincial associations. In recent years, promotions for the sport have included an incentive program that gives players who bring in a new recruit half-price registration or a free jacket. A newsletter, *The Ringette Review*, began in 1979, and by 1995 circulation had risen to 34,000.[20]

Despite its appeal, ringette has recently proven to be a training ground for future hockey players, especially in communities in the West where girls' and women's hockey did not exist in any substantive way in the early 1960s and 70s. Excited by the challenge of hockey, Albertan Judy Diduck gave up ringette in 1990 and went on to become a three-time member of the women's national hockey team. Diduck had signed up for ringette when she was ten years old and did not play on a female hockey team until she turned nineteen. "I didn't really know [women's hockey] existed," she said. "Certainly not in any organized way. I didn't realize there was a league of any sort until a friend told me about it."[21]

Interest in ringette is now fading. This is partly due to the fact that bodychecking was removed from women's hockey in 1986, which helped many ringette players who had wanted to play hockey but decided not to because their parents feared they would be injured. Registration for female hockey began to climb following the bodychecking ban, the world championship, and the inclusion of women's hockey in the Canada Winter Games. Between the 1990–91 and 1994–95 seasons the number of players more than doubled, going from 8,000 to 19,000. In the same time period, ringette added less than 900 players to its roster. Despite relentless organizing and promoting, ringette is still not fully accepted as a legitimate sport. The sport's advocates fight to get attention from the media for a game many now view as a quaint and outdated substitute for female hockey. In 1994 The Sports Network (TSN), Canada's only private all-sports broadcaster, ceased televising ringette's national championships due to poor ratings. Undaunted, ringette organizers produced and televised their own video of the 1995 championship using air time donated by TSN.

In the early 1990s ringette, like women's hockey, enjoyed the financial benefits of the Ontario government's policy of full and fair access for female sports. It received a windfall of $139,000 from the Ontario government in the 1994–95 season compared to the $89,839 women's hockey received. However, at the federal level of government, ringette has recently lost its funding. Although it received $160,000 in federal funding in 1994–95, beginning in 1996–97 it will receive no money. This loss of funding has been attributed to the fact that the sport is not represented at the Olympics and has limited international participation. The loss of federal funds, stagnant registration and the increasing acceptance of women's hockey could blow the final whistle on this sport anachronism.

While ringette gathered momentum in the seventies and early eighties, women's hockey inched along, largely at the senior level in most provinces. Minor hockey was virtually non-existent outside of Ontario, where registration surpassed the other provinces by climbing from 120 teams to 302 teams from 1979 to 1989. The cost of equipment and travel were inhibiting factors, as were parents' fears that their daughters would injure themselves. Bodychecking was a part of the game until the mid-1980s in most provinces. The misconception that girls are more fragile than boys and therefore more prone to injury was commonplace and highly effective in impeding girls and women from entering the game. Moreover, since the media had taken no interest in the sport since the 1930s, and since there was no national women's championship, many potential players were still unaware that women played hockey.

In the early 1970s women's hockey representatives launched associations in Alberta, Prince Edward Island and British Columbia within the male provincial hockey organizations. Ontario's female hockey representatives, inspired by the province's rich history, the growth of regional tournaments and strong leadership, founded a separate provincial women's hockey organization, the Ontario Women's Hockey Association which was instrumental in driving the game forward nationally. By the late 1970s spokeswomen for women's hockey from several provinces pressured the CAHA to commit government funding to national development seminars. Abby Hoffman, then director of Sport Canada, channelled money to the CAHA to fund a series of workshops to discuss the status of women's hockey across the country. These workshops dragged on into the early 1980s and accomplished very little. Finally, in May 1981 the CAHA created a Women's Hockey Council whose director would become a member of the CAHA Board of Directors.

In order to promote the women's game at the national level, advocates of women's hockey first had to overcome the attitudes of the CAHA and its branches. The OWHA was determined to reestablish a senior national championship with representation from all provinces. (In the 1930s only two teams, winners from the East and West, played off for the national title.) The OWHA began to lobby the CAHA to fund and support a national championship. Following a letter and phone campaign from women's hockey representatives across the country the CAHA finally agreed in November of 1981 to request funds from the federal government, which it would in turn use to launch a

national championship in April of 1982. The OWHA convinced
Shoppers Drug Mart to sponsor the event and donated two
cups, one for first place, the other for second place. The former
was called the Abby Hoffman Trophy, in honour of the
women's sports pioneer; the latter, the Maureen McTeer Cup,
named after the wife of then Opposition leader Joe Clark, who
had helped lobby for the championship. (A third place trophy,
the Fran Rider Cup, was added in 1984 to honour the OWHA
president.) Two months before the championship, the CAHA finally sent a letter of endorsement which sanctioned the competition as an official CAHA event.

The senior national championship was one of the pivotal
events that drove the women's game forward in the 1980s,
compelling each province to hold its own provincial championship. For example, the New Brunswick Women's Hockey
Association launched its first championship in March 1982 so
that it could send a team to the national championship. The
OWHA used the event to stimulate membership by stipulating
that any Ontario team that wanted to compete in the provincial and the national championships had to be a member of
the OWHA. Furthermore, the first few national championships
attracted major sponsors and generated media attention,
which had been absent from the women's game since the
1930s. Most importantly for players, they could now enjoy
the adrenaline rush triggered by the excitement of competing
at the national level, an experience their male counterparts had
long been able to enjoy. They could also test their skills against
other elite athletes and ultimately savour the accolade "the best
in Canada." Off the ice, this national event also provided
provincial leaders in the women's game with the rare opportunity to network. In fact it was during the national championship that the CAHA met with provincial representatives to
officially launch its first-ever female council, originally called
the Women's Hockey Council.

Despite the significance of the first Female Council in the CAHA, the council proved to have very little influence or power within the CAHA or its branches. Members encountered a firmly entrenched subculture, which has been aptly described by sociologists Richard Gruneau and David Whitson:

> Because women have always been excluded from hockey's institutional structure, even though women have been playing hockey-like games for almost as long as men have, organized hockey developed as a distinctly masculine subculture, a game played (at the organized level) almost exclusively by men and boys and a game whose dominant practices and values have been those of a very specific model of aggressive masculinity.[22]

What started as a game soon came to represent an exclusive male club at which women weren't welcome. This "club" represented a physical as well as cultural space, as most arenas have been monopolized by men and boys. As Gruneau and Whitson observe, "The increasing presence of girls and women in areas of life that were formerly all male really does reduce the spaces in our culture where 'men can be men' and male solidarity can be rehearsed."[23]

The Female Council director, Rhonda Leeman, had voting privileges on the CAHA board, but Leeman maintains the council's power was negligible. At her first CAHA annual meeting in 1982, she presented fifteen recommendations that called for financial assistance as well as a separate constitution that would allow the council to be independent, both in terms of its operation and finances.[24] None of these recommendations or others giving women's hockey more independence were ever passed by the male-dominated board.

Although the Female Council was allowed only a small degree of control over the women's game, it steadfastly maintained its priorities. Educating parents and young girls about the distinctions between women's hockey and men's hockey was a central component of the council's tasks. Another task that was critical to advancing the women's game was the establishment of training programs for referees, coaches, trainers and players. The council also assumed the task of managing the senior national championship in conjunction with the host city. In 1993, it also assumed the responsibility of managing the junior national championship.

Despite the overwhelming men's club atmosphere of the CAHA, the Female Council managed to accomplish some things. One of its most significant initiatives was winning approval to have girls' hockey included in the Canada Winter Games in 1991. The Games had been created in 1967 to encourage community development and participation in winter sports, but until 1991 hockey was limited to boys. With the inclusion of girls under age seventeen, these female players now had their first formal development program. The selection and training camps for the Canada Winter Games drew new players and sparked provincial participation in this underrepresented age category. (Prior to 1990 many provinces, with the exception of Ontario, had no hockey development programs for girls under the age of twenty.) A national program such as the Canada Winter Games drives the sport within small communities, where girls may want to play but may not receive any encouragement from parents or coaches. Indeed, the inclusion of girls' hockey in the Canada Games was largely responsible for the almost 40 percent increase in CHA registration for female hockey in 1991–92.

The Female Council's second major accomplishment, the launching of a national championship for the under-18 category in 1993, provided further motivation for provinces to develop programs for this often-ignored age group. Because of the small number of players in this age group, in 1993 only six teams competed: two from Ontario and one each from Alberta,

Prince Edward Island, Quebec and Saskatchewan. This championship will now take place every four years with the Canada Winter Games held in between. Some regional championships and jamborees have gradually been added to motivate these intermediate players. Although these are important advances, the CHA representatives — even those on the Female Council — are all too ready to justify the overall lack of equity. Karen Wallace, who has been the council director since 1991, defends the infrequency of the junior national championship by arguing that the CHA does not want to push young girls into competition too early and that the championships also strain the already low budgets for the teams. Wallace is correct in saying that women's hockey budgets are low; however, the CHA has done little to remedy this. Inadequate financing continues to hamper women's hockey. After six years of allowing volunteers to administer the women's game, the CAHA finally hired a coordinator on contract in 1988. Only following the success of the 1990 world championship did the CAHA hire a permanent manager for women's hockey, Glynis Peters.

Peters emits boundless energy and is intensely committed to the game. Coming from an athletic family, Peters participated in a variety of sports in high school and university, including a three-year stint on the Ontario provincial field hockey team. After graduation, while travelling in France, Peters had the opportunity to join a climbing expedition to Mount Everest. To do so, Peters raised money and even flew to Beijing to get the necessary permit. With only a few climbs in the French Alps under her belt, she and her partner joined three experienced climbers. They trekked to Base Camp 2 at approximately 6,500 metres (four miles) above sea level with no oxygen — a remarkable feat for a rookie climber. Peters returned to Canada in 1990 in time to apply for the job of manager of female hockey at the CAHA. The thirst for challenge that led her up Mount Everest and the teamwork required to cope

*Glynis Peters (left), manager of Canada's national team
and Shannon Miller (right), assistant coach at the
Athletes Village, Lake Placid, 1994 world championship.*

with the adverse conditions she encountered there serve her well at the CHA. Building a presence for women's hockey in a national sports organization in a country that is enthralled by men's hockey was and still is a daunting task.

When Peters joined the CAHA, women's hockey had just moved into the high-performance ranks. Her job description seemed better suited to a small department than to one person: as manager of the national team, she was responsible for producing a newsletter, tracking elite players, and directing all national team selection camps. She also met twice a year with the Female Council, which was comprised of volunteer provincial representatives. In January 1993, after several years at the CAHA, Peters commented on the inequities between male and female hockey. "Women are given a volunteer title and then given absolutely no power and no assistance or authority to do anything with it," she lamented. "I have seen so many of them frustrated and leaving. That was my first real exposure to that kind of situation. It really opened up my eyes and it's turned me into a real advocate and a real fighter. It has made me even a bit evangelical about the cause." Yet Peters also insisted that women's hockey had come a long way. "Definitely the people that I work with daily at the national level are really quite exceptional in their acceptance of the game," she said, "and are doing ... a great deal to try and help develop women's hockey. But there's a huge mass outside of that." [25]

That huge mass — including the media, sponsors, male hockey players, the general public, even the agency and its branches — is reluctant to accept the women's game. Because of this, the support of a national organization is essential to the sport. This is especially so when the sport is the country's national passion. Given its history and its monopoly over the game, the CHA could play a crucial role in elevating women's hockey to the same status as the men's game.

In 1995 the CHA outlined its plans for women's hockey. It

intended to provide more opportunities for women and girls across Canada to play hockey with their peers. It also saw the need for an improved system for player development and easier access for younger players; it also planned to offer specialized training programs for coaches and officials and to create national championships for an increased number of age groups and skill levels. Finally, the association expressed a desire to become more involved with women's hockey at the international level.[26]

These plans were and still are commendable but as of 1996 only one new national championship has been added and it is only held every four years. So far very little training is aimed at officials. However, in 1994 a pool of five female coaches was created to train for national team competitions, which is a start in the right direction. The most significant changes in women's hockey have occurred at the international level (see Chapters 8 and 9). Canada's leadership at this level can be attributed to several individuals: Frank Libera, former board member of the Female Council and member of the IIHF's (the International Ice Hockey Federation's) women's committee; to a lesser extent Murray Costello, president of the CHA; and most notably Gord Renwick, Canada's representative at the IIHF. By 1997, the CHA and its provincial partners will have hosted three international events since 1990. If the 1997 qualifying world championship for the Olympics is managed properly, it, too, could help to advance the women's game by attracting new sponsors and media interest. Only a few other countries have shown any interest in hosting these competitions, so the CHA has shouldered more than its fair share of the responsibility. Yet as the preeminent nation in women's hockey, Canada is expected to lead the way.

Despite the progress at the international level, the CHA could greatly improve its support of the women's game at the national level. The overriding influence of pro hockey is another contributing factor. In 1994, a floundering Hockey

Canada joined the CAHA. The organization, now called the Canadian Hockey Association, took on Hockey Canada's former responsibilities, which included managing the senior men's national team and the International Hockey Centres of Excellence (training centres for coaches and players) in five cities across the country. The addition of new members to the CHA board, such as the National Hockey League and NHL Players Association has served only to cloud the already blurry lines between amateur and pro hockey. The CAHA even deleted the word "amateur" from its name, a term that supposedly defined its mandate. Inherent in the word "amateur" are the values of participation, sportsmanship and the pursuit of excellence; one does not associate the word with the practice of developing future pro stars at the expense of young players. "They are so interconnected, the NHL and CHA," explains hockey analyst Alan Adams. "[The NHL is] like this locomotive: you ride it or you get out of the way because it will run you over."[27]

The NHL dominance in amateur hockey surfaced again in discussions with the IIHF and the International Olympic Committee (IOC) in 1994. At a time when amateur events are fast disappearing, the addition of pro hockey teams to the 1998 Olympics further undermines the amateur ideal. Hockey enthusiasts argue that fans want to see "the best against the best," which in their eyes means the NHL players. But the NHL's insertion of "dream teams" into the Olympics means that each country's regular national team has essentially been jettisoned from the Olympic Games by pro hockey parading under the banner of sport development.

Pro hockey's influence also affects the debate about what the draft age should be for junior male players. This debate has been ongoing since the 1970s. Many parents and coaches have lobbied for it to be raised from eighteen years of age to twenty in order to allow younger kids more time to develop both as players and as individuals. NHL teams, on the other hand, have pushed to sign up young talent sooner so that players can make an early entry into the pro ranks. Male hockey is still coping with these difficulties in the 1990s. "There are some problems with it [male hockey] at all levels," Glynis Peters acknowledged in 1993. "There are problems in minor hockey of too much pressure on the kids; too much ice time ... boys dropping out just because they don't make the NHL. In the NHL we've seen the violence, the checking from behind, the serious injuries, and players being tossed around from team to team."[28]

All this has a direct effect on the women's game. Peters would like to see women's hockey develop as a distinct game, not one that is trying to emulate the men's game to gain validity. "In hockey we don't want to be the same as the men. We don't want that game," she insists. "We play a different game and we think that there are values in our game and aspects to our game that should in fact be protected, and, to be quite frank, the men should probably adopt." But the men's game persists as the legitimate model, and the lack of appreciation for the female game continues to hinder national development. Women's hockey still lags years behind men's in key areas such as the development of female coaches, referees, officials, and volunteers. In order for progress to take place in these areas the CHA must make changes that allow women more control over their own game.

Aware of the paucity of leaders and volunteers, Peters and the Female Council introduced role model workshops in 1995. In 1996 Peters launched leadership seminars to attract and educate new volunteers. But it will take decades for these seminars, which are only held once a year, to develop the volunteer base that is needed to support the women's game. One obvious way to recruit more volunteers would be to add a women's hockey coordinator to the staff of each provincial branch of the CHA. These leaders could champion the game in underdeveloped areas such as high schools and universities within the provinces.[29]

While the decision to include representation from the Female Council on the CHA board in 1982 helped to further the women's game, the influence of one volunteer female director and one female hockey manager is relatively insignificant given that the forty-five members of the association staff are primarily devoted to male hockey, as are the branch presidents and directors and council representatives. Moreover, many of the volunteers and staff are men who are ex-hockey players or coaches who have little experience with women's hockey and resent the intrusion of female players into the game. According to Frank Libera, the officer for the women's high performance committee, "Women's hockey needs strong advocates on the board. The CHA culture needs work," he said in 1994. "If an organization wants to change, people have to give up power."[30]

In the case of women's hockey, power also means money. The CHA budget allocates very little to women's hockey. For the 1994–95 season the CHA's expenses totalled $8,860,837, of which $210,710, or less than 3 percent, was earmarked for women's hockey. The total CHA revenue was $8,825,865, which breaks down as follows: federal government grants totalled $1,218,400; the five Centres of Excellence, promotional and training centres sponsored by NHL teams, contributed $450,000; funding agencies contributed $528,200; the rest of the revenue came from sponsorships, gate receipts, advertising, hockey resource centres and various programs and branch revenues. According to the CHA budget, male hockey received $1,171,290 of the government-allocated funds, while women's hockey received $47,110 or a paltry 3.8 percent of these funds. Moreover, despite the high number of CHA staff members devoted to the male game and the male sport's aggressive marketing campaign, men's hockey lost $1,042,662, whereas women's hockey lost only $139,430 in 1994-5.

(Government revenue from these totals was excluded.)

The CHA is reluctant to discuss details of the budget and Peters refuses to even comment on it. The Female Council director, Karen Wallace, justifies the small percentage of federal funds allocated to women's hockey by arguing that 3.8 percent represents the approximate registration ratio of women's hockey to men's. But allocating funds to women's hockey simply on the basis of registration numbers doesn't take into account the historical imbalances between the male and female games or redress the fact that the women's game has been underfunded for the last eighty years. Thousands more young girls would be playing now if they had received the encouragement and the financial support boys get. Even Murray Costello, president of the CHA, acknowledged the association's shortcomings. "Fifty percent of our Canadian youth have been deprived of a wonderful experience for a long time by reason of us not moving earlier on this," he said in 1990. "I'm sure there were an awful lot of talented women who could have had that experience [hockey], but didn't because it was never organized."[31]

The success of the women's senior national championship in increasing the number of players in the senior age category points to the huge gap in opportunities for other age categories. It is indisputable that national championships are important cogs in the development wheel of any sport. Despite the Female Council and the CHA's involvement with women's hockey, only one annual national championship exists for women. Moreover, regional competition for women so far has only amounted to an annual Western Shield Senior Championship for the Western provinces. In the East, the Atlantic Shield (formerly the Eastern Shield) was relaunched in 1990, but this championship is not an annual event.

One extremely important area of growth lies at the university level. In 1994 the Canadian Interuniversity Athletic Union (CIAU), the governing body for university-funded

## OPPORTUNITIES FOR GIRLS AND WOMEN

ENTRY LEVEL (Initiation Program)

**COMPETITIVE LEAGUES**
**Peewee to Senior Levels**
When female leagues not available,
females integrated into male system.

**RECREATIONAL**
**LEAGUES**
**All Levels**

**JUNIOR (UNDER 18)**
**National Championships & Canada Games**
**(Biannual provincial team playoffs)**

**REGIONAL CHAMPIONSHIPS**
**ATLANTIC & WESTERN SHIELDS**
**Annual Provincial Team Playoffs,**
**Atlantic and Western Regions**

**SENIOR NATIONAL CHAMPIONSHIPS**
**Annual Provincial Team Playoffs**

**NATIONAL WOMEN'S TEAM**
**Olympics Starting in 1998**
**Biannual Women's World Championships;**
**Quadrennial thereafter**

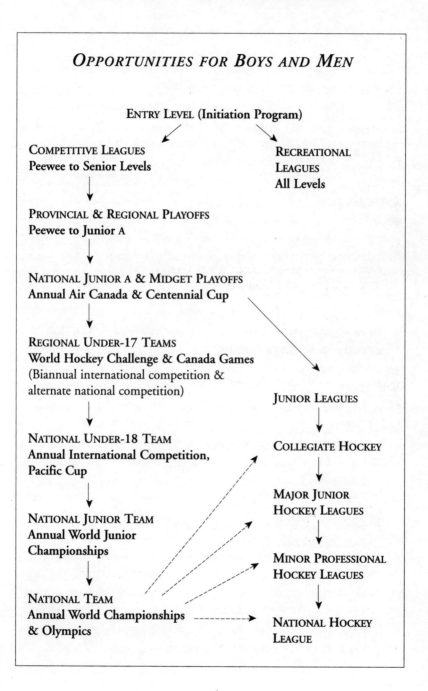

## OPPORTUNITIES FOR BOYS AND MEN

ENTRY LEVEL (Initiation Program)

COMPETITIVE LEAGUES
Peewee to Senior Levels

RECREATIONAL
LEAGUES
All Levels

PROVINCIAL & REGIONAL PLAYOFFS
Peewee to Junior A

NATIONAL JUNIOR A & MIDGET PLAYOFFS
Annual Air Canada & Centennial Cup

REGIONAL UNDER-17 TEAMS
World Hockey Challenge & Canada Games
(Biannual international competition &
alternate national competition)

JUNIOR LEAGUES

NATIONAL UNDER-18 TEAM
Annual International Competition,
Pacific Cup

COLLEGIATE HOCKEY

NATIONAL JUNIOR TEAM
Annual World Junior
Championships

MAJOR JUNIOR
HOCKEY LEAGUES

MINOR PROFESSIONAL
HOCKEY LEAGUES

NATIONAL TEAM
Annual World Championships
& Olympics

NATIONAL HOCKEY
LEAGUE

sports in Canada, joined the CHA board. A year later the CIAU, armed with a new equity policy, trumpeted plans to add women's hockey to its varsity sport roster. At that time almost forty universities reported having women's hockey teams, but only two provinces, Quebec and Ontario, funded varsity programs. Jennifer Brenning, director of international and community relations for the CIAU, believes women's hockey could take off as women's soccer has; women's soccer has flourished over the past ten years and now has varsity status at Canada's thirty-six of forty-five universities.[32] Not only does becoming a CIAU sport mean more funds for the women's game, it will also mean access to more ice time. Varsity players practise four or five times per week, which gives them a decided advantage over their club team counterparts, who only practise once a week. In anticipation of a CIAU championship, the universities of Guelph and Windsor added teams to the Ontario Women's Interuniversity League in 1994. Furthermore, Ontario and Quebec are planning a new regional challenge match between Queen's University, the University of Toronto, Concordia University, and the University of Quebec, at Trois-Rivières. (The CIAU requires that a sport have three regional conferences before it qualifies as a CIAU championship.)

But recent cuts in government grants to universities and the CIAU have forced both groups to reassess their priorities. Moreover, the CHA's lukewarm interest in the university game coupled with the lack of effective lobbying by representatives of university women's hockey makes it unlikely that it will become a CIAU-funded sport in the near future. "There are no champions for the sport [within the universities] and the CHA are not really keen," says Brenning. "The leadership should come from the bottom up. The CIAU executive were trying to push it from the top down."[33] In May 1996 the CIAU struck an ad hoc committee to develop a proposal for a women's hockey, participant-funded event that would take place in 1997–98.

Despite the paucity of championships for women, the CHA and its provincial counterparts have endorsed and supported ten annual events for male hockey: three national Junior championships; one Midget championship; three Bantam championships for the East, the West and Ontario, respectively; two Peewee championships, one for Ontario, the other for Atlantic Canada; and a CIAU Athletic Union Cup.[34] With the exception of the national senior championship, all of these male championships have sponsors. Lack of sponsorship is often the reason given for not creating more women's championships. When Shoppers Drug Mart opted out of the national championship in 1987, the CAHA was unable to find another sponsor until 1994. The CAHA said its inability to find a substitute sponsor was due to the fact that the registration figures for women's hockey were low compared to the numbers for men's hockey. If one compares numbers alone, women are indeed only a blip on the hockey map: there are 19,050 female players registered versus 493,787 male players. The picture begins to change, however, when one considers the growth rate of the women's game. Registration in women's hockey in 1984–85 stood at 5,778 players. In the last decade, that number has more than tripled. And while female registration grew, male registration dropped, from almost half a million players in 1983 to 401,482 players in 1990 — a loss of 88,283 players in seven years. In 1992, when women's hockey gained Olympic status, the 1993–94 registration figure swelled by another 30 percent. In the same year, male hockey lost 57,000 players. Even with only one annual national championship and three world championships under its belt, proportionately speaking the registration figures for women's hockey have exceeded the figures for the men's game.

This impressive growth rate, the success of the national team and the new Olympic status led to sponsors such as Imperial Oil signing a CHA sponsorship package in 1995 that at last included female hockey. The three-year contract infuses the women's national championship with $25,000 a year.[35] But sponsorship is only effective in tandem with media coverage. When she was asked in 1993 how long it would take for women players to get the recognition they deserve, Glynis Peters replied with a sigh, "I don't know. It's a huge job across the country. The network doesn't exist. The tools don't exist. The newsletters [and] the media don't exist right now to be able to allow these people to communicate and share ideas." As of 1996, this network still hasn't materialized, nor has the media coverage, especially in the critical form of television broadcasts. Indeed, neither the CHA nor TSN deemed the final game of the 1996 Pacific Women's Hockey Championship between the US and Canada — the two leading teams in the world — important enough to broadcast.

Yet the media tools do exist in male hockey. *Canadian Hockey Magazine*, the annual full-colour CHA magazine, is a product that includes the many factions that drive this amateur organization: pro hockey, national teams, international hockey and national championships. Previously known as *Hockey Today*, the magazine was launched in 1974 as a vehicle for spreading the CHA message about programs, for attracting sponsors and for merchandising products. The CHA controls the editorial content, which makes up 40 percent of the magazine, and the St. Clair Group sells the advertising, which makes up the remaining 60 percent of the publication and pays for production. The circulation is controlled, which means the magazine is sent to approximately twenty-five thousand coaches, each of whom receives seventeen copies to distribute to his team members. By the end of 1996 the CHA plans to expand *Canadian Hockey* to three issues a year. Up until this point in the 1990s women's hockey has been allotted only one article in each issue. These articles are invariably limited to summing up the recent success of the national team or repeating the standard history of the game.

In contrast, the women's hockey newsletter, *Go Overboard*, was axed in 1994 when the CHA revamped its newsletter program following its amalgamation with Hockey Canada. The newsletter had been launched only two years earlier. It was the first and only national vehicle for women's hockey and had received praise from hockey federations around the world. Because women's hockey has few championships and receives negligible media coverage, the loss of the newsletter cut off a vital national channel of information for players, fans and organizers.

Women's hockey is trapped in a catch-22 situation that is common to many women's sports. Lack of support from the national organization has led many people who are involved in women's hockey to question whether they should continue to work within the traditional male framework. What is needed, some argue, is a separate organization entirely committed to the women's game. Former marketing director for the CAHA, Larry Skinner is one advocate of more female control. "Women in the game should sell the game. The CHA needs a female technical director who understands and knows women's hockey," he says. "The Ontario Women's Hockey Association's success came from being a separate entity."[36] The OWHA accounts for close to 50 percent of the hockey played in the country. While Ontario has the highest population in the country, OWHA executive director Fran Rider is adamant that the growth of the women's game is due to its separate organization, which is fully committed to advancing the women's game.

Peters, however, believes the game must remain within the CHA. "Women's hockey is an integral part of the Canadian Hockey Association and that's who's going to drive it," she argues. "We've gone way beyond ever dreaming or thinking of a separate association."[37] One of the reasons for working within the male framework has to do with federal funding through Sport Canada. The policy concerning separate national organizations for male and female sports has shifted over the years.

In its funding decisions, Sport Canada now favours sports organizations that represent both genders rather than only one. It is unlikely that women's hockey would receive the same federal funding if it was a separate female organization.

For the time being, it is also unlikely that women's hockey will form its own organization at the national level. Although Canadian women have been playing the game for decades, strong, vocal leaders who will champion women's hockey are sorely lacking. While Glynis Peters works tirelessly to promote and control the direction of the female game, given her relatively scant resources and the dominant priorities of men's hockey within the Canadian Hockey Association, her effectiveness is restricted. So, too, is the efficacy of the CHA's Female Council, which possesses little real power. The council meets only twice a year and occupies a subordinate ranking within the CHA hierarchy.

We live in a society that, for the most part, honours and supports boys' and men's athletic feats while ignoring those of girls and women. As Richard Gruneau and David Whitson so rightly point out, men have monopolized the physical spaces where sport is played out, effectively transforming arenas into "men's clubs." And they have also laid claim to the cultural spaces of sport. This, coupled with the dominance of professional hockey in Canada, leaves little room for the women's amateur game to flourish. Truly supporting women's hockey, therefore, means challenging some core beliefs about the role of both men's and women's hockey. Is the "win-at-all-costs" mentality really creating winners? Or is it ensuring that large segments of the population, including girls and women, remain outside the game? Until those who support women's hockey challenge these central assumptions about our national game, women's hockey will remain in the second-class position it has been stuck in for decades, the "little sister" of Canada's national sport.

*Chapter Three*

# ONTARIO: VISION AND UNREST

ON FEBRUARY 9, 1995, the Ontario Women's Hockey Association (OWHA) celebrated two notable events: its successful bid to host the 1997 world championship in Kitchener and the opening of its new office in Mississauga. Huge red and white banners from the world championship sponsors adorned the walls, at this standing-room only event. The sponsors included Imperial Oil, Air Canada and The Sports Network. Hazel McCallion, mayor of Mississauga and longtime champion of women's hockey, and Anne Swarbrick, the provincial minister of Culture, Tourism and Recreation, both received Team Ontario hockey sweaters bearing the number ninety-eight, which represented the year women's hockey would first be played in the Olympics. Fran Rider, executive director of the OWHA, representatives from the Canadian Hockey Association (CHA) and from other area hockey associations basked in the glow of good will, along with members of Kitchener City Council. Winning the right to hold the 1997 world championship was a fitting reward for the OWHA, the visionary organization that had launched world competition for women's hockey a decade earlier.

Ontario has a remarkable legacy of intrepid women who defied social conventions by playing hockey in the early decades of the century. Women played a critical role in the early history of the game, organizing leagues and, when money permitted, regional and provincial championships. Ontario holds the distinction of being the home of the earliest recorded game in Canada. This game took place in 1891 at Ottawa's Rideau rink and received a brief write-up in the *Ottawa Citizen*. Thirteen women were reported to have played on two teams, identified simply as "No. 1" and "No. 2".[1] Unbeknownst to the majority of Canadians, until the 1940s hockey was a sport for both sexes. During the Victorian era of the early 1900s there was some resistance to women's involvement in the sport. However, women's hockey began to build community support and by the 1920s and 1930s, newspapers such as the *Toronto Star* reported regularly on women's hockey games. Given the current predominance of professional sports, it is refreshing to read that in the 1920s up to three thousand fans gathered at an outdoor rink to watch women's amateur hockey as far north as Fort William, Ontario.[2]

Ontario women played their first provincial championship in Picton in 1914, the same year the Canadian Amateur Hockey Association (CAHA) was formed. (As previously mentioned, the CAHA changed its name to the Canadian Hockey Association [CHA] in 1994.) In 1922 a group of mostly female players and coaches created the Ontario Ladies Hockey Association (OLHA), the first provincial women's hockey organization. The OLHA thrived during the 1920s and 1930s, hosting tournaments and provincial championships.[3]

At the community level the most revered team during these two decades was the Preston Rivulettes. This scant collection of about ten players reigned over women's hockey at both the national and provincial levels, losing only two games from 1930 to 1939. News reports of the team recall the rambunctious games — the players stuffed their socks with newspaper for protection — and the raucous crowds screaming for their favourite players. About six thousand people attended a two-game series in 1935.[4]

From 1890 to the 1930s university squads competed against both club and university teams in the South-Western Ontario area. As early as 1908–09 the Intercollege Ice Hockey Cup was awarded at the University of Toronto.[5] By 1922 the University of Toronto and McGill and Queen's universities began competing in the new Women's Collegiate Ice Hockey League for the Beattie Ramsay Trophy, named after a male player on Canada's Olympic hockey team.[6] The University of Toronto thoroughly dominated the league, collecting thirteen cups in fourteen years.[7] McGill withdrew in 1925 and Queen's in 1935. University competition ceased altogether in 1952 and was not revived until 1960.[8] The Depression, coupled with World War II and the rise of professional hockey, virtually wiped out the progress women's hockey had achieved in the 1920s and 1930s. By the 1950s many of the game's leaders in the province had retired. Men's hockey now dominated the media and the ice time. The sport had moved indoors to both private and public arenas with improved ice surfaces and facilities for fans. Team owners required indoor rinks to generate advertising and ticket revenue. Women continued to play in some leagues and tournaments, but the momentum was gone.

In the early 1960s a few women's leagues prevailed but they fluctuated in size, depending on finances and the availability of players. Since the media now focussed primarily on men's pro hockey, many women were unaware that female hockey even existed. "It was very, very difficult to play in the past," says Fran Rider, current executive director of the OWHA. "One or two key people on a team kept it together. There was no network or support. There were maybe three or four teams in a league. You played the same people week after week. The distances were great, you had to travel miles and miles to play a hockey game. So just as there was not enough competition, there was no variety of competition and there were great differences in ability levels on each team."[9]

But by the mid 1960s, interest in the female game resurfaced. Since competition in leagues was limited, key tournaments sprang up in small Ontario towns such as Wallaceburg, Preston and Picton. The first Dominion Ladies Hockey Tournament in 1968, organized by the Brampton Canadettes Girls Hockey Association, brought together twenty-two teams in Brampton, Ontario. The Canadettes' was the first organization to set up competition for players in a broad range of age categories. In the first tournament the ages of the players ranged from a grandmother in her sixties to a nine-year-old.[10] These events also functioned as an informal meeting place for the leaders in the women's game.

In 1975 the impetus to form a women's hockey association came from an unlikely source. Susan Dalziel, a senior level player from Prince Edward Island, wrote to the Ontario government for a list of teams she hoped might travel to PEI to play. Her letter landed on the desk of Jim Coutts, a sports consultant for the Ontario government. After reading about girls' hockey in his local Mississauga newspaper, Coutts contacted Joe Primeau, a female hockey coach in the area. Coutts was instrumental in arranging the first meeting with funding provided by the Ontario goverment. Coaches and female players soon gathered for their first formal meeting. The new Ontario Women's Hockey Association (OWHA) was founded at the Dominion tournament in Brampton. Kay Cartwright, a lawyer and former Kingston Red Baron player, was elected president. Cartwright, along with participants from the Central Ontario Women's Hockey League (COWHL) and other parts of the province, spent a year consulting with team representatives to determine membership benefits and to draft a constitution for the new organization. Once the association was formed, it took a year or so for teams to adapt to the rules imposed by the new organization and to convince them of the benefits of joining.[11]

The decision to create an independent hockey organization was a critical step for women's hockey in Ontario. Female proponents of the game contended that the issues in women's hockey were very different from those in men's hockey. Foremost, was selling the sport as an appropriate game for girls. Furthermore, the OWHA did not want to be encumbered by a male bureaucracy that would be unlikely to take the female game seriously. Female hockey quickly became known as the "outlaw sport" by the Ontario Minor Hockey Association because of its resistance to male hockey's governing bodies. "Men's hockey had high membership costs, no benefits and they kept telling you what you can't do," says Bev Mallory, one of the founding members of the OWHA.[12] Fran Rider, president of the OWHA from 1982 to 1993, remembers the obstacles in that era. "It is important to understand that support from the [male] minor hockey community did not exist for females," Rider explains, "so any progress was in spite of discouragement by male hockey. We had to deal with problems like bad ice times, few leagues and no support systems."[13]

Despite these problems, membership in female hockey slowly began to expand within the new organization. The OWHA was the only hockey organization in the province that assisted female players and provided both opportunities and a structure for the sport to grow. From 1977, its first year of registration, to 1979, membership in the OWHA almost doubled; the number of teams grew from 65 teams to 120 with 6 divisions. These numbers could easily have been higher, but many girls and women still didn't know the game existed; of those girls who did, many had parents who considered hockey too rough.

Negative attitudes towards the female game were one of the serious challenges facing the fledgling association. Although most people were familiar with male hockey, the

OWHA realized it had to educate all the partners in the female game, including parents, potential players and the hockey community. With the help of government grants, the OWHA hired a development coordinator in 1981, who began to travel to towns and cities across the province in order to visit schools, set up tournaments and conduct leadership camps. In the late 1970s the OWHA had also launched a newsletter to keep isolated women's hockey communities across the province informed about the sport. To stimulate new membership the OWHA required all teams to join the new association if they wanted to play in the provincial championship, which had been reactivated in 1977, and other sanctioned tournaments.

In 1980, five years after it had been founded, the OWHA joined the Ontario Hockey Association (OHA). With its membership growing, the OWHA could now more comfortably take advantage of male hockey's expertise and officially join Ontario's hockey community. The OHA, one of the sport's three governing bodies in Ontario, was the OWHA's link to the CAHA. The OHA coordinates junior and senior male hockey in Ontario in conjunction with the two other provincial branches of the CHA, the Ottawa and Thunder Bay District Associations. (In 1990 the Ontario Hockey Federation [OHF] incorporated, replacing the OHA as one of the three governing bodies in Ontario.) As a new member, the OWHA was allotted one vote on the OHA board of directors. In the same year the OWHA executive established a board of regents to advise its volunteer board of directors. Hazel McCallion, the mayor of Mississauga, acted as the first member of the board of regents and would prove to be a loyal and influential friend to women's hockey in Ontario. McCallion had herself been a hockey player in Montreal during the 1940s.

Although the OWHA membership was growing steadily, senior hockey accounted for the largest registration. To encourage more participation at the minor and junior levels, the first leadership development camp for girls between the ages of fourteen and eighteen was held in 1983. But one of the most important events in terms of increasing registration took place in 1985 when the bi-annual Ontario Winter Games accepted girls in the Midget A category (under 17). The same year, the OWHA hosted provincial championships in five age divisions and sanctioned an unprecedented thirty invitational tournaments. Between 1979 and 1989 the number of teams registered with the OWHA increased from 120 to 302.

However, two significant issues slowed the progress of women's hockey in Ontario. First, the OWHA joined the OHA in a legal battle to prevent twelve-year-old Justine Blainey from playing on a boys' hockey team. The OWHA maintained that allowing girls to play on boys' teams would destroy female hockey. (See Chapter 6 for a more detailed discussion of this incident.) For at least three years, from 1985 to 1987, the OWHA allocated their limited resources to presenting briefs, writing letters, appearing in court and researching the effects of girls leaving female hockey. By 1990 the OWHA was still paying off its portion of the total bill for the Blainey case, which came to approximately $100,000. The legal battle also fractured the association since many members believed girls deserved to play with boys if equitable opportunities did not exist for them.

The second issue that stalled the development of women's hockey was the delayed elimination of bodychecking. In 1989, three years after bodychecking had been prohibited in national championships, Ontario finally banned the practice in all age categories. This decision helped the game immensely: fewer injuries resulted, players were forced to be more creative and the image of the game improved.

With these two issues behind them, the first world championship in 1990 and the announcement of Olympic status in 1992, OWHA registration skyrocketed to 612 teams in the

1994–95 season. This figure does not include girls who played on boys' teams or female teams in high schools and universities, which are distinct from the OWHA community teams. Ontario also sent two teams to the first under-18 national championship launched in 1993 (and held every four years). By 1995 the OWHA had seven minor hockey categories, ranging from intermediates (20 and under) to tykes (7 and under) and boasted more female divisions than any other province in the country.

The proliferation of female hockey schools is further evidence of the rapid growth of the sport in Ontario and burgeoning leadership in the 1990s. For example, in 1996 national team players Angela James, Natalie Rivard and Margot Page ran hockey schools throughout eastern and southwestern Ontario. These national team players are vital role models. Their schools, which operate in the summer, are open to girls of all ages and some schools include leadership training for young girls. Another outstanding role model is Geraldine Heaney, a defensive star in the Senior AA league and five-time national team member. Heaney teaches at hockey schools in both Canada and the US and as a result of her national team profile, Heaney's responsibilities in 1995 included working as a women's hockey consultant for Lauridon Sports Management. The company is building York University's new ice hockey complex, which opens in the fall of 1996. Heaney, originally from Ireland, started playing hockey at age ten at a North York girls' hockey club. Famous for her acrobatic game-winning goal in the 1990 world championship, Heaney attempts impossible plays. Described by the press as "a fluid, effortless skater and skillful puckhandler," Heaney was voted to the all-star team in the 1992 and 1994 world championships.[14] She is also a member of the Canadian roller hockey team. Her eclectic sports background includes ball hockey, soccer, Gaelic football and running. Hockey has even helped

*Geraldine Heaney (centre) at the 1996
Pacific Women's Hockey Championship.*

Heaney reap some financial rewards along with the opportunity to heighten the profile of female hockey.

Although Ontario university hockey developed outside
the OWHA, it was revived in the early 1960s, at about the same

time as community hockey. A group of students at Queen's University canvassed other institutions and eventually won approval from the Women's Intercollegiate Athletic Union (WIAU) to set up a varsity women's hockey league for a two-year trial period. The first universities to join the league were Western, McGill, Queen's and McMaster as well as the University of Toronto and the Ontario Agriculture College (now the University of Guelph). In 1971 the almost fifty-year-old WIAU merged with the Ontario–Quebec Women's Conference of Intercollegiate Athletics to form the Ontario Women's Interuniversity Athletic Association (OWIAA). Once again female leaders decided that a separate women's sport organization would best serve its constituents. "There was an interest in promoting sport for women and [the OWIAA] felt the growth would be faster," reports Sheila Forshaw, executive director of the OWIAA. "It would also develop female leaders. I think there is a real need for role models in women's athletics."[15]

Despite the newly formed OWIAA, varsity women's hockey in Ontario continued to struggle for support from the university community and specifically the university athletic departments. For example, in 1975 eight teams faced off for the Judy McCaw provincial championship. (Judy McCaw had been captain of the University of Guelph team in 1967.) Two years later, however, three universities cancelled their programs. Western's team only lasted from 1972 to 1977, the victim of an indifferent athletic department.[16] By the late 1980s the OWIAA schedule dwindled to only ten games a season and by 1991 only the University of Toronto, the University of Guelph and York and Queen's universities remained in the league. With the possibility of a national varsity championship looming, the University of Windsor and Laurier University joined the OWIAA league in 1994–95, boosting the league to six teams.

Sport equity, namely, fair distribution of funding to both male and female sports, is still a contentious issue in Ontario universities in the 1990s. Despite a separate women's sport organization, male sports account for the lion's share of the budget at university athletic departments. Although male and female university students each compete in about twenty provincial events, inequities also persist in the number of universities that finance women's varsity sports. In 1995–96 in Ontario, twenty-four universities financed men's varsity hockey teams while only six of these funded women's teams. Women's hockey exists at five other universities in Ontario, but women either play in the intramural program or operate much like Western's team, the Fillies, whose members compete in tournaments and exhibition games at their own expense.

But support for varsity women's hockey is slowly building in Ontario, with the University of Toronto leading the way. In 1992 the University of Toronto's women's hockey program was nearly cancelled due to budget cuts. After a huge outcry and support from the women's hockey community, the team was reinstated. As a result of the new gender equity policy that was introduced in 1993 at this university, the women's hockey budget has been significantly bolstered and access to ice time has improved dramatically.

One area that offers a glimmer of hope is alumnae fundraising. In 1996 supporters of women's hockey at Queen's University launched an alumnae drive, having anticipated that future funding cuts might easily lead to the demise of women's hockey. The Queen's group hopes to build some financial stability and community support for the program. At the University of Guelph during the 1995-96 season, an influential alumnae donor and father of a varsity player urged the university to provide more financial equity for women's hockey and pledged to demand more support for the women's game.

High school hockey will also play a role in the development of the university game. "Different sports have different feeder systems. High school participation will drive university participation," says Sheila Forshaw, executive director of the OWIAA. Nonetheless, girls' high school hockey lags far behind boys' hockey. Without leadership within the schools or an association to champion the game, competition inched along in the 1980s. But the acceptance of women's hockey in events such as the Canada Winter Games and the Olympics is attracting new players. In the 1991–92 season, 67 percent of the Ontario Federation of School Athletic Associations (OFSAA) offered girls' hockey, which amounted to 1,230 players.[17]

A private high school hockey championship for girls, first hosted in 1992, has also shown some promising results. In 1992 eight teams played in the three-day tournament sponsored by Canadian Tire and sanctioned by OFSAA; by 1994 the number of teams had grown to forty-eight.[18] While this growth is noteworthy, boys' high school hockey has been thriving since the first provincial hockey championship in 1948. Each boys' league crowns a regional champion who competes in the OFSAA provincial championship. Close to 9,000 boys competed in 1994–95 and sixteen teams faced off for the high-profile championship.

Because hockey is still a male-identified game, girls' hockey needs to be promoted within the high schools. As girls enter puberty, they often abandon sports, because they believe that boys won't be interested in them if they play sports. "There are all these messages that your body is ornamental," says sociologist Helen Lenskyj. "The idea that your body could be a physical asset, that it's something you can use and do things with, do exciting stuff with, and feel strong and empowered, that just doesn't enter into the learning. And it gets worse as time goes on."[19]

The exception would be female-identified sports such as volleyball, which is the most popular girls' high school sport in Ontario; more than 20,000 girls played volleyball in 1994–95. By offering girls more opportunities to play sports schools send the message to girls that their participation in athletics is important. Girls' high school hockey is still developing and needs regular events such as skills clinics or jamborees to drive it. The majority of teams don't play in a league; tournaments and exhibition games are the norm. For the 1994–95 season only 2,000 girls were playing in Ontario's 774 high schools. In some high school regions, such as Ottawa-Carleton, ringette is the only high school-sanctioned ice sport for girls, effectively precluding those girls who want to play hockey.

Establishing an OFSAA provincial championship would be one way to improve the sport's visibility and to motivate students in high school. At the time of writing, in order for a sport to be granted an OFSAA championship, at least 50 percent of the member associations must have girls playing and one association must nominate the sport to OFSAA. As well, an invitational event must be conducted and evaluated by OFSAA. Of the nineteen associations in OFSAA, eleven offered girls hockey in 1995. As of March 1996, however, no association had contacted OFSAA to sponsor a girls' hockey championship. In June 1996 OFSAA approved a new process which would make it easier to develop and manage championships. The process now includes gender equity as one of the new criteria.[20]

The OWHA is the logical choice to advance girls' hockey at the high school level. But the organization has not taken on this challenge. If it did, there would be benefits for both OFSAA and the OWHA: girls could learn the game in high school and move on to community teams within the OWHA. Bev Mallory, vice-president of development for the OWHA from 1988 to 1993, encouraged both high school and university hockey but, as Fran Rider explains, "Our jurisdiction is not the high school system. Our focus is on developing community hockey."[21]

However, the OWHA went beyond its jurisdiction twice in the 1980s, producing both national and international offspring. First, it established the national championship in 1982.

*Fran Rider (left), OWHA president and Hazel McCallion (right),
Mayor of Mississauga with the McCallion World Cup at the
first world tournament, April 1987.*

Women's hockey was back in the spotlight for that first national championship thanks to the lobbying efforts of the OWHA and prominent patrons such as Maureen McTeer. The OWHA also raised the profile of women's hockey within Sport Canada and CAHA branches across the province when it finally persuaded the CAHA to endorse the national championship. The OWHA realized that a national championship was essential to drive grassroots development in the provinces. So rather than waiting years for the CAHA to grasp the significance of this, the OWHA took matters into its own hands, and ultimately proved that women did indeed want to play the game if given the right opportunities.

The second event initiated by the OWHA was the 1987 world tournament, which set women's hockey on the road to the Olympics. For Fran Rider, acceptance into the Olympics represented the ultimate dream for women's hockey. As OWHA president from 1982 to 1993 she steered the organization through a tumultuous decade of change and growth. Rider considers the 1987 world tournament "the key event in the history of international women's hockey" and her greatest accomplishment.[22] This unofficial world tournament finally forced the International Ice Hockey Federation (IIHF) to take notice of women's hockey. The world tournament also spurred the CAHA into taking action at the international level on behalf of women's hockey. After negotiations with the IIHF, the CAHA agreed to host the first world championship in 1990. Against resistance and with no financial support from the CAHA or even some members of the OWHA board, Rider championed this tournament, knowing that world competition was the first step towards the long-awaited goal of Olympic status.

Today Rider's name is synonymous with the OWHA. After almost twenty years of volunteer work with the association, Rider has become instrumental in shaping the modern saga of "the little sport that could." As a girl she only played shinny hockey in a rink in her backyard. However, when she turned sixteen she discovered women's hockey through her local newspaper and promptly joined a team. After graduating from high school in Etobicoke, Ontario, Rider worked in a variety of jobs until she decided to create her own courier company in the mid-1970s. She became the OWHA Toronto representative in 1977. The following year Rider began to direct the highly successful Brampton tournament until 1988. She had joined the OWHA board in 1981, and the next year she was voted president. The soft-spoken yet determined Rider soon became a ubiquitous presence at arenas in the province.

Her volunteer time with the OWHA mushroomed when she took over as president in 1982. Rider's commitment to women's hockey was partly due to her parents' influence: they had both served the community for more than forty years, Rider's mother as a volunteer with Save the Children Canada and her father as an employee of the Toronto fire department. Rider thinks of hockey as a way to contribute to society and also considers it her life's work. On one of her many late nights alone at the office, she acknowledged softly, "I can stay this late because I don't have a family that relies on me."[23] Her work has not gone unrecognized: in 1992 she received the Gold Stick award from the Ontario Hockey Association, the first woman in forty-five years to receive this order of merit. To be eligible for this honour, the recipient must have worked for a minimum of ten years in the hockey world. In 1994 Rider also received the CHA Order of Merit for her contributions.

Rider's orchestration of the world tournament and her long history with the only independent women's hockey association in the world has given her a unique status in women's hockey. She has become the spokesperson and leader of the women's game well beyond Ontario's borders.

Although Rider has undoubtedly contributed much to the game, some OWHA members think she has become too personally immersed in hockey politics. Members depict Rider as unwilling to change her views despite criticism and upheaval from within the organization she controls. Low morale, internal squabbling and ineffectual management have characterized the OWHA in the 1990s. Rider brushes off the criticism,

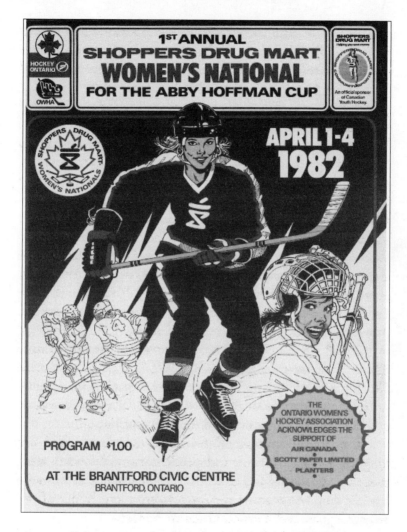

*Program cover for the 1982 national championship.*

maintaining that every organization has its detractors and critics. While this is true, there is much evidence to suggest that her critics have a point. The 1996 provincial Senior AA championship provides a recent example of the OWHA's poor management. This championship is a highlight for women's hockey fans, especially since the winner of the Ontario championship represents the province at the national championship. Players who participated in the 1996 championship found it difficult competing in both the semifinal and the final on the same day. As well, there was little publicity for the event and the results of the final game were not reported in the newspapers. In a similarly frustrated vein, Ken Dufton, coach of the North York Aeros, had four years earlier bemoaned the state of the provincial championships. "I had two guys from the OWHA organizing the Senior AA provincial championships and they have never seen an AA game."[24] After the 1996 championship, the Central Ontario Women's Hockey League (COWHL) vowed to run the Senior AA championship in 1996–97. They plan to book their own arenas and handle promotion and scheduling themselves.

The COWHL's Senior AA league, which was founded in 1980, is the highest-calibre senior hockey league in the province. The COWHL draws from the largest pool of players in the country and has dominated national championships, having won six times since 1982. Ontario players, such as Geraldine Heaney, Angela James and Marianne Grnak, continue to be a significant presence on Canada's national team.

But financial constraints and the lack of junior player development still plague the women's Senior AA league. Even by 1996 the COWHL consisted of only six teams, despite the fact that two new teams had joined the league in 1995. The number of Senior AA teams has consistently hovered around 6–8 teams in the late 1980s and 90s. The Hamilton Golden Hawks, launched in 1980 with their "friendship-first" philosophy, proved to be a winning combination. This group of talented athletes became friends on and off the ice, partying together and sharing their passion for hockey. Winner of five provincial championships and the 1987 world tournament, the Golden Hawks, at one time the "best women's team in the world," folded in 1992–93 because of financial problems, player turnover and the absence of minor hockey development in Hamilton. The Golden Hawks returned to the league in the 1993-94 season with a new manager.

Ambitious organizations such as the North York Aeros (formerly the Toronto Aeros) have taken advantage of the weak leadership within both the OWHA and the COWHL. This organization ushered in a new breed of management and philosophy in women's Senior AA hockey. In 1987 Ken Dufton became the head coach of the Senior AA team, the Toronto Aeros, after a ten-year stint in male hockey. Both Dufton and owner/manager Colin MacKenzie treat the game like a junior male hockey team that is strictly in the business of winning games. The Aeros can be commended for being one of the few Senior AA teams to bring both promotional savvy and financial discipline to the Senior AA league. For example, in the 1990s, the minimum annual cost to ice a Senior AA women's team is about $20,000. The Aeros raise approximately $35,000 by enlisting the aid of seventeen sponsors. Players also help to raise money by attending events for sponsors, including autographing photos for young players. After watching the Aeros in the Eastern US in the early 1990s, a St. Louis coach for a men's Junior B team gushed, "They can skate and shoot as well as any men's Junior A or B players. As a team, their discipline and position play is awesome!"[25] In 1996 the Aeros won their seventh provincial championship, losing the national championship to the Quebec All-Stars in overtime. As well, the Aeros organization holds training and selection camps and aggressively pursues players to continue to build its program. The provincial dominance of the Aeros has forced other Senior AA teams to improve both their team skills and management.

The Aeros' organization, however, is not without its critics. According to Julie Stevens, a former player who has written her master's thesis on women's hockey, "They have forced teams to shut down due to stacking and player tampering." Tampering occurs when a coach persuades a player from another team to join his or her team. Although three thousand senior players compete in Ontario, elite players at the Senior AA level are a rare breed. So rare that in 1992 the Aeros organization established the Junior Aeros to develop players for its senior team. There were so few intermediate teams at the time that the Junior Aeros were forced to play in the Senior AA division initially. Developing the intermediate age category, which languishes at about 600 players, the second-lowest age category in the OWHA, would help to solve the reputed tampering problem. The COWHL is also considering limiting the age at the Senior AA level to eighteen years or over to deter the drafting of Bantam and Midget players to senior teams, which depletes these minor levels.

In the meantime, the proper management of Ontario leagues is hampered by the OWHA's kitchen-table approach to operating. Until 1994 the OWHA had only one paid employee, a development coordinator, despite the fact that the organization represents about 10,000 players, or almost 50 percent of the female hockey players in the country. "We didn't [even] have an accountant for ten years," laments Cathy Lehman, who was the development coordinator from 1989 to 1991.[26] (Lehman is still an OWHA member and is also the founder of the Oshawa Ladies Hockey Association.) While a part-time secretary and a new office have improved the situation somewhat, there is still a reluctance to hire professional staff.

Nonetheless, its financial status has changed dramatically since its 1979 budget of $3,500. Revenue for the eleven months ending May 20, 1995, was more than $500,000. The increase in funds derived from insurance and registration charges from players as well as grants from the Ministry of Culture, Tourism and Industry. However, the new office and staff salary increases noted for the 1995–96 budget were two of the reasons the association was left with a projected deficit.

Although membership has increased dramatically in the 1990s, the OWHA must generate new revenue from a variety of sources, especially sponsorship. The organization had some success with sponsors but only for the first national championship. The OWHA has been unable to find a major sponsor for its provincial championship or any OWHA events. Given the explosive growth of women's hockey in Ontario during the past five years and the province's image as the hockey hot spot in Canada, the lack of sponsorship money is surprising. But the OWHA seems unable to take advantage of marketing opportunities presented to it. For example, in 1993 the Hockey Hall of Fame contacted the OWHA to establish a women's hockey week. The OWHA agreed to this plan. Having a presence at the shrine of professional hockey may have been a good idea, but the event was poorly executed. Within the high-tech, glitzy Hockey Hall of Fame, the OWHA set up the same dull display of outdated photographs and flyers that it features in arena foyers at its tournaments. Not surprisingly, the media's response was lukewarm and attendance at the week's events was poor. In 1994, in an attempt to increase revenue, the OWHA ordered three thousand copies of a thirty-dollar pictorial women's hockey book to use as a fundraiser. Close to two thirds of the stock remained unsold by March 1996. The OWHA's marketing consultant, hired on a contract basis in 1996, seems to have his work cut out for him. One of the problems facing this consultant will be persuading the executive to accept new ideas. "Marketing and public relations should be [the] number one [priority] for the OWHA. We need leadership in that area," insists Cathy Lehman.

Political infighting also has taken its toll. Volunteers are leaving the association because they are frustrated with an executive. Between 1993 and 1995 a vice-president, three regional directors and the registrar left in protest. Kathleen Bevan, who lasted one year as regional director and marketing committee member, had this to say about the OWHA: "As a player and coach I didn't see what went on. There was very rarely an election; usually the executive was acclaimed. There is great reluctance to put your name forward for election because of the bad reputation and great distrust of the executive among the membership."[27]

During the past few years, the friction over both leadership and control of women's hockey within the OWHA has left members feeling wary of the association. Both former and present members of the OWHA are concerned about the organization's future. "There is a reluctance to change," says Bevan. "[The attitude is] 'it worked well before so let's keep doing it.' The intention is there but they don't deliver. Even when a decision is made there are still no changes."

Some members have repeatedly asked the executive to permit nominations from the floor for executive positions, and to limit the number of years a person can hold office. "The OWHA is a closed shop," according to longtime member Georgina Raynor. "People don't feel they have ownership in the OWHA."[28] In 1993 some members believed Fran Rider, who had been president for eleven years, should step down. Unwilling to lose control, the executive (which is sympathetic to Rider) appointed Rider executive director for five years. This appointment was never ratified by the membership and is not part of the constitution, according to Bev Mallory, treasurer of the Hamilton Girls' Hockey Association and former vice-president of development for the OWHA. Details surrounding Rider's appointment remain contentious because few people wish to speak up for fear of being ostracized by the executive. As well, many don't want their organization's dirty laundry aired in public. Furthermore, the president's position is now confusing, since Rider, the new executive director, has many of the powers of the president but no voting privileges. Since 1993 three token presidents have been acclaimed by the executive.

## · ONTARIO: VISION AND UNREST ·

Membership dissatisfaction with the OWHA executive prompted a strategic-planning process, which began in June 1994, but with a consulting group chosen and directed by the executive. Questionnaires concerning values, goals and priorities for the OWHA were sent to more than seven hundred randomly selected managers, coaches and individuals. Six areas emerged as priorities (these areas were once again determined by the executive): communication, marketing, administration, regional responsibilities, role redefinition and gender equity/facility access. Initially the strategic planning generated both excitement and reservations from the members. In the workshop evaluations, members made comments concerning their reluctance to speak openly about problems in the presence of the executive and their misgivings about the ability of the OWHA to execute the new plans.

Ironically, after a year of these workshops, the same old problems were still embarrassingly obvious at the AGM in May 1995. The executive declared that the AGM would run only from 9:00 AM to 1:00 PM, despite members' requests for more time to discuss the numerous issues on the agenda and past complaints that one day was not sufficient for an AGM. The chairperson suggested that any further discussions could take place at workshops that afternoon. Some members noted bitterly that this would mean any business conducted in the workshops would not be part of a formal AGM vote. The subject of new area representatives in the regions generated a heated debate since the executive wanted to appoint the representatives instead of allowing the regions to choose them. Several of the discussions became very acrimonious, with both the executive and members making personal attacks on individuals.

While the OWHA falters in its vision, players in Ontario need a strong organization to manage the rapid growth of the game and address the key issues. Rider herself acknowledges that four universal problems persist: "Ice time, money, credibility and control. The public exposure is absolutely critical," she says. "If there's a girl or a woman in this province or this country that wants to play the game, she should be able to. That's one of our long-term goals."[29]

But to date, the ice-time problem refuses to go away. Many of the arenas across Ontario are owned by cities and municipalities. Women's hockey leagues are tiny fish in large ponds when it comes to competing with male hockey organizations. For example, the Metro Toronto Hockey League, one of seven leagues in Ontario, spent more than $1 million dollars in 1994 for approximately 16,000 games for its 388 male minor hockey teams. In comparison, the entire budget for the OWHA and its seven hundred teams is around $600,000. Finding ice time has become a problem for both sexes, but male hockey players have the precedents, professional staff and financial clout to continue to dominate arena managers. The problem is exacerbated by the fact that men tend to stay in the game longer than women do since they can play in a variety of industrial and recreational leagues. These teams can also afford the expensive prime-time rates for ice. As well, boys' minor hockey accounts for huge amounts of ice time. This is especially true of travelling representative teams, which play many more games and require more ice time than house league teams do. With the high demand of boys and men for ice time, female players find it difficult to make any headway.

So far the most successful way to deal with the problem has been to take public arenas to court. Another approach would be to follow the example of Minnesota, where women's hockey lobbied for a state-authorized ice-time policy that stipulates minimum amounts of time allocated for female hockey. However, Fran Rider contends that in Ontario such a policy would have no clout with the arena managers or their board of directors. So far her approach has consisted of attending meetings with the arena's board of directors to try to persuade them to give more ice time to female hockey teams. Rider's timid approach partially stems from her fear of male hockey. She maintains that the OWHA shouldn't air its grievances publicly or criticize male hockey. Her reluctance is based on her ever-present apprehension that male hockey will ultimately take over female hockey in Ontario. Rider argues that male hockey has a vested interest in controlling the women's game now that women's hockey has shown it is a viable sport. Her fears are not unfounded: at the annual general meeting for the CHA in May 1995, a male hockey organization raised a motion to give two Ontario male hockey branches, Ottawa and Thunder Bay, control over women's hockey in their districts. The motion was defeated when it came to light that a written agreement struck in the early 1980s gives the OWHA control over the female game in Ontario. However, the agreement also states that this will remain in effect "until notice is given by either party to the other at least six months before the date upon which dissolution shall become effective."[30]

The incident is a prime example of the "little sister" status the women's game is accorded. Male organizations have no problem allowing women to manage the female game when its membership and influence are relatively insignificant, but once it becomes a threat to the male game — in this case, a threat to ice time — then previous arrangements can be set aside.

The successful bid for the 1997 world championship has given the OWHA a perfect opportunity to address what Rider considers its other "universal problems": money and credibility. The OWHA is working with two partners, the CHA and the city of Kitchener, to host the 1997 world championship, which is a qualifying tournament for the Olympics. It should attract thousands of people, who will be able to watch teams from China, Europe and the US, and it should also make money for the OWHA and its partners. The women's hockey community is expecting not just a tournament but an international hockey festival: a place to network, to buy female hockey products, or to attend a coaching or refereeing symposium, and to watch a panoply of women's hockey.

Although the world championship should provide the OWHA with more opportunities, some members claim the organization is facing serious problems. "I think within the next five years there will be a blow-up. It will [either] make the OWHA strong, put them out of business or split the province," predicts Joan McCagg, a fourteen-year member.[31]

So far this internal unrest has had some predictable results. A number of member associations, such as the Mississauga Girls' Hockey League, have become so strong that they operate almost independently of the OWHA. They hold their own clinics for coaches and referees, and promote and run their own tournaments. Many discouraged members see the situation where regional associations are operating more independently from the OWHA as the norm, since so many of these associations cannot depend on the provincial organization for consistent advice.

These regional associations have realized that times have changed: the new generation of players requires more professional management from both its leagues and the provincial organization. Fran Rider and the OWHA have been the driving force for the women's game in both Ontario — still the hotbed of women's hockey in Canada — and the world. For the women's hockey community it is critical that a strong and distinct voice be maintained. The community must operate independently from male hockey organizations. But a new vision is needed now, especially as the game heads into the dynamic post-Olympic period. Whether the OWHA will seize the opportunity to share its power with the membership will determine its survival as the game's visionary force. It is time for the world's leading women's hockey organization to welcome the energy and ambition of the next generation.

*Chapter Four*

# RISING IN THE WEST

*"We plan to build girls' ice hockey into one of the greatest ice attractions on earth. One of the 'big' [events] that plays all the big arenas here and elsewhere .... This will take earnest application and organization .... It will take high morale and vitality and determination. We know your girls possess all that .... They are magnificent — fast and skilled and full of teamwork — jet propulsion, no less."*

> — Margaret Williams Parker of Encino, California, to Pearl Wylie, organizer of women's ice hockey in Moose Jaw, Saskatchewan, 9 January 1953, in reference to the formation of a professional women's hockey league in California.

HOCKEY IS AS MUCH A PART of a prairie town as the wheat elevator. For decades it has been one of the few, if not the only, outdoor activities in which people of all ages and from all classes and both sexes can participate. In the West, as in towns across the rest of Canada, hockey is the metaphorical hearth of winter life, kindling community warmth and fervour. It is a way to celebrate winter, rather than to simply survive it.

For decades girls have played alongside boys on the frozen sloughs or town rinks of Western communities. Isolated from one another by an endless expanse of frozen fields, female players have regularly braved bitter winter storms and hours of travel to meet raucously — joyfully — on a patch of ice. They have approached hockey with a hardy, frontier relish, which to this day characterizes their game.

Because the game springs from the small towns, the rural values of cooperation and inclusion are reflected in Western hockey. Female teams here do not possess the star quality of Ontario and Quebec teams; in fact, up until very recently, just a handful of players made it to the ranks of the national team. Rather, Western teams exhibit a collective work ethic not associated with more urbanized regions. Many of these players grew up on farms; they are mentally and physically tough and place more value on working cooperatively than on their individual performances.

After years of merely surviving, albeit with a pioneer verve and defiance, the female game in the West is ascending rapidly. Not only is the number of players rising, but so, too, are the quality and aspiration of these players. The first high performance centre for women's hockey in the world was established in Calgary in 1995, the first female head coach of the women's national team is a product of the West as are several of the highest-ranked players in the country. But as any prairie farmer can tell you, for something to grow so well, the roots must be strong. Thus any account of women's hockey today in Western Canada necessarily begins with the Edmonton Chimos, a team that has endured and inspired for more than a quarter of a century. With their hardy union of prairie grit and flamboyant daring, not only have the Chimos set the standards for women's hockey in the West, but they have also planted the seeds for its recent growth.

The Chimos came together as a team in the fall of 1971 after a local hockey organizer put out a call over an Edmonton radio station for women who were interested in playing hockey. The call netted enough women to form two teams, ranging from ages seventeen to fifty. While most of them had not played hockey since childhood — some couldn't even skate — many had dreamed of being part of a real hockey team. The simple pleasure of slipping on team jerseys and lacing up their hockey skates thrilled them.

The Chimos originally referred to themselves as the "Tuesday night girls' hockey team." In the first season they met only a few times to face off against their competition, "the Sunday night team." After games and practices, the women gathered at a local bar where they clanked their beer mugs together and shouted *Chimo,* an Inuit greeting, which means hello. The cheer evoked the affable spirit of the group and was adopted as the team's name the following year.

What began as an assemblage of eager, if not particularly able, hockey players, rapidly evolved into a team of players with extraordinary determination. Commitment was vital. Although female hockey began to show signs of a renaissance in the early 1970s, public support for the sport was not widespread. This had not always been the case. From the turn of the century until well into the 1930s, female hockey in the West had enjoyed a host of tournaments. Rivalry was especially intense between the Calgary Grills and the Edmonton Rustlers, who both vied for the title of the Western Canadian Championship. The players left husbands and children behind to travel by train to the tournaments, booking several box cars in which they slept and changed for the duration of the championships. Crowds of up to three thousand cheered on the athletes for the more important competitions. With World War II, however, women were shut out of the rinks and encouraged to put any extra energy towards the war effort. The popularity of the game suddenly ceased to expand.

The renewed popularity of female hockey in the 1970s hardly matched that of the 1930s. Indeed, the Chimos encountered no such enthusiasm — not in their early years at any rate, and certainly not in larger centres such as Edmonton. As the team struggled to master basic skills, it did so at rinks in small towns outside the city; these were the only rinks that would allow it ice time. Practices were invariably scheduled during left-over ice time, often from 10:00 PM to midnight. Most of the players accepted that they were playing a male sport and gratefully took what they could get. The last thing the women wanted to do was compound the ridicule or scorn that they encountered when they revealed to acquaintances that they played hockey. As late as 1990, when a Chimos member told a co-worker that as part of the first Team Canada she was going to be on The Sports Network, he scoffed, "Why are they wasting air-time on female hockey?"[1]

Finding a coach who would take the team seriously was also no easy feat. After several years of half-hearted instruction from a variety of coaches, the team welcomed Dave Rehill, who reciprocated the Chimos' devotion to improving themselves. Under Rehill the team honed its skills, pulling together into a tight, well-balanced unit. The Chimos learned to play intelligent hockey, always choosing crafty dekes over body-checking. Team captain Shirley Cameron also helped raise the level of play. Two decades later, she would take on the role of the team's coach. Cameron had grown up in Bonneyville, a town several hours northeast of Edmonton. As a girl in the late 1950s, she had played shinny on a pond with her brothers, but had not been allowed to join an organized boys' team. Like many of the Chimos women, she had never expected to play on a women's team, let alone one that would eventually prove to be so successful. On ice, this tiny woman flew from end to end, digging ferociously in the corners when the puck slid into the defensive zone. "Every time Shirley took a face-off, it was like the last face-off she would ever take," recalls a former opponent. "She wanted to win every little one-on-one battle with you. She would never quit."[2] Cameron took it upon herself to train off-ice as the level of competition rose, feeling fortunate she had the chance to put her skills to use. She set the goals for the team and through her own resolve, drew out commitment in others. If team members had partied late the night before and were lethargic on ice, for instance, Cameron would berate them in the dressing room between periods until their play improved. The players who initially lagged far behind caught up and the even calibre of the team soon became its key strength.

After several years of playing local men's teams, the Chimos branched out into the rural areas in 1975, taking on men's old-timers' teams. In a manner reminiscent of the 1930s, the Chimos travelled around in an old RV gutted and outfitted with seats and a bathroom. On weekends the team set off to play as many as three games in a town. Word spread through rural Alberta about the "ladies' team" and soon the arenas were packed with fans, the most ardent of whom were the local women, who hollered from the stands for the Chimos to

*A proud Western legacy: the Edmonton Chimos, 1978.*
*Shirley Cameron stands on the far left, second row.*

cream their husbands. At the end of the event, a hat was passed around to cover the team's travel costs. The Chimos invariably set off for home exhilarated and exhausted.

The weekend excursions proved invaluable to the evolution of the team. While ignored or ridiculed by urbane Edmontonians, Chimos members were treated as celebrities by rural Albertans. Hockey, after all, had its deepest roots in rural life. While city dwellers are generally viewed as more forward-thinking, people in the small towns far more readily accepted the idea that women could play. The rural support not only enhanced the team's confidence, but also led to more competitive games. By the late 1970s the team had improved to the point of dominating the old-timers' teams. The novelty aspect consequently wore thin and the light-hearted play that had characterized the early matches hardened into tense competition. In one game in the town of Glendon, a Chimos player decked a member of the old-timers' team, who just happened to be the town's mayor. Infuriated, the mayor slugged the player in retaliation as fans booed from the stands. "When we started to win the majority of the games, the men got angry," sums up Cameron. "That's when it stopped being fun."[3]

Lack of sponsorship also detracted from the fun. The costs of equipment, gas, food en route to games and registration could tally as high as $3,000 in the mid-1990s. "Any men's team that has been as dominant as we have I don't think would be scratching for sponsorship," says an agitated Cameron. "They'd have sponsors knocking down their doors to jump on board."[4] As late as 1996 — twenty-five years after the Chimos' launch — the largest donation the team had ever procured was $1,000 from the Cheemo perogy company. It was enough to cover the expense of team hockey bags.

Throughout the 1970s most contact with other female teams took place at tournaments. In 1973 a rival team from Calgary called the Alberta Wild Roses formed and vied with the Chimos for the Alberta and Western championships. The next year the Wild Roses revived the Canadian Western Shield of the 1930s, which attracted sixteen teams from four Western provinces and twelve hundred fans for the final game. The Sweetheart Tournament in North Battleford, Saskatchewan, where female hockey had been extremely popular in the early 1900s, was also launched in the early 1970s. The Sweetheart's appeal was fast, hard, full-body contact hockey, an element that propelled the tournament until 1986, when national rules were passed forbidding bodychecking.

Dozens of female teams from across the West flocked to North Battleford to take part in its February 14 Sweetheart Tournament. Townspeople embraced the event, hosting parties and dances and guaranteeing a packed rink of almost four hundred fiercely pro-Saskatchewan fans. Although the teams were there to play hockey, they hardly shied away from the social aspects of the event. All the women's team members took rooms at the dilapidated Beaver Hotel, crowding the hallway as they waited at the antiquated stand-up register for their keys. A roomy bar downstairs served as the teams' meeting place. There post-game parties carried on until sunrise.

For the Melfort Missilettes, the dominant Saskatchewan women's team, the North Battleford tournament provided a rare opportunity to take on the Chimos, their staunchest competitors, before a partisan crowd. The Missilettes had formed in 1972 in Melfort, a farming community southeast of Prince Albert and a couple of hours' drive from Saskatoon. On ice the Missilettes' moves were basic, consisting of mainly chasing, dumping and forechecking. But the players were passionate about the game and as dedicated as the Chimos. Most of the Missilettes travelled long ribbons of icy prairie road just to make practices. Facilities were primitive: the temperature inside the team's home rink often dropped lower than the temperature outside. The Missilettes wore toques under their helmets and rushed to a heated hut halfway through practices to thaw their frigid feet. The rink, called The Four Seasons, was soon dubbed "The Four Freezins."

Most of the Missilettes' games consisted of encounters within the Western university league — a league that resurfaced in the mid-1970s after an almost thirty-year hiatus. As in the rest of Canada, organized female hockey in the West was played first at universities. The University of Saskatoon iced its inaugural women's team in 1913. The team competed both in a city league and in the Western Inter-Varsity Athletic Union until the league shut down during World War II, when the armed forces took over the rinks.[5] The university league revived in the mid-1970s with the University of Saskatchewan team, the Huskiettes (later the Huskies), facing off against other Western teams in tournaments held at the universities of Manitoba, Calgary, Minnesota and British Columbia, and at their own tournament, the Labatt Cup. The Huskiettes, like the other teams, received no funding from their university, and wore uniforms handed down to their players from the men's team.

While the university league provided some tournaments, no club league existed in Saskatchewan until 1982. In search of further challenges, the Missilettes would often drive to Winnipeg or Calgary, leaving at 5:00 PM on a Friday and arriving at dawn on Saturday. They would play all day and then turn around to go home. Because of the lack of funding or support from the provincial amateur hockey association, the Missilettes folded in 1979, only to be reactivated in 1982 under the name of the Maidstone Saskies. The next year the Saskies went on to represent the province in the national championship for the first of eight consecutive times.

In 1987 the Saskies even managed to compete against Finland and Sweden. To get to Scandinavia, members signed personal guarantees for a sum total of $26,000 and held bingo fundraisers for two years after the tournament to pay off the loan. They could hardly afford ice time at home and would often practise late into the night on a frozen lake in Bud Miller Park in Saskatoon. Coach Bill Thon, a stern man who demanded discipline, oversaw the outdoor practices. "It'd be ten o'clock at night and Bill would have us just skate and skate and skate. We thought of ourselves as Rocky," recalls former Saskie Cindy Simon with a chuckle. "We'd always wonder what the teams in Ontario are doing right now. And certainly the Chimos weren't outdoors!"[6] Occasionally the Saskies managed to get some ice time in "an ugly little arena" in a town call Hillmont. Driving home late one night in freezing cold weather, Simon's car broke down. She and a teammate pulled their gear out of their hockey bags and put it on to keep warm. They trudged through the snow towards the nearest farmhouse — hockey sticks in hand to protect them from any dogs. When they finally arrived, the farmer refused to open the door because he was afraid. His wife at last let them in and served them cups of hot chocolate while her husband went out to fix their car. In the end the cost of playing and travelling to games made it impossible for the Saskies to continue. The team disbanded in 1990, leaving a legacy of physical and mental toughness.

One team that did not struggle to exist from year to year, at least initially, was the Canadian Polish Athletic Club (CPAC) team from Manitoba. Although CPAC never matched the talent and fame of the Chimos, it set the pace of hockey in the province's five- or six-team women's senior league. The team was spawned in the north end of Winnipeg at the St. James Bord-Aire community club in the early 1970s. While other teams in the West grappled with financial worries, the Polish club raised funds through bingo games to pay for the CPAC's equipment, ice time and travel costs. At the end of each year, the club even threw a banquet for the team. As former team member Sandy Rice, now in her thirties, comments, "You just thought, 'Wow! This is what it would be like playing in the big time.' You just had to sign your name at registration and never worry about money." [7]

Many of its members were in their early teens, the core of the group formed by the three Sobkewich sisters and a then thirteen-year-old Rice. Dawn McGuire, who would later become the prominent defence for both the Chimos and Team Canada, also played on CPAC in the mid-1970s. McGuire grew up north of Winnipeg. She participated on boys' teams until she was thirteen. A this point a coach barred her from the local team because she was a girl. Determined to continue, McGuire commuted forty minutes to Winnipeg, where she participated in the thriving girls' league composed of almost seventy teams. Most of the games were held outdoors, the wind blanketing the ice with snow. The temperature often dipped so low that after certain games McGuire and teammates had to roll jam jars filled with hot water over their frozen feet as they wept from the cold.

CPAC took part in the Winnipeg Women's Hockey League and played a thirty-game schedule against the Panthers, Angels, North Ends, and its fiercest rivals, the Rebels. The team also competed in the Sweetheart and Western Shield tournaments, as well as the Mid-Canada Tournament hosted by Manitoba, which ran from 1975 to 1981. With their youthful devotion to the game, CPAC members were provincial champions until the team folded in 1987, a victim of the declining numbers in girls' hockey and the Polish Club's decision to sponsor boys' minor hockey.

By the late 1970s the Chimos, too, teetered on the verge of extinction. The team so overwhelmed its opponents — by as many as twenty goals a game — that all the other teams were placed in the B division. As the lone entry in the A division of the Northern Alberta Ladies Hockey League, the team became a virtual outcast in the league. Its members were now separated from the very thing they had sought when they joined the team: competition with other women.

In 1978 the Chimos turned to the east in search of higher stakes, the first to do so. By combining their savings and making up the rest through bingo games, raffles and dances, the players gathered enough money to fly to Wallaceburg, in Southern Ontario. It was a brave move given the trepidation the team felt towards its Eastern counterparts. Most of the Chimos had grown up in small farming communities and felt intimidated not only by Ontario's bravado but also by the big-city sophistication — some would say arrogance — of its players. But the Chimos surprised themselves and everyone else by placing first in the competition. Although the players lacked the flashy moves of the Ontarians, they worked harder, passed more skilfully and performed more cohesively as a team. In short, their emphasis on cooperation and inclusiveness — values that stemmed from their rural background — ultimately paid off.

If the contact with the East did much to boost the morale of the Chimos, the first national championship held in Ontario in 1982 saved the team. The new level of competition supplied an invigorating challenge to the other Western teams as well. It also indirectly transformed the Western Shield into a B championship and maintained a high-level tournament for the teams that did not win the provincial championship. While the winning A team from each Western province proceeded to the national championship, second-place teams carried on to the Western Shield to face off against the winner of the B league. A Midget division was added soon afterwards, further expanding the event's scope.

The 1970s and early 1980s also saw a substantial growth in girls' minor hockey, much of which took place in rural areas. "Every small town had a team of girls in the 1970s," remembers

Lila Quinton of the Saskatchewan Amateur Hockey Association (SAHA). "Even the town of three hundred where I grew up [in rural Saskatchewan] had a girls' team. It was a lot more acceptable than it is now. Our parents didn't worry as much if it was womanly or not, and we never had the hassles that I've had as a senior player [with men] putting us in our place verbally if we did good against their team."[8]

By the mid-1980s, however, the numbers began to decline. The drop in registration reflected a growing awareness of the violence in the male game, more than the existence of problems in the female game. A federal investigation into violence in hockey was launched, and soon hundreds of teams disappeared across the country as parents pulled their children out of the game. Coinciding with the protest against the violence in hockey was the introduction of ringette, a relatively new low-contact game touted as the "feminine alternative" to hockey. Droves of girls traded in pucks for rings. Behind the defection lay the wishes of the parents. Many wanted their daughters to play a safer, more acceptable game, as well as one that did not compete directly with the boys' game. "It has often been the parents who are livid about girls playing hockey," says Sandy Johnson, a prominent coach in Saskatchewan. "They'd say, 'They're taking the place of somebody's boy. If she wasn't playing, my boy would be. Go play ringette, that's a girl's sport.'"[9]

In 1990 the lull in female hockey abruptly ceased with the first official world championship whose final game flickered across a million and a half TV screens. Four of Team Canada's members were from the West. Of these women, the three who were or had been on the Chimos shone in the media: thirty-seven-year-old Shirley Cameron was lauded as the oldest player; as the sister of the New York Islander Gerald Diduck, Judy Diduck was closely observed; and Dawn McGuire was celebrated as Team Canada's most valuable defence player in the championship. In 1992 the announcement that women's hockey would at last be included in the Olympics only enhanced the game's visibility.

These events had profound repercussions for female hockey in the West. Numbers suddenly ballooned. By 1995 more than fifty senior women's teams were competing in Alberta alone. Just as significantly, however, the players began to perceive themselves differently. No longer were they in the game simply for friendship and fun: they were also in it to win.

This shift in attitude has been considerable and is manifested in players' approach to nutrition, off-ice training and mental preparation before games. The rowdy partying that often followed games in the late 1980s has given way to tame outings that wrap up by 10:00 PM. The family atmosphere with its inherent requirements of group sacrifice and devotion — the linchpin of the Chimos' success — has steadily dissipated. "In the 1970s and early 1980s, you structured your life around hockey and made sacrifices and that was that," explains Cameron, who now coaches the Chimos. "But now it's very hard to sell the younger players the idea of team commitment."[10] The younger players are instead focussing on personal goals. In doing so they are raising both the athletic calibre and the stakes of women's hockey.

It is no coincidence that at a time when the nature of the game and its players are transforming, national level coach Shannon Lee Miller has emerged as a powerful presence both in the West and nationally. As assistant coach Miller helped guide the Alberta team to victory in the first Canada Winter Games, which were held in 1991. After acting as assistant coach for Team Canada during the 1992 and 1994 world championships, Miller became the first female head coach of the national team. Also, in 1995, she led an inexperienced Calgary senior team to victory against the unbeaten provincial champions, the Chimos, and then helped the same team win third place at the national championship.

Miller is a short woman with jet-black hair and calm, penetrating blue eyes. She drives a sleek sports car that reflects her own high energy level. As a coach Miller projects composed authority and is most frequently described by players as intense and intimidating. "Sometimes it's just the look she gives you," says player Hayley Wickenheiser, blushing and laughing. "She sure speaks her mind!"[11]

It's a description that both puzzles and pleases Miller. "I hear all the time that players think I'm intimidating, and on the one hand I don't understand it because I go out of my way to be approachable," muses Miller. "But I think part of it is that women aren't used to coaches taking them seriously, even if a coach is excellent. It somehow comes out that male coaches don't expect quite as much from the female athletes [as they would from male athletes]."[12] Heather Ginzel, a former national team member, puts it this way: "It's a trust thing. You know, we grow up thinking that men know more about hockey, which is true because they have more opportunity. But when Miller was coach, you'd get off rink and she'd make you feel so good."[13]

Miller demands the utmost from her players, an attitude that stems from her own upbringing. Born in 1963, Miller grew up in the farming town of Melfort, Saskatchewan, the daughter of a high-school gym teacher. When Shannon was a girl, her father would take her to the park where he coached football and would encourage her to play alongside the boys. "In his opinion there wasn't a difference between a little girl and a little boy," says Miller of her father. "He never made me feel like there wasn't anything I could do. Even today, I feel I can do anything."[14] While still in grade school, Miller spent her time after school training with the high school track and field team, which her father also coached.

At a provincial track meet when Miller was in Grade Seven, her father cautioned her to keep her eyes focussed forward on the curves or she would lose her lead. During the race Miller looked back — and was passed. As father and daughter walked from the track towards their car, Miller's father placed his hand around her shoulder and asked, "Well, so why do you think you're holding the silver medal?"

"'Cause I looked over my shoulder," replied Miller, sheepishly.

Her father simply let out a gentle laugh. "He was demanding," recalls Miller, "but always supportive and positive."[15] It would be the last time Miller was to be coached by her father; the next year he died of cancer.

At seventeen, Miller left Melfort to attend the University of Saskatchewan, where she coached and played on its club team and then played for the Saskies. Five years later she moved to Calgary, where she trained to become a police officer. In motivating players, Miller employs the most valuable skill that she acquired from crisis situations in policing: timing. "Everything in life is timing," she declares. "When you speak, when you learn to listen, when you take action."[16] Miller is highly proficient at the technical side of coaching, but her real forte is motivating players, a skill that relies on this sense of timing. "She'll give people a chance," explains one player, "but if you cross the line and screw up, you're in trouble."[17]

In many ways, timing has been on Miller's side. Sent by the Alberta Amateur Hockey Association (AAHA) to assess the first women's world competition in 1990, Miller witnessed a talented Team Canada, one that she knew immediately she would like to coach one day. The championship motivated her to improve her coaching skills, or as she puts it, "to set goals and dream a bit."[18] Miller soon realized that it was within her reach to coach the national team. She offered her services on a volunteer basis and passed up many opportunities to advance within the police force in order to dedicate herself to hockey. The police force encouraged her to write a set of exams that would enable her to become a sergeant or detective and eventually fulfill her dream of working undercover. Instead, she opted to invest even more time into hockey schools across the West. She also made a commitment to continue developing Calgary's freshly launched girls' team. Miller had put the city's only female Peewee team together in the 1988–1989 season. She remembers the team's first game, in which it lost 19–0, as the most fun game she has ever coached. "Some of the girls could hardly skate three steps without falling over," Miller recalls, grinning and shaking her head. "After the game, mothers were taking pictures and coming up to me crying with joy."[19]

Miller invested two years of long hours to establish the team. The Calgary Minor Hockey Association initially resisted the idea of a girls' Peewee team. It refused to help finance the team or give it ice time, although it provided these services to boys' teams. The association endorsed the idea of girls' hockey once the team was set up, only then permitting it to take part in the boys' league.

It was through this team that in 1990 Miller met twelve-year-old Hayley Wickenheiser. A small, wildly aggressive player who had just moved to the city from Shaunavon, Saskatchewan, Wickenheiser had skated since she could walk. She showed finesse with the puck and an ability to anticipate plays that was beyond her years. She was also a firecracker on ice, explosive and greedy with the puck. Accustomed to playing with boys only, Wickenheiser felt frustrated by the level of this new girls' team. After shifts she would smack her stick against the boards and swear, angry that a teammate had missed a pass or failed to score. Miller, who herself had been a testy player in her youth — once, she had removed her glove on mid-ice to give the crowd the finger because it had cheered after she had been hit and knocked out — kept Wickenheiser on the bench when she needed to cool down. When Wickenheiser played for Team Canada in the 1994 world championship, her temper again flared up. Although bodychecking was officially banned, Wickenheiser got slammed into the boards. From the ice she hollered at Miller, "I thought there was no fucking bodychecking!" "Apparently there is," Miller laughed, "so go out and hit somebody."[20]

While Wickenheiser's temper at times has detracted from her ability on ice, off ice she is impressively mature and focussed. At school she receives high grades and at home she is precociously independent. "You never have to get on her and say, 'Let's go, work hard,'" says her father, Tom. "She works at a top level all the time."[21] Wickenheiser's drive, however, concerns her mother, Marilyn, who thinks her daughter is growing up too fast. Tom worries about this, too. "It's been a lot harder on her being isolated as the only girl [on boys' teams]," he explains. "She missed out on a lot of socializing and that was tough. She'd have to get changed in the skate sharpening room or the bathroom or some place. She was never really with the team except on the ice."[22] Tom Wickenheiser's fondest memory of Hayley is connected to a scrimmage in Shaunavon. The town had rounded up a team to play against a team from Medicine Hat. "Hayley played in net by third period because after scoring goal after easy goal, I realized we couldn't let her skate," recalls Tom. "I told the guy from the other team that I'd move her back into goal, but she had fun. It was light and there was no pressure and it was good for her."[23]

In her Calgary home, Wickenheiser inhabits a basement bedroom that she chose for its privacy and autonomy. Its walls are checkered with posters of legendary hockey players and motivational messages handwritten on cue cards. "Focus awareness! Be mindful in tough situations," "Fake it!" "Energize! Pump!" "Intimidate and Annihilate!" "I have made the choice to be positive," the slogans exclaim. Similar messages are found scribbled in the margins of Wickenheiser's journal: "Relax!" "Explode!" "Focus!" "Bang!" "Snap!"

After two years with Miller's Peewee team, Wickenheiser switched to an elite AAA boys' Bantam team. Now that she had turned fifteen she wanted the challenge of full-contact hockey, which came with the boys' league. Wickenheiser was no longer the petite player who darted frenetically between her opponents: she was growing into a towering, broad-shouldered woman — she would be 5 ft. 9 in. (174 cm) 170 lbs. (75 kg) by 1996 — who could return the toughest bodycheck. In 1993, the year in which Wickenheiser returned to the boys' league, she received an invitation to try out for the Canadian national women's team. After some hesitation about her age — at fifteen she would be the youngest player to make the team — Canadian Hockey Association officials decided she was too talented a player to pass up. In winter 1994 Wickenheiser joined Team Canada in Lake Placid for the third world championship and brought home her first gold medal.

The next season Wickenheiser returned to Miller's female team after being cut from an AAA Midget boys' team. When she received the news that she had not made the team, she was bitterly disappointed. In her diary she wrote:

> Today was the last game of try-outs. They posted the list of the forty-five guys that would continue on from this camp. My name wasn't on it!! I got shafted big time! Politics sucks! I shouldn't have been so naive. I should have expected this. No matter how good I played, the coaches couldn't pick a first-year sixteen-year-old GIRL! There were guys that were picked that I surpassed last year. I trained all summer and was in better shape than most guys there![24]

Once she returned to Miller's team, however, Wickenheiser became a role model for other young women in the sport. "Hayley has been a very long project," says Miller. "It's been like taming a wild horse."[25] During games Wickenheiser is now less selfish with the puck; during practices she will team

*Hayley Wickenheiser, now one of the top players in Canada,*
*takes instruction from coach Shannon Miller.*

up with weaker players, pointing out improvements they can
make. Now that she has crossed over into the world of
women's hockey, she is less wrapped up in her performance.
The intensity that Wickenheiser feels for hockey is no longer
manifested in childish outbursts. Instead, it is poured back

into the game. Under the guidance of Miller, and others, Wickenheiser has sharpened her game. At the national team selection camp in the fall of 1995, she was ranked as the top forward in the country. Still in her teens, she is an imposing presence in the game of women's hockey.

A surprising turn of events has also offered Wickenheiser the training that she hoped she would get with the top Midget boys' team. In September 1995 Shannon Miller left her policing job to become a full-time coach in the first-ever high-performance female hockey program at Calgary's Olympic Oval. There Miller provides an intensive training program to Wickenheiser and five other high-performance female players, as well as eighteen Midget-aged girls. Not only does the program provide an unprecedented opportunity for both the players and Miller — who is the first full-time paid female hockey coach in the country — but it also indicates just how pivotal Alberta has become to women's hockey. Numerous players from the Olympic pool are planning to move temporarily to Calgary to train under Miller, who will also most likely be appointed as head coach of the Olympic team.

The elite program for female players in Calgary is only one of the West's success stories. Girls' minor hockey has developed rapidly in other parts of Alberta and the West since 1990. Albertan female leagues have tripled in size since the late 1980s. In 1995 there were more than 2,200 senior and minor female players. In the same year fourteen teams attended the Midget provincial championship, up from three the year before. In Edmonton nine girls' teams compete within the city's minor league and seven female Midget teams have formed their own league.

The growth is in part due to the inclusion of female hockey in the Olympics. Its effects reverberate throughout minor and senior hockey leagues across the country: a new legitimacy has been cast on the sport, replete with some of the dreams and aspirations of male hockey. But in the case of Alberta, other factors have come into play as well. In 1992 the women's national championship was held in Edmonton, exposing many girls and their parents to the female game for the first time. Following the championship, a Fun Day was held. Any girl who wished to play hockey was invited to do so. Five hundred girls showed up, and organizers were obliged to book ice time to accommodate the numbers. The inclusion of girls' hockey in the semi-annual Alberta Winter Games in 1994 and in the Canada Winter Games in 1991 also opened the doors for girls. The training programs for the games helped Alberta Hockey track its promising players. Moreover, it allowed girls to play with their peers; in smaller communities the only option available is to play with boys' or senior women's teams.

The unpaid work of women such as Judy Colpitts, the CHA Female Council representative for Alberta from 1991 to 1994, and Melody Davidson and Marilyn Wickenheiser, the past and present girls' minor hockey representatives, has provided the impetus for these events. Davidson, in particular, has made a significant contribution: she has coached, held clinics, written manuals, run jamborees and served as a well-respected spokesperson for the sport. "Everything comes down to leadership," Davidson says of the recent growth. "Ten years ago, senior [hockey] women were not involved. Then they started to see that their teams couldn't survive without minor leagues. That's when things started to take off."[26] Now senior players, including many current and former Chimos members, act as coaches, referees, administrators and instructors at summer hockey camps. With younger girls playing again, parents have become more involved, increasing the momentum of expansion.

Since girls' minor hockey took off in the early 1990s, the minor system in Saskatchewan has emerged as one of the strongest in Western Canada. Most of Saskatchewan's inhabitants have grown up in small towns or on farms and despite long distances between these communities — some girls play on teams that are based up to one hundred kilometres from their home — a love of the game at the grassroots level has persisted, ensuring its survival. "We don't get mass population," explains the female hockey representative for the province, Lila Quinton, "but we do get ones who are dedicated and driven. The girls are very good because they want to play, not because parents push them."[27]

Currently, more than six hundred girls are registered with the Saskatchewan Amateur Hockey Association (SAHA), most of whom play on girls' teams. Including girls who belong to recreational leagues, there are now almost eight hundred female players, whereas during the mid-1980s there were only one hundred. In the province's biggest city, Regina, the women's division of the Queen's City Hockey League included twenty teams in 1995, an increase from two teams in 1991.

While the popularity of ringette helped produce a ten-year gap in the development of girls' hockey in the 1980s, since 1990, ringette has begun to serve as a training ground for girls who later go on to play hockey. In the mid-1990s, for example, entire ringette associations in North Battleford and Swift Current switched to girls' hockey. But as in Alberta, the development program for the 1991 Canada Winter Games, called Sask First in this province, has proven to be the main attraction for new members. Saskatchewan has done well at the Games, taking home the silver medal in 1995. The rising number of female players reflects the program's success, reports Games coach Sandy Johnson, because its development camps offer girls from six to sixteen a much-wanted chance to play against each other.

The Sask First program notwithstanding, the SAHA has generally ignored the female game. Lila Quinton, the chair of the association's Female Division and the Female Council representative for the CHA since 1992, has fought hard to make her voice heard at meetings over the years. Quinton is equally critical of both organizations for their failure to support female growth at the grassroots level. "The CHA is very elite driven," says Quinton. "All its energy and money seems to be going to the elite program. The cream always rises to top, but you need to look at the milk: it's the milk that supports the cream." Indeed, this province of only a million people has fostered its share of outstanding female hockey players and coaches in the country. These include Shannon Miller and Olympic team contenders Hayley Wickenheiser, Carol Scheibel, Fiona Smith and Kelly Bouchard. Ironically, however, Saskatchewan's senior female leagues are among the weakest in the country. Most talented players head to Alberta in their late teens, where the level of competition and training is far higher.

Within Saskatchewan the central obstacle remains locating the myriad girls who play on boys' teams. The SAHA has compiled lists of these female players in the Sask First program, but refuses to give them to anyone outside the organization. Consequently communities who wish to start a girls' team have found it difficult to locate players in the surrounding area. Furthermore, rural boys' teams are now urging girls to join their teams in order to boost their shrinking rosters. "It's going to be a fight in rural Saskatchewan," says Quinton. "The population is going down and the boys are going to want these girls to go make their teams [to help keep them afloat]. But our numbers are so low that we [female hockey] need them." To ensure that girls do not end up playing only on boys' teams, Quinton managed to pass a rule in 1995 that bars girls from joining boys' teams unless they register with a girls' team first, provided there is one in the area in which they live. The rule has caused some confusion, and promoters of the female game such as Sandy Johnson think it may put too much pressure on youngsters. "I understand it's to build numbers," says Johnson, "but you're forcing the girls to do something they're not making a decision on. Many of these kids live in rural centres where they drive forty-five minutes in the winter when it's blowing and snowing to play a game."[28] Quinton, however, insists the rule is the only way to guarantee that female hockey will continue to thrive in the province.

Next door in Manitoba, twelve hundred girls registered on approximately fifty female teams in 1994–95. Only two years earlier, as few as five hundred girls had played hockey. These figures do not include the number of girls on boys' teams: as is the case across the country, this number is unknown because provincial associations do not keep track of these girls. Manitoba included female hockey in its provincial Winter Games for the first time in 1990 and this event, combined with the Canada Winter Games program, led to the resurgence of the game. Bev Drobot, the representative for female hockey in the province, predicts the female game will continue to grow as girls' ringette teams in smaller towns switch over to hockey. In rural Manitoba, the first female hockey league was formed in 1995–96, partly in response to the rapidly spreading interest in the game, partly in reaction to the discrimination many of the girls' teams faced in boys' leagues. "It just didn't work out with girls' teams playing boys'[teams]," says Cathy Allen, an organizer of rural girls' hockey in southern Manitoba. "When the girls showed any aggression on ice, it was taken the wrong way. It seemed like it was O.K. for the boys to go after pucks aggressively, but girls couldn't. The better girls were singled out by the players, parents and coaches of the boys' teams and were called all sorts of names — 'bitch' was a favourite. That's the main reason we formed the female league."[29] Another reason why Allen formed a separate girls' league was that the mixed minor leagues continually cancelled the girls' ice time if a senior men's team needed the rink for a tournament — a practice Allen says is not unique to her area.

Although advocates of the female game are pleased that

the sport has grown in Manitoba, they worry that its roots are not strong enough. "The system is still fairly fragile," explains Bev Drobot, "because we just don't have the volunteer base yet. When I was watching the girls' Provincials, [I noticed] all the coaches have a daughter on their teams. I wonder what will happen when the girls leave. Will the coaches leave, too?"[30] This dearth of volunteers outside players' immediate families threatens the game's future. While the provincial amateur hockey association, now called Hockey Manitoba, has paid for skills clinics for girls, female organizers find they can only offer five or six clinics a year because there are so few people to help run the clinics. Most of those who do contribute to girls' hockey are women playing on senior teams. Their time is already stretched thin.

Nonetheless, Manitoba has managed to produce a stable, if somewhat mediocre, senior league. Eleven teams play in the Winnipeg senior league. Two are classified as A teams: the University of Manitoba's Lady Bison Team and the Sweat Camp Storm of Winnipeg, the 1995–96 provincial champions. The rest are B teams. Manitoba has so far produced only one national team member (excluding Dawn McGuire, who was playing for the Chimos by 1979): Susana Yuen. Yuen played on the national team in 1990 and now manages the Lady Bison team. Currently, the only contender for Team Canada is Tracy Luhowy, who is now training with Shannon Miller in Calgary.

The situation could well change within the next five years thanks to the unexpected burst of female hockey on Native reserves in northern Manitoba. Without any tradition of organized female hockey, Cree communities such as Norway House and Cross Lake have fostered a thriving recreational league of girls' and women's teams. Located at the junction of several water routes 30 km (20 miles) north of Great Winnipeg Lake and over 500 km (300 miles) north of Winnipeg,

Norway House was a hub of the Hudson's Bay Trading Company fur-trade and supply lines in the early 1800s. It is now an Indian reserve with a population of five thousand. Since the time in 1991 when two young girls on the reserve expressed an interest in playing hockey, the community has spawned a Midget, Peewee and five senior female teams. Teams now practise up to four times a week on one of the reserve's two ice rinks, an almost unheard-of luxury for female hockey players. The top players from the five women's teams in Norway House also play on a senior all-star team. The team travels in the northern region, playing the ten other Cree teams from Cross Lake, Opasquiak Cree Nation (The Pas), Grand Rapids, Easterville, Split Lake and Pine Creek. Another Native team from Prince Albert in northern Saskatchewan hosts a tournament in early April, but so far the Manitoba teams have been unable to attend the tournament because it is too risky to cross the Nelson River East Channel, which may be partially thawed by that late in the spring. Due to distance and the prohibitive cost of travel, only the Midget team has ventured south to tournaments. That team most recently won the Borden Female Midget Hockey Tournament in March 1996, in which ten teams participated. The Norway House coach and organizer, Eric Halcrow, plans to put together an all-Native all-star minor hockey team to compete in the next Manitoba Winter Games. He and Jim Leary, another man who has been instrumental in the development of the female teams, say that given the drive and dedication of many of the twelve year olds, they would not be surprised if a Cree team soon represents Manitoba in the national championship. While both men are ambitious for the teams, they make their priorities clear. "We made a conscious decision to develop our kids as opposed to setting up a regional team and taking only five here and the rest from elsewhere because only those five will get us the title," says Jim Leary, whose daughter Jaymie now plays at the University of

Manitoba. "Female hockey is very closely tied to community development. Everyone involved is either friends or relatives. It's an investment in our kids."[31]

In other Native communities in the Northwest Territories, the first-ever championship for women of the Northwest Territories took place in March 1991. Seven teams met at an arena in Rankin Inlet to vie for the region's title. The arena was not equipped with the amenities that arenas in the rest of the country have. It did not have an ice-clearing machine, and before they could skate, the women swept down the ice grasping ends of plywood to clear off the snow. Most of the players had small children, whom they brought to the tournament.[32]

While geography binds British Columbia to the other Western provinces, BC's mild winters and laid-back culture mean female hockey holds nowhere near the significance it holds for its closest neighbours. Not only does the warmer climate mean that a host of sports is available to the population year-round, but the mountainous terrain and ferry crossings make teams think twice about travelling to tournaments in other areas. To drive from Prince George to the lower mainland, for example, takes twelve hours; to travel by ferry between the province's two major cities, Vancouver and Victoria, costs about $40. As a result, many of the female teams are restricted to playing in small pods and experience little exposure to other teams in the province. Furthermore, the province suffers from a shortage of public rinks. Private rinks, which were built to exploit this shortage, charge as much as $200 an hour. This represents a rise in price of more than 50 percent since the early 1990s. Families who are worried about securing a place for their sons on the local hockey team (this is still many parents' main priority with regard to hockey) have begun putting their boys on waiting lists when they are as young as age two. More often than not, women's and girls' teams end up taking whatever practice time is left over.

Karen Wallace, the current director of the CHA Female Council and a former director of the British Columbia Amateur Hockey Association (BCAHA) has focussed most of her energy on building the female sport from the bottom up. She believes in promoting the sport at the grassroots level in order to ensure the future of female hockey, and also to give girls the sporting opportunities they are not getting elsewhere. "When hockey started growing, the expense went up," says Wallace. "At the same time, [subsidized] school sports programs were being wiped out and this especially affected girls. If you weren't there pushing to get your daughter in hockey, she wasn't going to be there."[33]

Currently almost two thousand girls and women play hockey in this province which has a population of over three and a half million. Sixty-five percent of the female players are under eighteen. Since the early 1990s, the thirty-six Lower Mainland League girls' teams have been facing off against each other. Other Peewee and Midget teams have also sprung up in Kamloops, Fernie, Cranbrook, Prince George, Victoria and other Vancouver Island communities, although these teams play against boys.

While the numbers appear encouraging, BC has consistently lacked senior players who are committed to developing younger players. Few senior women have shared their skills with the girls who are moving up the ranks. However, there are a few exceptions. Both Christine Gardner, a Midget coach and winner of the CHA volunteer award in 1991, and Becki Bookham, BCAHA female hockey representative from 1990 to 1994, have helped younger players. While more senior women have coached younger teams since 1993, the relatively low involvement of older players attests to a lack of tradition of the kind the Chimos have brought to Alberta. The fact that BC was not represented on the national team until the 1995 Pacific Rim tournament reflects this lack of tradition of older players bringing along younger ones. The senior system in BC has also suffered the same affliction that hindered Quebec's league for many years: players have shown more interest in playing for the team that has the most promise of representing the province than in building up a solid league. Each new season has been characterized by a scramble to join the best team, which has in turn led to a disabling imbalance within the league, with the same few teams going to the national championship each year. In 1995–96, one team finally laid tampering charges against a coach in an attempt to end the team hopping. The BCAHA suspended this coach for six weeks for allowing players to participate in his try-outs without the properly signed CHA registration cards from their previous team. This action sent a message to coaches and players that ignoring the regulations designed to curb team-switching would no longer be tolerated.

The BCAHA has only recently begun to fund the girls' game, sponsoring leadership and officiating programs. As all representatives for the female sport will contend, it has been a long struggle to get provincial associations to commit any funds to the female game. Bill Ennos, the technical director for the association, says it would be impossible to cite the exact amount of money that goes towards developing the female game because some girls participate in the association's mainly male programs. His answer echoes those by representatives from other provincial associations across the country, most of whom refuse to release any figures that pertain to female hockey. Indeed, even most representatives of female hockey are not privy to their associations' budget. Ennos does say, however, that the overall budget at BCAHA for development is more than $600,000 and that some of that money is put towards female development. "Our philosophy is that membership is membership," he maintains. "All our clinics are open to anyone and we really don't discriminate against male or females. But we certainly promote the female game more than the male game."[34]

While Becki Bookham acknowledges that clinics are open to women, she nonetheless contends that the BCAHA is not spending enough money or time on female hockey. "Right now, there are not enough players simply because not a lot of money is spent on finding them and promoting their participation,"[35] says Bookham. Johnny Misley, project coordinator for the BCAHA and a supporter of female hockey, defends the amount of money going towards its development, although he, too, says he cannot say how much money the BCAHA allots for the female game. "We do things to promote it [female hockey] and develop it, no question," asserts Misley. As proof he points to the annual female hockey brochures and posters the association prints to promote the sport as well as the three female hockey seminars it has sponsored in the last five years. "But to put more money into it means we have to cut elsewhere and we're already on a shoe-string budget and our funding's getting axed more every year. To fund the girls' program more might mean pulling out a special program on the boys' side."[36] The same remark is repeated across the country: promoting the girls' game takes directly away from the boys.

In 1990 the BCAHA initiated the province's first-ever female development program, which runs every four years in conjunction with the Canada Winter Games. As in other provinces, the program has helped train and track athletes between the ages of thirteen and seventeen. The inclusion of girls' hockey in the Games has certainly made girls feel that they are taken more seriously as hockey players. However, they still do not receive many of the perks the boys are given. For example, the boys competing in the Games benefit from an annual elite program called Best Ever. Their expenses are paid by the association and their equipment is provided by the program's sponsor, CCM. A comparable program does not exist for their female counterparts.

The one girls' program in the province that does enjoy sponsorship is the annual Dairyland Sportsmanship Jamborees. Eight- to thirteen-year-old girls partake in these yearly tournaments. Since the program's first year in 1992, the number of participants in two of its events has risen from 137 to 300 in 1996.[37] The Jamborees, which are sponsored by Dairyland milk producers to encourage clean play, functioned as a boys-only program for years. Players register individually — teams are not permitted to enter — and points are awarded to individuals for incurring no penalties as well as for scoring. Most importantly for the girls, the Jamborees provide them with the rare opportunity to play against other girls. During the regular hockey season, most of the participants compete against boys' teams, or in the case of those who live in rural areas, on boys' teams.

Also growing in popularity is British Columbia's first female hockey school. Director Becki Bookham, the former BCAHA director for female hockey, launched the camp in Summerland in 1993 with two other women, Linda Fedje and Nancy Wilson. The camps offer women the chance to act as role models for girls and to develop their coaching skills, allowing girls who have felt ignored or not taken seriously at boys' camps to improve their ability on ice.

As hockey camps and teams for girls and women proliferate across the West, it is important to recall that what has made the future so promising is the legacy of the past. Teams such as the Chimos planted the firm roots of Western women's hockey, and their legacy has ensured its growth. For years teams such as the Chimos persevered with little or no support. Provincial hockey associations have been slow, painstakingly so in most cases, to back the female game. To this day, these associations' attitude to the female sport remains highly ambivalent. But their resistance has not deterred the myriad female teams in the

West. For perhaps more so than in any other Canadian region, hockey has not been just a recreational option here, but a way of life — an integral part of every prairie town.

So the small-town and big-city hockey leagues continue to survive and, with the hope the Olympics inclusion has injected into the female game, to grow. But even as female players become more numerous in the West and in the rest of the country it is important to recall the past. The fact that so many of the women who promote the game sprang from teams such as the Chimos and its rivals attests to the historic importance of this province in the development of the game. So, too, does the fact that Shannon Miller and Hayley Wickenheiser pursue their hockey careers here. And so, finally, does the fact that the first female high-performance program in the country has been established in Calgary. Female hockey is taken seriously here, more seriously it would seem, than it is by its reputed promoter, the Canadian Hockey Association. One thing is clear: female hockey is indeed rising in the West, and in renegade Western tradition, it's not waiting around for the rest of the country to approve.

*Chapter Five*

# QUEBEC AND ATLANTIC CANADA: PASSION AND SURVIVAL

INSPIRED BY THE SPIRITUAL and cultural traditions that permeate hockey in Quebec, Québécoise players tackle the game with a passion that has swept them to the forefront of women's hockey in Canada. While the female game has a long history in Quebec, the powerful national position of the province's female players is nothing short of extraordinary given the comparatively low number of women who play hockey here. Ontario bustles with more than ten thousand female players, some of whom have been on the ice since the age of six. Quebec, which has seven million inhabitants compared with Ontario's ten million, has just slightly more than four thousand female hockey players, most of whom did not join the game until late in their teens. Yet Quebec has consistently supplied a plentiful crop of talented women to the Canadian national team. In addition its own teams have offered increasingly fierce competition to those of Alberta and Quebec's archrival, Ontario.

The tradition of hockey runs deep in this province. The first covered rink in the world was raised in Quebec City in 1852, followed ten years later by the Victoria Skating Rink in

Montreal from which North American hockey took its standard size. There the first world hockey championship for men was hosted in 1883. In this once overwhelmingly Roman Catholic province, hockey has taken on a quasi-religious meaning and, in more recent decades, nationalist overtones. Both these elements are apparent in the fact that the old Montreal Forum in which Quebec's "national" team, the Montréal Canadiens, played for so many years was exaltingly referred to as *le cathédral.*

Female hockey, too, reflects Quebec's history, mirroring its linguistic and regional divisions. At the turn of the century hockey was essentially a game of the upperclass and, in Quebec's case, of English Canadians. Most women who played in an organized capacity did so as part of a university team. In the late 1800s McGill University women competed against women from Queen's and the University of Toronto and then in 1900, as part of a Quebec women's league, the first in Canada. Although some French-speaking women played in the anglophone leagues, the English dominated the circuit, as they did the province's politics and economy. In the late 1960s when women's hockey was in the throes of its first renaissance since the 1930s, hockey thrived in Montreal. The dominant east-end Aces Hockey League enjoyed sponsorship that covered the full cost of its equipment and expenses; the league included on its teams both francophone and anglophone women. Francophone teams, however, did not emerge as a force until the late 1960s when Quebec nationalism reached a feverish peak.

Québécoise players present an emotional and intense likeness of their region. Their style is a potent brew of small-town inclusion and defiant, individualistic flair. On ice the Québécoises are freewheelers; they make razor-sharp passes, take audacious shots and perform outlandish dekes. At national championships their team chants and songs before games are attacked with a gusto that could only come from those particularly intent on proving their worth — a sentiment that once again stems from the province's uncertain position in Canada. Off ice they often resist outward signs of conformity such as wearing team jackets, which they view as a constraint on their personal expression.

Since the mid-1980s, France St. Louis has been the unyielding luminary of women's hockey in Quebec. Born in 1958 in Laval, Quebec, St. Louis was the captain and one of the oldest members of Team Canada in both the 1992 and 1994 world championships. Her talent has won her many accolades: since 1984 St. Louis has been a member of nine senior national hockey championship teams, taking home six gold medals and winning MVP in 1988, 1990, 1991 and 1993. She has frequently acted as captain of the Quebec team at national championships and often has been the best female scorer in her senior league. In 1994 St. Louis inaugurated the École d'hockey France St. Louis, the first female hockey school in Quebec. She was also a remarkable lacrosse player. In 1985, just two months after first playing the game, St. Louis was selected as a member of the national lacrosse team and became its pivotal player in two world championships and five national ones. She has helped lead the way not only for Québécoise athletes; she also has set the standards for any female hockey player who dares to call herself an elite athlete.

St. Louis first took to the ice in a pair of figure skates in the well-to-do Montreal neighbourhood of Ahunstic, where she grew up. She hated figure-skating lessons and soon quit, preferring to spend her time playing shinny hockey at an outdoor rink with her brother, Bernard. Late one night when St. Louis was sixteen, she slipped out of the house with Bernard's skates and sped around the deserted rink down the hill from her home. It was an intoxicating moment — the solid hockey skates hugging her ankles as she pursued the puck on the moonlit rink. Shortly after her parents bought France her own pair of hockey skates and Bernard joined her in the late-night outings.

When France joined her first organized female hockey team at nineteen, her parents, Lise and Guy, initially attended all the games. During games Guy paced anxiously behind the opposing team's net. He was well-intentioned, but his presence caused France to lose her focus. After games he would chatter excitedly for hours, barraging France with tips and strategies. Eventually he understood the effect his presence had on his daughter and stopped coming to her games.

Since 1983 St. Louis has worked at the private Montreal high school, the Académie Michèle Provost, first as a Physical Education teacher and later as the athletic director. Her teaching and coaching style is exacting. "Play like you practise," she has often advised the girls' basketball team. "If you don't do anything during practise, you won't accomplish anything during the games."[1] Rather than alienating her students, her tough approach has won her admirers. After the 1994 world championship, the school's principal, Michèle Provost, presented St. Louis with a $100 gold coin from the 1976 Olympics in front of a gym full of cheering students. Provost has also granted St. Louis the time off she requires to fulfill her hockey commitments. Although such support may seem standard for a world-class athlete, most Team Canada members are docked pay from their jobs while away at world championships. Others have risked losing their jobs entirely by taking time off.

Unlike many of her provincial teammates, St. Louis is not a flashy player. At 5 ft. 8 in. (172 cm) and 140 lbs. (64 kg), her tall, svelte body travels the ice with studied rigour. She reads the play well, capitalizing on opportunity with her decisive passing. Her precision on ice is merely an extension of her off-ice persona. St. Louis is almost fanatical about promptness,

*France St. Louis, captain of Team Canada, 1994.*

fastidious about her equipment, and can be regimented even when on holidays, rising at the crack of dawn to train. "She's kind of nutso sometimes," sums up her close friend and former Ferland–Quatre Glaces teammate, Therese Brisson, with a laugh. Brisson recalls the time at a tournament in Trois-Rivières when St. Louis' skates were returned late from the sharpener's. St. Louis had asked Brisson to pick them up from the shop and bring them to the tournament. When Brisson was delayed due to traffic, St. Louis panicked; pacing frantically up and down the aisles, she asked everyone in earshot if he or she had an extra pair of skates. "By the time I got there," recalls Brisson, "the whole arena knew France St. Louis needed a pair of size seven skates. I mean her nervous energy had the whole place on edge."[2] Teammates have often had fun with this side of St. Louis' character, hiding her skates just to watch her go into a frenzy. She responds good-naturedly to the teasing. Despite her finicky side, she is even-tempered and displays an ironic sense of humour refreshingly free of putdowns or barbs. She is also a master at galvanizing her teammates with enthusiasm. "France makes you want to buy into it," says Brisson. "She makes you feel like you can be like her."[3]

All of St. Louis' decisions — from selecting an office with a shower so she can go directly from the gym to work to carefully monitoring her diet, sleep and fitness — are centred on her goals as a hockey player. She is never without a goal, forever measuring her objectives against tangible contributions she can make to her team. But as with many elite athletes, her self-worth as a person often depends on her athletic performance. The perfectionism, teammates say, also reflects a fear of letting go of her drive — a drive that at times has worked against her. In the 1987 national championship, St. Louis experienced the perils of overtraining, pushing her body so hard that it lost its much depended-on resilience. She was plagued by exhaustion. On ice she found she couldn't catch her breath and off ice she lacked her usual enthusiasm and interest in others. "It was basically a lack of maturity," explains St. Louis in retrospect. "I just didn't listen to my body."[4] The experience forced her to reconsider her approach to training and gave her the necessary maturity to grow as an athlete.

Now after a stressful week St. Louis goes home and relaxes in front of the television rather than pushing herself to train. She spends an average of only eight hours a week training, including two hours every other week skating. (It is not by choice that she spends so few hours on ice, but rather because of the prohibitive cost of renting ice time and the lack of ice available for senior female teams.) The perspective St. Louis now possesses does not detract from her focus. Indeed, with the Olympics hovering in the near distance, St. Louis has fused her dedication and maturity to redefine just what is possible for her as a player in her late thirties. For St. Louis the race to Nagano, Japan, the 1998 Olympic site, is not just a race against younger players, but a race against the clock. Prior to the national team tryout camp in the fall of 1995, coach Shannon Miller doubted St. Louis could triumph over such odds. "She has the talent and leadership," Miller had contended, "but it's a matter of her age slowing her down. It just does. That's life."[5] To Miller's delight St. Louis proved her wrong. The player performed remarkably well at the camp and consequently was ranked as one of the top ten players in the country. "What can I say?" says Miller, beaming. "She's an amazingly dedicated athlete."[6]

Since the early 1980s St. Louis has been the mainstay of the senior club team Ferland–Quatre Glaces (formerly Repentigny) of Brossard. The twenty-four team Repentigny Regional Female Hockey League (League Régionale du hockey au féminin) just north of Montreal boasts the strongest competition in the province. For a twenty-year period beginning in the mid-1960s, the Montréal Titans — composed of both French- and

English-speaking women — dominated the league, representing Quebec in the early years of national championships. Since the mid-1980s, however, Ferland–Quatre Glaces and its rival, Jofa-Titan (formerly Sherbrooke), have formed the heart of the league.

Ferland–Quatre Glaces is distinguished by a handful of star players and a sentinel of "plumbers," those less skilled players who work hard following a system laid out by the coach. The team trains under the inspired coaching of Danièle Sauvageau, a member of the national coaching pool who works nights as a narcotics detective. National talents such as goalie Denise Caron, and defence Therese Brisson, one of the first anglophones to join a club team, have also played for Quatre Glaces. (Brisson now lives in New Brunswick and plays on its only Senior A team.)

Jofa-Titan, on the other hand, is rife with exceptional talents. It has included national team members Nathalie Picard, Nancy Drolet, Diane Michaud, Danielle Goyette, France Montour, goalie Marie-Claude Roy and, for a brief period, even Manon Rhéaume. For many years the team was held together by captain Nathalie Picard, known affectionately by other players as "Picou." On defence Picard had a clear grasp of how games unfold. She acted as the team's backbone, curbing its tendency towards individual play through her understated leadership. Picard's influence, combined with the talent of the players, carried the team from playing in the B league in the early 1980s to stealing the gold at the 1988 national championship. As team captain of the first official Team Quebec in 1993, Picard introduced the team's motto, *Fière d'être québécoise et hâte de gagner* (Proud of Being Québécoise and Set On Winning.) When Picard retired from hockey in 1994, Nancy Drolet of Drummondville took on the role of team leader, becoming its manager. Still in her early twenties, this young player has displayed remarkable skating skills on ice and an

*Québécoise members of Team Canada celebrate another*
*gold medal at the 1994 world championship. From left to right:*
*Nancy Drolet, Therese Brisson, France St. Louis, Laura Leslie,*
*Danielle Goyette, Nathalie Picard.*

off-ice knack for organizing team finances and attracting sponsors. She was instrumental in leading the Quebec junior team to a bronze medal in the 1991 Canada Winter Games and awed fans at the 1992 world championship with her hat trick. In 1993 Drolet was named Junior Athlete of the Year by the Sports Federation of Canada and the "next great women's player" by *Inside Hockey* magazine.

Drolet began playing female hockey at age fourteen after nine years on boys' teams. She is naturally gifted and with the frequent practices and superior coaching of the boys' league she was able to hone her liquid acceleration and brazen shots on net. Drolet and teammate Danielle Goyette, the most effortless and creative scorer in Canada, form a lethal pair. As members of Jofa-Titan, the two carefully observed one another on different lines for four years. They finally played on the same line in the 1992 world championship. When they played together, instinct took over; Drolet and Goyette wove throughout the games as if attached by an invisible thread, uncannily anticipating one another's moves.

The intuitive style of Drolet and Goyette aptly characterizes Jofa-Titan. The team does not practise, relying instead on the natural talent of its players and its experience together. Jofa-Titan clearly outweighs its chief rival, Ferland–Quatre Glaces, in terms of skill. But when key players from the team retire or move on, it has to struggle on ice to maintain its advantage.

By 1995 twelve senior leagues consisting of fifty teams were registered with the Quebec Ice Hockey Federation (QIHF). This almost represented a doubling in the number of players since 1991. These leagues do not include the teams of Concordia University, University of Quebec at Trois-Rivières, St. Laurent College or McGill University. Concordia female hockey has enjoyed varsity status (which means it is financially supported by the university) since 1975 and equitable funding since 1985. The money channelled into the program has translated directly into better coaching and higher calibre hockey. This is because the program attracts players with higher goals, who in turn demand higher standards. The university teams have proven to be particularly important in developing players between the ages of sixteen and twenty-five, while the club teams for the most part offer opportunity to women who are twenty years old and over.

While the Quebec women's senior teams have produced a superb yield of national athletes, until 1992 the system was plagued with troubles. Each year teams such as Quatre Glaces and Sherbrooke set out with the primary goal of winning the provincial championship and the right to represent Quebec at the national championship. "Stacking," the best players flocking to these few teams, became regular practice. This resulted in the near ruin of the competitive network of the A level (now called AA). One team after another dropped out after consistently losing games to the dominant two or three teams by as many as twenty goals. The problem was by no means unique to Quebec: stacking had hindered senior league development in Ontario, Alberta and British Columbia, as well. But to further detract from the stability of the Quebec league, the leading teams played with skeletal rosters of twelve or thirteen players in regular season. The better players understandably wanted more ice time and saw the limited number of players as a way of spending less time on the bench during games and more time in play. At the 1990 national championship hosted by Quebec, the province featured the lowest number of registered players in Canada. To mask the reality, the team representing Quebec placed "ghost" players on the list: coaches, managers and retired players — one of whom was born in 1936 and was in fact the mother of a player. Although the Quebec team won that year, the skeletal rosters worked to its disadvantage at the national championships since it competed against full teams of nineteen highly skilled players.

The selection process for the national team also proved to be a muddled affair across the country and Quebec was no exception. Provinces were not notified by the CAHA of the 1990 championship until mid-October 1989. A quota system of recommending players to the national team tryouts was set up and Quebec was asked to list ten players by November. Given the short notice, a committee headed by Quebec female council representative Lucie Valois decided to target the four teams officially registered in the Senior A league. These players were sent forms that asked them if they were interested in attending national team tryouts. According to Valois two of the senior teams boycotted the process as a way to force the

CAHA to change it. Instead, says Valois, they wanted the same selection process that had been used for the unofficial 1987 world championship in which the winning team from the national championships had represented the country. In the end six players reversed their decisions, four of whom were eventually chosen for Team Canada, Valois reports. "I am still bitter about that episode," she says, "where Senior A players were so misled by their coaches and some influential players [into boycotting the event]."[7] Players, however, tell a different story, saying they were more confused than anything by the process and that the significance of the event was never properly explained to them. When the Québécoises who played in the first world championship returned, those who had opted out also felt bitterly led astray.

Valois, a medical doctor and headstrong member of the CAHA female council from 1985 to 1993, was irked by the flaws in the senior leagues. In 1993 Valois worked with the QIHF's Excellence Commission, where she developed a scheme to both remedy the ills of the senior teams and foster growth within minor hockey, where female numbers had just begun to rise. She designed a program whose main thrust was to develop a provincial team. Valois modelled the program on the female under-18 Program of Excellence that had been set in motion for the first Canada Winter Games in 1991 and had continued for the 1993 under-18 national championship. She presented the elite program to the QIHF, which in turned requested a grant from the federal government to launch it. It was approved, most likely because it complied with Sport Canada's point system, which favours the funding of sports benefitting both elite and largely underrepresented female athletes. In 1993–1994 Quebec competed in the national championship with its first all-star team, making it the only province to be represented by its best players rather than the winning team of the provincial championship.

Outside of Quebec, the program was not widely appreciated. Alberta and Ontario especially resented the advantage an all-star team gave to Quebec. Ontario argued that such a system denied less talented members on the winning provincial teams a chance to play in national competition. Within the province, however, the program has been an unequivocal success. Not only has it solved the stacking problem by offering all the better club players a chance to play on the provincial team, it has also cleared up the selection process for the national team, guaranteed a full roster of provincial team players and provided a tangible goal for younger female players in the province.

Team Quebec's budget totalled $25,000 in 1995–96, a considerable sum for a provincial elite female program. This figure is particularly striking given that other senior provincial championship teams scramble to raise the money simply to attend the national championship. Up to $12,000 is supplied by the provincial hockey federation, several thousand by the CHA and the rest is made up through player fees and fundraising.[8] Despite the relatively generous funding, the program is run entirely by a volunteer staff consisting of one director of operations, three coaches, one physiotherapist and one equipment manager. When the director of operations, France Lajoie, has inquired about receiving an honorarium for the hours of work she and others devote each week to the program, federation managers have said, "That's how it works; there's nothing we can do about it."[9]

Lajoie, formerly the president of the Repentigny senior women's league, took over as the voluntary director of operations of the program in 1994 and added a pool of three advanced-level coaches to work with the team. The pool includes Danièle Sauvageau and Concordia University coach Julie Healy, both part of the CHA coaching pool. Healy was head coach of the under-18 provincial team in 1993 and of Team Quebec in 1995. The addition of coaches to the program reflects Quebec's commitment to developing a corps of expert female hockey coaches, a priority that is absent in the rest of Canada. The percentage of women coaching female teams is high in Quebec because the hockey federation has made coaching certification mandatory for the intermediate and elite level teams. Since 1986 the federation has organized coaching courses exclusively for women, many of whom have felt daunted by the traditionally male terrain. The courses paid off and by 1995 women coached all AA teams, six of the seven senior club teams and the majority of the sixteen BB teams. The varsity teams, which represent the best-paid positions — or, in the case of women's hockey, the only paid ones — are still largely coached by men. So, too, are teams at the minor level, where the concern has been not so much to develop female coaches, but simply to provide girls with decent coaches.

While the provincial team program has undoubtedly raised the skills and aspirations of elite players in Québec, until recently the province has failed to offer much to the majority of young female players. Girls have been playing in the minor hockey leagues in Quebec since the early 1980s. They began to play following the 1978 court decision in the *Québec (Commission des droits personne) c. Fédération québécoise de hockey sur glace Inc.* case that forced the federation to allow female players into its leagues. By 1995, seventeen years later, only 990 girls played on female minor teams and 1,012 on boys' teams, making up 5 percent of the minor players in the QIHF. While the Ontario Women's Hockey Association has been providing opportunities for girls since 1975, the Quebec federation only began to actively promote female participation in 1990. Ontario's provincial Winter Games have included girls since 1985. Quebec's Winter Games didn't embrace female teams until 1996.

Marc Beaudin, manager of female hockey at the QIHF,

insists that girls' hockey is now a priority. According to Beaudin, in addition to the elite program between $20,000 and $30,000 is spent annually on female hockey, a sum that is spread out over salaries, administrative costs and a number of programs. Like so many of the provincial associations female program directors, Beaudin becomes defensive when asked for the portion of the overall budget of minor hockey that goes to girls. Indeed, many associations refuse to release figures pertaining to female hockey or else claim that such figures are impossible to calculate given that some girls participate in their mainly male programs.

As part of its strategy to offer more opportunity to girls who wish to play hockey, however, Beaudin points to the Quebec federation, which held its first minor hockey leadership seminar for regional representatives in 1994. Representatives from all fifteen hockey zones in the province attended to discuss ways to promote female participation. Foremost among the suggestions was the need to publicize the sport to girls, particularly given the high level of resistance to female players in communities that are strapped for ice time. This is no small point, as it is the local associations that decide whether or not they will accept girls' teams. In some cases, however, when the local towns refuse to form girls' teams, female organizers have turned to one of the fifteen zone (or regional) associations to launch the teams. This is because the zone associations permit their players to come from larger geographical areas. For new, struggling female teams, the chance to draw players from a larger pool often determines their ability to survive. To further increase the competitive opportunities for girls, in 1995–1996 the federation launched a new provincial championship for girls under-16 called the Chrysler Cup at which an all-star team from each of the fifteen zones competes.

Senior players now await a similar championship. Although senior tournaments are held about once a month, with

the formation of the Quebec all-star team program, club competition among leagues has fizzled since there is no longer a
provincial championship where teams vie to represent Quebec
at the national championship. While the all-star programs provide the better players with proper training, the system has also
brought out an individual approach to the game. Players are
now less concerned about playing as a team and instead focus
more on accomplishing their personal goals. As the stakes are
raised in the province, a significant shift in values — from collective to individual — is emerging. Some have suggested that
to restore the once important team incentive, Quebec should
launch a new senior championship in which all levels of teams
compete.

Quebec female hockey may have only recently begun to receive the funding and tournaments it deserves, but it is strides
ahead of its fledgling Eastern neighbours. This is not to say
that Atlantic Canadian women's hockey is a new phenomenon. It possesses a proud and spirited history that extends
from Newfoundland's undefeated Bay Roberts Roverines and
PEI's Crystal Sisters of the 1930s to the enterprising PEI
Spudettes of the 1970s. Nonetheless, it has been an ongoing
struggle for female players in the region to make even a dent
in national competition. In each of the four Atlantic provinces
— New Brunswick, Nova Scotia, Prince Edward Island and
Newfoundland — the survival of the female game has fallen
on the shoulders of solitary individuals, who, without support
from local hockey associations or parents, have propelled the
game forward. The broader lack of interest in promoting girls
in the sport has created a fragile system, one that has crumbled
when lone organizers leave in exhaustion and frustration. This
situation is exacerbated by the geography of the provinces:
major centres are few and far between and travel between

provinces often involves a costly flight or ferry crossing. These are expenses many of the depressed communities cannot afford. Consequently, the sort of tournaments and jamborees that have thrived in the West have been small and sporadic in the Atlantic provinces. Even the Atlantic Shield (formerly the Eastern Shield), a tournament for junior and senior teams, has been held only once since its rebirth in 1990.

Despite these obstacles, a tradition of female hockey has survived in the East, and it is due to the hard work of a handful of women and men. By far the most well-known and admired leader is New Brunswick's Stacy Wilson, who has been a member of Team Canada since the first world championship in 1990 and is also captain of the New Brunswick provincial team. The similarities between Quebec's France St. Louis and Stacy Wilson are striking. Like St. Louis, Wilson teaches Physical Education and has used her background to painstakingly prepare herself for international competition. She has been instrumental in launching the first female hockey school in the region and has demonstrated a deep sense of regional loyalty as assistant coach in the Canada Winter Games and through her involvement in female jamborees and clinics. But while St. Louis is surrounded by players of similar talent and drive in Quebec, until very recently Wilson has been peerless in Atlantic women's hockey. Rather than moving to another province, where she would undoubtedly face more and stronger competition, Wilson has remained in the region. There, almost single-handedly, she has raised the calibre of female hockey.

Wilson would deny her pivotal role in female hockey in the Atlantic provinces. She is a shy, unassuming woman with a slight build; her blue eyes, set against coal-black eyebrows, startle with their transparency. Teased by her friends and teammates for refusing to drink or swear — her harshest expletive is "Geepers creepers!" — Wilson is, however, anything but moralistic. At parties she is invariably the last one to leave, often overcoming her timidity to pick up her guitar and play. Wilson, nonetheless, remains firmly reticent with the press: attention leaves her uneasy. Often after a story appears that portrays her as a star, she will grimace to teammates and ask, "Do you think that article was O.K.?"[10]

Her reserve, just as much as her commitment to building confidence in female hockey players, has won her a coveted place in the hearts of Maritimers. Born in Moncton in 1965, Stacy Wilson grew up in the tiny nearby village of Salisbury, the youngest in a family of three children. Although she is an all-round athlete — an Atlantic champion in badminton and an accomplished golfer and swimmer — hockey won out over these other sports. The sense of freedom skating brought her, the cleansing mental effect of the cool rink air, even a feeling of patriotism at playing Canada's national sport seized Wilson's imagination as a child.

Much of her love of the game also sprang from her belief in team work, a value instilled in her by her parents and a community that celebrated her struggles and victories as its own. Wilson's mother, Betty, accompanied her to every game when Stacy played in a minor boys' league. Betty, who like her daughter is uncomfortable with the braggadocio that goes with many competitive sports, sat apart from the other hockey parents during games to avoid their hostile bellows. If she overheard someone deriding Stacy, she would diplomatically defend her. Stacy's community was behind her, too. When Wilson returned from the 1990 world championship — the only Team Canada representative from the Atlantic provinces — Salisbury held a reception for her in its community hall and declared her Citizen of the Day.

Wilson became a force in hockey in the Maritimes in 1984 during her second year at Acadia University in Wolfville, Nova Scotia, when she helped form a team. The next year Wilson led this group of inexperienced players to a provincial victory against the seasoned Dalhousie University team, which had defeated them the year before 18–0. She returned to the Moncton area to teach in 1987 and joined the Jaguar women's hockey team, now known as the Maritimes Sports Blades. In the 1980s the team played in a small league, usually competing against the University of New Brunswick in the provincial finals. In the early 1990s the Sports Blades became the only A team in the province and has since acted as the provincial team. It draws players from all around New Brunswick. Most commute hours each weekend to Moncton to be part of the team. Because the Sports Blades team is literally in a league of its own, it lacks a fixed schedule, organizing ad hoc games against men's teams from week to week. Practices are held in a small arena outside Moncton late on Saturday nights and on Sunday mornings.

For years the Sports Blades wallowed in what it came to call "the toilet bowl" of fifth or sixth place nationally. At the 1994 national championship, after a particularly bitter defeat against Alberta in a preliminary game, Wilson penned her frustration in a journal:

> Feeling a game slip away is a horrible, sickening feeling. I have lost ... games before, but this one really hurt, I guess because I believed in our team. I'm proud of the team, but can't quite express it in the dressing room, as everyone silently takes off the gear more slowly than usual, like they are still trying to slow down the clock. We know we are in the "toilet bowl" again. We have been in this game so many times and so close to breaking through that I think we have earned the right to call it that. We own it. It's the first time I've cried after losing at Nationals.[11]

Determined to escape the toilet bowl, Wilson conducted a closed-door visualization session with her teammates before the final game at the 1995 national championship. As the players drew together in the dressing room, Wilson quietly handed each member a small piece of gold, asking her to tape it to her body or slip it into her skate. The day before the gold bits had formed an individual achievement medal, which Wilson had been awarded after an earlier game. At her request the team's equipment manager had spent three hours slicing the medal with a hacksaw into nineteen pieces so that Wilson could literally share her medal with her teammates. Although the team lost to Quebec, New Brunswick took home its first silver medal in the national championship. It was a fairy-tale victory for Wilson.

While Wilson's presence on the New Brunswick team has transformed its members into contenders for the national championships, Team Canada has performed a similar alchemy on Wilson. Before she was selected for the national team in 1990, Wilson did not regard herself as a serious athlete. This only changed just before the 1992 training camp. During workouts on a Nautilus machine at the local gym, Wilson stared at a poster someone had hung on the wall. It displayed a quotation from the German poet Goethe. "Until one is committed, there is hesitancy, the chance to draw back, always ineffectiveness, concerning all acts of initiative (and creativity)," its first lines read. "Whatever you can do or dream you can do, begin it. Boldness has genius, power and magic in it. Begin it now," it ended. Contemplating these words, Wilson realized she must now give absolutely everything over to the game of hockey. Either that or stop playing altogether.

Since her transformation in 1992, Wilson has not been without doubts or fears. Attending national tryouts for Team Canada is always intimidating, particularly as more younger players, who have had better opportunities, are invited to attend. Although she stands out on ice with her stalwart forechecking and willingness to fill any necessary role, Wilson

*Stacy Wilson (back left corner) with players at her hockey camp.*

worries about her lack of ice time and insufficient exposure to tougher competition. She must also deal with the stress of juggling work with hockey: when she plays for Team Canada, Wilson forfeits her teaching salary and also must pay the substitute who replaces her. Furthermore, when Wilson played at the 1994 Lake Placid world championship at the age of twenty-nine, the media dogged her with questions about her age, implying her retirement was imminent.

While most of Wilson's energy goes into training as a player, she has also coached girls since 1990. Along with Michelle Belanger, who has been the New Brunswick representative for the CHA Female Council since 1992, and teammate Joanne Vautour, Wilson founded a hockey camp for girls in 1995. The school means a great deal to Wilson, who is resolute about giving girls the opportunities she never had as the only girl on a boy's team. Wilson's presence has also meant much to young hockey players in the region. It meant so much to one girl that she burst into tears of joy when she first sighted Wilson at the camp.

Currently in this province of 750,000, almost 300 girls participate in minor hockey. In 1995 the New Brunswick Interscholastic Athletic Association formed a league of high school teams, which Michelle Belanger registered with the provincial hockey association. This gave a much-needed boost to girls' minor hockey. By 1996 fifteen female high school teams were competing in the province. Three all-girls' teams have also registered since 1995. Having succeeded in increasing the numbers from year to year, Belanger's current goal is to ensure female representation in the province's eight hockey zones. Already six committed representatives have begun to promote the game in their zones.

With a population of 132,000, Prince Edward Island presents an impressive example of female inclusion in hockey within Atlantic Canada. In 1991, the year of the first Canada Winter Games held in PEI, only four minor girls' teams played. By 1995 more than thirty-five female teams competed, twenty-five of which were minor; the rest were senior or recreational teams. Fifteen percent of the minor hockey players in the province are female, 90 percent of whom belong to all-female teams.

Several elements have combined to make PEI the female minor hockey leader in the region. First, the island boasts the highest number of indoor rinks per capita in the world at twenty-five and thus, with the exception of its major centre, Charlottetown, ice time has been readily available to girls. Second, the number of boys playing has dropped in the last decade, and hockey associations have eyed girls' participation as a way to revitalize the sport. Third, and most important, PEI has been blessed with one of the most committed promoters of female hockey in Canada: Susan Dalziel. Dalziel's love of hockey blossomed in 1973 when she played on her first organized team, the Kensington Spudettes. The team sprang from a long tradition of female hockey on the island, which took root with the famed Crystal Sisters and Charlottetown Abegweit Sisters (the Micmac name for PEI, meaning "cradle on the waves") at the turn of the century. Member Kay McQuaid played nets for the Spudettes from 1968 until 1984, when she joined a rival team, the Island Whitecaps, and ended the Spudettes' winning streak in the East. McQuaid's girlhood practice sessions embodied the whimsical essence of PEI life: she took shots from her brother behind her family's barn on a dark, layered rink formed from the moisture drainage of a manure pile; she used potato bags stuffed with straw and fastened to her legs with old binder twine to protect her shins. In the Spudette's early years, members played without helmets, and more than once a bouffant wig worn by a player would fly off — bobby pins and all — following a solid bodycheck.

The Spudettes travelled to tournaments in the East and Ontario in an old Ford camper van, which had to be jump-started after the ferry crossings. McQuaid's mother followed the team religiously — literally. She cheered players on with an old cow bell, intermittently fingering her rosary beads and whispering Hail Marys to protect them from injury. In 1976 the Spudettes won the B championship at the Dominion

*Spudettes, 1976. Goalie Kay McQuaid sits second from left in front row. Susan Dalziel, one of the sports' most committed proponents, sits on the far left, second row.*

Ladies Hockey Tournament in Brampton and placed second the next year in the A championship. The highlight of the team's career came in 1976 at the same tournament, then the largest women's hockey tournament in the world. The team was chosen from among seventy Canadian and American teams as the recipient of the Roy Morris Sportsmanship Award, and the choice was unanimous. After losing the final game of the tournament, the Spudettes took to the dressing room, stood along the benches and burst into song. "We're PE-Island born and we're PE-Island bred," they belted, "and when we die, we'll be PE-Island dead!"[12] "The island is small and people feel closer than they do other places," reflects Mc-Quaid. "A lot of people didn't have a lot when they started out and when you get something it means a whole lot to you."[13] The coach from the opposing team, the Mississauga Indians, remarked wryly about the singing, "What do they do when they win?"[14] By 1980 travel had become too expensive for the team and with no minor hockey teams from which to draw talent, PEI stopped competing in the Dominion Tournament. When the national championship was launched in 1982, PEI managed to send a team until 1989, when lack of money again forced the province to forego the event until 1995.

Dalziel, a modest schoolteacher, first became involved in organizing female hockey in 1977 when she came across an announcement in the local newspaper for a Canadian Amateur Hockey Association (CAHA) seminar about the future of female hockey. Dalziel attended the seminar, an early version of the Female Council that was formed in 1982, and has since been a driving force of the sport at most of the Female Council's yearly meetings. Also in 1977 Dalziel became the PEI girls' coordinator and then, in 1980, the director of Female Hockey in the province.

The late 1970s and early 1980s were prosperous years for female hockey and Dalziel worked intensively on the sport's behalf, staging coaching clinics for women, putting out a newsletter and encouraging communities to include girls in their leagues. Despite her efforts the number of female players dropped drastically by the mid-1980s, as the violence in both the amateur and professional game turned many parents off hockey. For almost a decade, Dalziel laboured single-handedly to keep what was left of the female sport alive. She began to wonder whether she had wasted years of her life on a pipe dream and was on the verge of abandoning the game when, in 1988, the provincial hockey association asked her to coordinate female hockey for the 1991 Canada Winter Games. The Games were to be held in PEI in what would be the inaugural year for female hockey. At last Dalziel was able to put her experience and wisdom to use to promote a game whose reputation had been restored. Parents soon came aboard to help her, although financial support from the local association is still not forthcoming. "I used to find with the hockey association in general, the funding would go to different male programs," says Dalziel. "I didn't ask and they didn't volunteer. There's not as big a discrepancy now as there used to be, but that's because money is dropping all round."[15] Nonetheless, PEI's minor female hockey leagues have become a beacon for its neighbours, a luminous example of what can be achieved with the proper conditions and the work of a tenacious leader.

In Nova Scotia Lynn Hacket, the first representative of female hockey in the province, attended her inaugural CAHA meeting in 1983. At the time Nova Scotia sustained only a three-team senior league. "It felt like I was in a foreign country — that the national border stopped at Quebec," Hacket recalls of the CHA Female Council. "I couldn't fathom that Ontario had three hundred teams. I could only laugh. I was too embarrassed to even open my mouth about our little league. I had absolutely no idea that so much was going on."[16]

From 1973 to 1978 the densely populated area of Halifax-Dartmouth had supported a league of six senior teams. In 1976 the demise of the local league was set in motion when a competitive team, the Fairview Acettes, was formed to challenge the Halifax university teams of Dalhousie and St. Mary's. The Acettes stripped the other club teams of their best players and quickly overwhelmed the rest of the teams in the league. But the league's coup de grâce came in 1978 when the City of Halifax suddenly refused to subsidize ice time for the league, claiming it had just discovered that girls over the age of eighteen were playing, which was against the city rules for boys' hockey. League members were outraged and claimed that the age restriction rule was simply an excuse to get them off the ice: what city officials really wanted was to free up more ice time for the swelling boys' league.

From the early 1980s to 1990, the three university teams from Acadia, Dalhousie and St. Mary's carried women's hockey forward in Nova Scotia. A recreational team from East Hants, a town in the Sidney Mines area just outside of Halifax, was formed in 1986 and joined the university league for exhibition games. Ice time cost the university teams nothing, but access was haphazard, with the women being slipped into the spaces in the men's schedule. In 1982 St. Mary's University won the provincial championship and went on to the first national championship. The next year Dalhousie represented the province, followed the year after by Acadia University, which has dominated the league since. At the national level the Nova Scotia teams never fared better than eighth place. In 1989 Dalhousie folded due to lack of leadership, and for the remaining teams competition dwindled to an occasional regional tournament. A Nova Scotia team did not return to the national championship until 1995 when two all-star teams competed against one another to represent the province.

By 1994 the Canada Winter Games program at last rejuvenated the women's league. The league of four teams, which had floundered since the late 1980s, was now bolstered by three other teams: the Halifax Breakers, Shearwater, and the Nova Scotia Natives, a team composed of women from two Micmac reserves in the north-central Truro region of the province. An eighth team from New Glasgow, a former steel industry region two hours northeast of Halifax, joined the league the next year.

It was no coincidence that the New Glasgow senior team sprung up when it did. Since the first Canada Winter Games in 1991, New Glasgow has boasted the fastest-growing girls' minor league in the province. Brenda Ryan, the first woman in the province to attain the Advanced level of coaching, saw a long-awaited opportunity to kick-start the game in her region. Four girls from the area were selected for the 1991 Nova Scotia team, and two years later, when the program for the 1995 Canada Winter Games began, minor hockey officials decided to base the training in the New Glasgow area. Ryan used the girls who had made the provincial team to entice others to join. After the provincial team was selected, its members travelled to the six towns that populated the region, playing games against boys' teams. Ryan drew local girls into the game by encouraging them to drop the puck at the start of games, distribute prizes and sell tickets at the doors. "I just kind of jumped all over it [the opportunity the Games offered] and took it home,"[17] Ryan recalls. By 1995 seventy girls formed an active league of three minor teams and one senior team; five years earlier none had existed.

The success of the Canada Winter Games showed to young women — many of whom had been herded into ringette at an early age — that they could be an active part of Canada's national game. The local minor hockey association helped to set the necessary conditions for the growth of the female sport by giving female players a magnanimous reception. The Pictou County Minor Hockey Association opened its league to the female teams in 1991 and even banned bodychecking from male-female games at the bantam level to help the Games' team train under the no-intentional bodychecking rule, which governed female hockey. Consistent ice times have ensured the league's continuation.

The revival of the female game in Nova Scotia has also attracted hockey scouts from American universities. Some of the province's better players have been enticed south with lucrative scholarships. Other talented players have gone west to attend Concordia University's exceptional hockey program or have moved on to the high-performance female hockey program at Calgary's Olympic Oval. The better players who do not leave the province generally compete on boys' teams. In Halifax, for instance, girls have been permitted to play on boys' teams since 1973 and many prefer the male teams to which superior coaches traditionally have been drawn.

A persistent barrier to the female sport's expansion, however, remains the indifference of the Nova Scotia Minor Hockey Council, particularly with regard to ice time for girls. As Gary Smiley, the representative of female hockey since 1992, puts it, "They support it where it is but haven't done anything to promote it. Their attitude is, 'You deal with it.'"[18] Although the council has officially backed integrated hockey province-wide since 1984, it has done nothing to reach girls who may want to play but do not realize they can join the boys' leagues. Of the total sixteen-thousand registered minor players in the province, one thousand are girls. Sixty percent of these girls play on the girls' teams that have been formed since 1991.

The passive resistance to female participation in minor hockey is particularly pronounced in the Halifax-Dartmouth-Bedford area, a ringette stronghold in Nova Scotia. While female hockey has spread southwest down and across the province from Cape Breton to Shelburne, it has completely bypassed the metro area. The metro area's hockey association, the Sackville Minor Hockey and Ringette Association, automatically guides girls who approach the league into ringette. As a result, not one minor female team exists in the urban centre. When Smiley expressed his concern over the lack of opportunity local girls have to play hockey, association representatives responded that they did not want to sap ringette. "It was just an excuse and a pretty lame one," says Smiley, whose daughters play hockey. "I said we're in this for hockey, let ringette look after themselves."[19]

Of all the Atlantic provinces, Newfoundland, a province beleaguered by economic depression and isolating winters, has experienced the greatest difficulty in fostering the growth of female hockey. Its senior team has not competed in the national championship for eight years, mainly due to inadequate ice time. In 1988 its league consisted of five teams. But by 1991 the number of teams had dwindled to three as practices and games were pushed later and later into the evenings to accommodate men's teams. The prohibitive costs of flights — it costs more than $10,000 to fly a team of twenty to another Atlantic province — has meant that female players cannot compete outside the province. Travelling between cities on the island itself is problematic: a ten-hour drive separates the two largest centres of St. John's and Corner Brook.

Because senior teams have not fared well, Georgina Short, Newfoundland's female hockey representative since 1991 and its highest qualified female coach, has directed most of her energy into the minor level. Since 1995 Short has received no financing for girls' hockey from the Newfoundland Amateur Hockey Association. Although the association has never restricted her efforts to include girls in its leagues — boys' minor teams in the province have been open to girls since 1970 — forming girls' teams has proven problematic. Fifty-one local hockey associations dot the island, but distances between communities can be offputting to a girl whose only all-female option is a two-hour drive away. For the girls who were selected for the Canada Winter Games team, distance proved to be even more of an issue. Some live in Gander, which is a four-hour drive from St. John's; others live in Badger, a six-hour drive from the capital. The team's talented goaltender, Bonnie Stagg, resides in Labrador and was fortunate enough to hitch a ride on an Armed Forces flight to try out for the team.

In 1995 approximately 400 girls played hockey in this province of 580,000, compared with almost 10,500 boys. Forty percent of the girls play on one of twelve female teams;

four are senior teams and eight are junior ones. Interestingly, in 1995–96 the minor hockey association in St. John's agreed to rid the female minor teams of the upper age limit of nineteen in order to ensure that women could continue playing at the convenient time scheduled for minor hockey. Georgina Short says that many of the fathers involved with the association now have daughters who want to play and at last comprehend the need for unique guidelines to protect female inclusion.

Compared with their Western neighbours, hockey enthusiasts struggling to gain opportunity for female players in the Atlantic region have endured a long and often discouraging battle. Not only have they had to contend with the adverse elements and the isolation that come with the geography of the region, they have also had to face indifference to the inclusion of girls. It is heartening that the number of players is now on the rise. But what is most meaningful is the undying belief in the need for sports equity. The legacy of female hockey has survived and been passed on to the present generation, but so, too, has the conviction that girls should and must be given the same chances in life as their brothers. In a region of small victories, these are not insignificant ones.

Nor are the victories of Quebec female hockey. While the number of Quebec players is still low in relation to the province's population, female players' talent and zest has had a pronounced influence on the sport nationally, propelling the level of play to new heights across the country. Women's hockey organizers in Quebec have initiated a bold all-star program to nourish this talent, a program that those in other regions have not dared to request. With the Quebec Ice Hockey Federation at last supporting female inclusion, Quebec is pulling ahead of the game at the elite level. It not only supplies the national team with exceptional players, but it has also triumphed at the national championship since 1994. The lesson Ontario and the rest of Canada would do well to learn is that extraordinary things can be accomplished when women — athletes and organizers alike — demand as much from the game as they do from themselves.

*Chapter Six*

# PUTTING ON THE HEAT: EQUITY ON ICE

*Girls have to take the left overs. From bantams to seniors, the boys get the preference in rinks throughout the province. And when the boys' teams have completed their schedules, then the girls get the opportunity to take the ice. Even in Preston and Galt, where the girls last year drew the largest two crowds to be seen there in a decade, even there the girls must wait until the men's playdowns are all over.*
— Alexandrine Gibb,
*Toronto Daily Star,* 1938

WHILE THE ISSUE OF SPORTS ownership and control underlies women's struggle for equity in all sports in Canada, in the case of hockey it cuts to its core. Canada's national pastime has come to epitomize an almost gross caricature of maleness: on-ice violence and off-ice wheeling and dealing all too often characterize the game. At an amateur level, many organizers approach the sport as a feeder system for elite levels rather than attempting to make it an enjoyable experience for a child who wants to play.[1] The intense pressure on boys to "make it," and in doing so, to mimic the disturbing aggression of the professional leagues, has been partly responsible for driving them away from the game.[2]

The thrust to groom boys for the elite levels also has allowed male hockey organizers to ignore girls' desire to play the game. If girls don't have a chance of making it to the big league, the prevailing attitude is, why waste valuable resources and ice time on them? "There's a whole rationale to exclude women from the sport and this argument is just one of them," says Nancy Theberge, a sociologist at the University of Waterloo and a fiery proselyte of the women's game. Theberge is part of a movement of sociologists that has existed since the mid-1970s that studies the way in which traditional male sports exclude women. Resistance to female participation is particularly severe in the case of hockey, she says, because the sport typifies those characteristics associated with manliness in our culture and acts as what she calls a "signature of masculinity."[3] "Sport is very important culturally and socially," Theberge explains. "Historically it has been a way to give very clear messages about who we are. If you were a male you did sport, and if you were a woman, you didn't. Now there's a lot of ideological confusion, and men are holding on to any argument they can use."[4]

Despite its shortcomings, hockey continues to hold mythic status in Canada. In all the glorified references to "our common passion" and "the language that pervades Canada," little attention has been paid to its troubling aspects. Even less note is made of the fact that "the game of our lives," until very recently, has been almost exclusively the game of boys' and men's lives.

Although female hockey has survived since the turn of the century, it has done so with virtually no support — and, in fact, much opposition — from supporters of the male game. Recently, however, a shift has occurred. Thanks to those lobbying for sports equity, the high profile of goalie Manon Rhéaume and the advent of international competition for women, including the new Olympic status, female hockey is no longer just surviving. It is flourishing. Unprecedented numbers of women are lacing up their skates and charging onto the ice. Between 1990 and 1996 alone, female participation in hockey rose 200 percent; the total number of players was more than twenty thousand by 1995–96.[5] Ontario, a hub of women's hockey in Canada, boasted over eight hundred teams in leagues outside of schools in 1995–96 — a dramatic rise from fewer than two hundred in 1980–81. Also in 1995–96, the number of players registered with the Ontario Women's Hockey Association surpassed the thirteen thousand mark, a number that does not include girls who play on boys' teams or in most high school leagues.[6]

With this unprecedented surge of women into the sport, the pressure is now on those whose attitudes towards female athletes lie frozen in the past. But the resistance is proving difficult to overcome. Women and girls continue to be dealt fewer resources and programs than men and boys, as well as inferior facilities for competitions. Furthermore, their games are still scheduled in undesirable time slots. When female players do manage to get on ice, many are mocked, harassed and intimidated by the parents, fans, players and organizers of male hockey. Off the ice, women hold only a small share of sports administration positions, have little voice in policy-making and occupy just a tiny percentage of coaching positions across the country. With a few exceptions, female hockey players have been virtually overlooked by the media and sponsors.

Nowhere is the lack of equity between men and women more apparent than in the allocation of ice time. The average female hockey player receives a fraction of the time that a male player receives. This is mainly because large and small communities alike have obstinately resisted opening the doors of their rinks to girls and women. In some cases the opposition takes the form of assigning a girls' team a one-hour time slot late on Friday nights. In other instances the effort to organize a female team has triggered acrimonious debate in communities that claim they need to "protect" the ice time of boys, who at least have a shot at the revered NHL.

In order to grasp just how fundamental ice access is to equity for female hockey players, an overview of the hockey equity debate and the different forms it has taken is necessary. The debate first made headlines in 1955, and on the surface, at least, centred on the issue of girls playing on boys' teams. Eight-year-old Ab Hoffman registered with the Toronto Hockey League and played in it for one season. Officials, her teammates and coach assumed Ab was a boy, an assumption neither she nor her parents bothered to correct, knowing full well she would be expelled from the team if the truth was discovered. Hoffman proved to be an exceptional player, and it was not until she made it to an all-star team that it came to light that Ab was a girl. While the discovery launched Abby Hoffman into short-lived celebrity status, it also put an end to her hockey career. The following year Hoffman was persuaded to play on a girls' team. When the female league ran into difficulties setting up a schedule, Hoffman quit to pursue track and field. She went on to become an Olympic-calibre runner.

By the early 1970s participation in female hockey had picked up, but the dearth of girls' teams placed many players in the same situation as Hoffman. In urban areas more female teams existed, but the meagre practice schedules and long hours spent travelling to play other female teams prompted many girls to turn to boys' teams. Three court cases in the late 1970s involved girls seeking to play hockey on boys' teams: *Forbes v. Yarmouth [Nova Scotia] Minor Hockey Association, Québec (Commission des droits de la personne) c. Fédération québécoise de hockey sur glace Inc.* and *Cummings v. Ontario Minor Hockey Association.* In each case, the organization attempting to bar the girls from boys' teams claimed to be subject to Canadian Amateur Hockey Association (CAHA) regulations, which limited membership to males. In the Forbes and Quebec cases, the judges involved broadly interpreted the associations' mandate of offering services to the public. They ordered both hockey associations to open their programs to girls. The Cummings case was not as straightforward. After the Board of Inquiry decided that the Ontario Minor Hockey Association had discriminated against Cummings, the Ontario Divisional Court reversed the decision and held that the OMHA was private and did not provide a public service. The decision was upheld by the Ontario Court of Appeal.

It was not until 1986, when twelve-year-old Justine Blainey and her mother took the Ontario Hockey Association (OHA) to task, that this ruling was challenged. Blainey had successfully tried out for a boys' hockey team in the Metropolitan Toronto Hockey League, an affiliate of the OHA. Her reason for choosing to play with boys was simple: it meant more ice time, less travel time for games and better practice hours. "I used to watch my brother's games and practices and realized that he was playing twice as often and getting more practices," recalls Blainey, still exasperated. "My practices would be at 5:30 AM, his would be at 11:00 AM. My tournaments would be a four-hour drive away, his would be close by. Mine would be outside, his would be inside. And there was a huge difference of what was expected in terms of quality."[7]

To register with the boys' team, Blainey needed a CAHA player's card, which could only be obtained through the OHA. The rules of the OHA restricted eligibility to boys, however, and Blainey was banned from joining the team. She challenged the ban. In her challenge, Blainey asked the Divisional Court of Ontario to find the OHA regulation contrary to the Canadian Charter of Rights and Freedom. On behalf of Blainey, the Women's Legal Education and Action Fund (LEAF), with the help of the Canadian Association for the Advancement of Women and Sport (CAAWS), argued that provincial sports associations were subject to the equality provisions of the Charter, just as government agencies were, because they were heavily funded by the government. The court rejected this view. Instead, it held that both the CAHA and OHA were private, autonomous organizations that were not subject to the provisions of the Charter. Blainey also asked the court to declare section 19(2) of the Ontario Human Rights Code, which allowed athletic organizations to restrict activities to the same sex, contrary to section 15 of the Charter. The court agreed that the Ontario Code did violate the Charter but held that based on evidence of physiological differences between girls and boys, the impact on the local league in which Blainey played, and historical precedent, section 19(2) of the Ontario Code, and hence the rules of the OHA, were justified. The evidence of physiological differences was particularly absurd given that Blainey had tried out for and made the team.

Blainey appealed this decision before the Ontario Court of Appeal. This time the court found that section 19(2) was "grossly disproportionate to the end sought to be served" and struck it down. "In substance, it permits the posting of a 'no females allowed' sign by every athletic organization in the province,"[8] Justice Charles Dubin said in the majority decision. The Supreme Court of Canada upheld the Ontario Court of Appeal's decision, and Blainey took her original complaint back to an Ontario Board of Inquiry. The board ordered the OHA to allow any girl to compete for a position on a boys' team and to display prominently on its materials a statement to the effect that both girls and boys are eligible to play. It also forced the OHA, which spent more than $100,000 fighting to keep Blainey out, to pay her $3,000 for the mental anguish it caused her to suffer.

The Blainey case achieved two important results. First, it eliminated an exemption in the Ontario Human Rights Code that had permitted sports organizations in Ontario to discriminate against women. Second, it established that a private sports organization discriminated against girls when it did not allow them to participate in its programs. A less beneficial result of the case, however, stemmed from the Divisional Court of Ontario's rejection of CAAWS's argument that provincial sports associations should be subject to the equality provisions of the Charter because of the funding they receive from government. The court's rejection of the argument has meant that predominantly male organizations, such as the CAHA (now the CHA), have no obligation to include girls and women in their programs. In 1987, the year that Blainey won her case, the CAHA received over $1 million from Sport Canada, with an additional $560,000 going to Hockey Canada to fund the men's national team. Funding for the Women in Sport category within the CAHA was non-existent for that year.[9]

In hindsight the Blainey campaign was clearly aimed at broadening girls' opportunity to play hockey. Surprisingly, however, Blainey's plight led to a bitter rift among female hockey advocates. The Ontario Women's Hockey Association (OWHA), barely a decade old, feared the outcome of the Blainey case would destroy its fledgling league. If girls had the option of playing on boys' teams, President Fran Rider argued, the female teams would be drained of the better players — or worse, most girls would simply quit if faced with mixed competition. CAAWS, on the other hand, supported Blainey's aim and fought hard to have the Ontario Human Rights Code changed.

Time has proven Rider's predictions to be unfounded. Nonetheless, the controversy sparked by the Blainey case set off a larger debate about the very nature of the female game. Inherent in the OWHA's campaign against the Blainey case was its desire to preserve the women's game as not only separate, but distinct from the men's game. In its promotional literature, the OWHA stresses the safety and recreational aspect of female hockey, placing great weight on its rule against intentional bodychecking. "Female hockey is one of the fastest growing participation sports in the world. It's fun; it's fantastic exercise; it's safe and it's a great way to make friends," the OWHA brochure proclaims. In a coaching manual for female hockey the CHA also stresses "Friendship ... fun ... [and] social bene-fits ...."[10] Fun and friendship are undoubtedly important to young people. But by trumpeting these aspects, the OWHA and CHA do what promoters of women's sports have done since the turn of the century: they assure girls and, more importantly parents, that the sport is gentle, non-competitive and, when stripped of all its protective gear, essentially feminine.

Most advocates of female hockey wholeheartedly support the option of recreational hockey, but some have criticized what they consider to be a palatable version of the female game. Sociologist Nancy Theberge contends that Fran Rider does a disservice to players, especially to those striving to be-come elite athletes, by continually emphasizing the fun and social nature of the women's game. "All the talk about sports-manship is an evocation of the Play Day philosophy," she says, referring to programs developed by physical educators in the 1930s to expunge hazards of aggressive play from women's sports.[11] "It's belittling a bit. Everyone should be able to play sport to win. There's nothing wrong with that."[12] Or, as Abby (formerly little "Ab") Hoffman, director of Sport Canada in the 1980s has bluntly stated, "The game is being sanitized for women as a reaction to the violent play of men. The response should be to clean up men's hockey, not limit women."[13]

Helen Lenskyj, a well-known feminist sports sociologist who assisted Blainey with her case, concurs. Lenskyj is one of the sharpest critics of the "female deficit" model of sport that upholds traditional male values and attitudes as ideal,[14] but she also stresses the need for a range of options. "Not everyone wants to play a recreational [sport]," says Lenskyj. "If they [women] are serious players, they are very frustrated by the fact that it's mostly fun. It doesn't aim at winning and the competition is downplayed. And that doesn't serve all women's interests. So there have to be all sorts of choices available."[15]

Bodychecking was one such choice that was hotly debated by the female provincial representatives of the CAHA in the 1980s. While it continued to be a part of the game in some provinces, the CAHA phased it out for the national championships in 1986 in order to lower the high number of injuries due to the uneven skill levels of female players across the country. Female players rarely received proper coaching and most were not taught the art of safe bodychecking. An injury during a game could mean time off work and a loss of income. Unlike male Junior A players, a level comparable to the women's senior level, women players receive no financial incentives or perks to make this risk worthwhile. The elimination of bodychecking has also proven to be detrimental to the promotion of the game. Promoters and fans of the men's game consider bodychecking to be an essential element of the sport, one that defines "real" hockey. Its absence in the women's game has provided those who object to women playing hockey with one more reason to dismiss the female game.

Bodychecking was banned in world championships in 1992 by the International Ice Hockey Federation. The move has reduced injuries, but it has obscured the root cause of injuries: the lack of access to top-quality coaching and the limited availability of ice time for women. Girls and women simply do not receive the proper training to learn how to bodycheck and receive bodychecks. Practices for girls' and women's teams continue to be squeezed into the gaps between male teams' practices and games; community rinks still ignore women's requests for more ice time, claiming there is nothing they can do to alter the decades-old rules of first come, first served. Because men have traditionally played the game, they have established connections with rink managers and can often secure prime-time ice by simply calling these managers. Women and girls, then, get stuck with undesirable ice times. Furthermore, players on adult teams which are mostly male, are unregulated, unlike their minor hockey counterparts, who are permitted to play on only one registered team. As a result, many men have monopolized the ice, playing on several different teams whose games are all at prime time — the time safest for young girls to travel to and from rinks.

The Toronto area offers several examples of the resistance mounted against women and girls who want to play hockey. It also offers examples of different strategies that can be used to ensure that female players get a fair crack at ice time. In the spring of 1995, Fran Rider of the OWHA and Phyllis Berck, recreation manager for Toronto's Parks and Recreation Department, met with the city's rink managers to discuss the need for more ice time for girls. "It was basically a closed door," Rider recalls.[16] The women were told by these managers that for decades the ice time had been allocated based on who used it the year before. "They said it worked for them, so they saw no reason to change,"[17] says Rider, appalled. Berck, however, did not stop there. Spurred by community groups' demand that city-owned rinks serve their residents more fairly, she made numerous recommendations that explicitly required Toronto's seven rink managers to respond to female needs. The recommendations called for ice-rink management boards to give ice time, freed up when teams disbanded, to female leagues before offering it to male teams and to report yearly on what had been done to give females increased access to ice time.

The recommendations also called for changing residency restrictions, which require a certain percentage of women's team members to live within city limits. (Residency rules within the male leagues are not adhered to; many players simply give fake addresses in order to play in a certain area.) Instead of the 75 percent requirement for men's teams, the Parks and Recreation Department suggested a 50 percent requirement for women's teams. This would help to foster the growth of women's hockey. In Toronto, and in other parts of the country, residency restrictions have essentially prevented new female teams from playing on community rinks. This is due to the fact that in many communities there are not yet enough women to form full teams, which makes it necessary for new teams to draw players from a larger geographical area. Coaches find themselves caught in the difficult situation of attempting to promote the sport's growth while being unable to provide players with facilities. Cheryl Harper, president of the Toronto Red Wings Ladies Hockey Association, faced this dilemma in 1994 when she was asked by the William Bolton Arena in downtown Toronto to launch a girls' house league. Harper, who had requested ice time at sixty-two arenas in greater Toronto, had managed to negotiate only a tentative promise of two hours per week at one rink for the five girls' teams she already ran. She therefore jumped at the chance to form a league at the Bill Bolton Arena, quickly pulling together three girl's teams. But arena officials changed their mind about the girl's league when they discovered that many of the players did not live within city limits. They ultimately cancelled the league and told the girls to join teams elsewhere. Harper, who reports she almost has to harass arena managers to get even a few hours of poor ice time, says residency restrictions for girls serve only to keep them away from the sport. Berck agrees: "Sport develops with opportunity. That's the catch-22 of women's hockey. People don't join hockey and then not have a venue to play."[18]

In April 1995 Toronto city hall approved the recommendations, in theory paving the way for more female participation. City Councillor Pam McConnell captured the essence of the issue at the meeting. "I can recall having to walk one and a half hours to get a chance to skate in an outdoor rink as a girl. Then I'd have to put on those skates with picks on the toes that I was constantly tripping over," she recounted, her

voice thick with irony. "We girls were sort of like Bambi —
shoved to the margins of the rink while the boys skated and
played their hormonal games in the middle."[19]

The city's approval of the recommendations did not resolve the access issue, however. By August, four of the seven
city-owned rinks had done little or nothing to make ice time
available for female hockey. Once again, on the table at the
Neighbourhoods Committee were recommendations designed
to open the ice to female hockey. This time, however, the
council named the guilty rinks — Forest Hill, Ted Reeve,
George Bell and North Toronto Memorial — and approved a
recommendation that required each of these rinks to make
two hours of prime-time ice available for women's groups by
1996–97. The council also requested that the Budget Review
Group look at how well the rinks were serving female hockey
players when considering their annual operating budget. Since
the arena boards are appointed and funded by city council,
city council is essentially their landlord. By threatening to pull
the arenas' purse strings, city council was at last endorsing the
recommendations. "It was clear that [we] were getting
nowhere, that arenas weren't adhering to the [April] requests,"
says Councillor McConnell. "Some had no difficulty, but the
other four put the blinkers on and dug their heels in and basically said we don't have to and we won't do it."[20]

Judging from a lengthy letter accompanying a half-page
Metro Toronto Hockey League (MTHL) advertisement published in the *Toronto Star*, arena managers were not the only
ones digging in their heels. MTHL President John Gardner had
also put on the blinkers. In a letter entitled, "New Season
Starts with Old Issues on Burner," Gardner depicts the amateur hockey community in Toronto as "being targetted by
Councillor McConnell [sic] war games computer."[21] Utterly
misinformed about the issue, Gardner accuses McConnell and
other city councillors of having demanded that 50 percent of

all ice time allocated for hockey be handed over to women, rather than the meagre two hours a week. He then writes:

> Now before ... a few mothers or feminist groups start sharpening their knives, let me explain that this isn't meant to be an anti-female hockey editorial. So put the blades away and let's pose some legitimate questions that should be addressed ... before Councillor McConnell decides which of, or if each of the existing user groups in the arenas under attack are forced to give up currently contracted ice.
>
> First, has she checked to see if the local community-based hockey associations have taken steps to determine if there are a sufficient number of young girls in the respective communities to justify the formation of female teams? If there aren't, then what's all the fuss about? And if there are, then I find it exceedingly difficult to believe that the requirements wouldn't be responsibly handled.[22]

When later questioned about the inaccuracies in his letter, Gardner admitted he never attended the city council meeting or read its minutes, but instead based his editorial on a small article that had appeared a week earlier in the *Toronto Star*. He did not, however, back away from his accusations. "It's almost gotten to abuse and intimidation," he says of women vying for more ice time. "In essence, girls get the better run of it by being able to play on boys' and girls' teams .... And the women's aggressive approach lessens the will to cooperate with them."[23] Gardner cites a meeting with North York's city council concerning ice time for female hockey in which the OWHA's Fran Rider, renowned for her fear of appearing too radical, "showed up with the representative of some ladies' rights group. They weren't there to listen, they were there to say, 'To heck to the rest of them.' The OWHA takes a very aggressive stand and boy, it was man the guns, no subtlety at all."[24]

Gardner was referring to a February 2, 1995 meeting in which women from the Newtonbrook's Senior Women's Recreational League voiced a complaint after Newtonbrook rink officials unilaterally took away two of their hours and re-allocated the time to an AAA boys' team. As a result of this move, the twenty-year-old league had been forced to cut four of its twelve teams. At the meeting, the representatives from the league, some of whom were lawyers, also requested that residency requirements similar to those passed by Toronto city hall be implemented. According to Fran Rider, the reaction of many male hockey players was exceptionally hostile. "'Why should women have any ice at all?' was the mentality," says Rider.[25]

Although the City of North York Parks and Recreation Department seemed amenable to lower residency require-ments for women, when the Parks and Recreation Committee of Council voted on the issue in May 1995, it reinstated the original 75 percent level. Members of one of the league's teams, the Apotex Bombers, responded in December 1995 with a human rights complaint. Paige Brodie, a lawyer and the Apotex Bomber who officially filed the complaint, calls the residency requirements discriminatory and wants them struck down. This is particularly the case for senior women's leagues, she says, which will not benefit from the influx of girls for some years to come and cannot possibly meet a 50 percent re-quirement, let alone a 75 percent one. Currently, the highest percentage of senior female team members who reside within North York is 40 percent. "Women need to be more aggressive and to take a strong stand on this issue," says Brodie. "Some people think the way to get things done is not to make waves and be nice and the arenas will not take anything more away. This approach hasn't gotten us anywhere."[26]

Women's hockey teams in smaller communities have faced the same willful ignorance. In Parry Sound in 1989, the

## · PUTTING ON THE HEAT: EQUITY ON ICE ·

Bobby Orr Community Centre manager, Jack Lawson, gave the women's team's traditional 6:15 PM slot on Sunday to a men's industrial league and moved the women to 5:00 PM — without their consent. While the time slot represented 100 percent of women's hockey scheduling in the arena, the men's industrial league were allotted two blocks of prime-time ice on Sunday and Thursday evenings. Outraged, team representative Chris Cardy and other women approached town council to reinstate the original time. The councillors refused to reverse the rink manager's decision, informing the women's team, the Trilites, that the men who played in that time slot "owned it." Cardy and teammates then filed a complaint with the Ontario Human Rights Commission. While the decision was pending, the team was obliged to drive thirty miles out of town to a smaller rink where they were permitted to play. "It went on and on," says Cardy, recounting the ordeal with bemused annoyance. "Every time we tried to set up a meeting, the guys would say, 'We can't have it then, that's hunting season, or that's when the guys work.' As if the women don't work!"[27] At one point a male hockey player attempted to launch a counter-case, claiming that the men were victims of discrimination at the hands of women usurping their ice time. "You know," Cardy comments wryly, "they only could play on three teams each, six times a week. Real tough."[28]

After a three-year wait, Cardy and teammates won the case in August 1992 and they can now claim Tuesday nights at 8:30 for their one-hour practices, an improvement from the original Sunday night time. But the resistance did not end with the commission's decision. The Trilites were subsequently harassed by leering male players and this harassment did not abate until Cardy sent a letter of complaint to the arena management, the police and town council. Furthermore, the human rights victory has brought no sense of security to Cardy and her teammates: their ice time was taken away again in the fall of 1995 and reinstated only after Cardy sent a letter warning town council that she would take action.

The Orillia Girls Hockey Association in Ontario has endured a similar trial. The league was set up in 1991 and by 1995 it had attracted more than sixty girls. Its players, whose ages range from nine to seventeen, share a Friday time slot of 8:45 PM to 11:00 PM, a slot that was given to them by the boys' minor league. The former treasurer of the Orillia association, Roger Czerneda, approached the Parks and Recreation Department of the City of Orillia to request a better time. Officials told him they would not make room for anyone, girls or boys, because it would mean bumping men who had played at the same time for years. "The whole thing is very brutal," says Czerneda with contained frustration. "It's been detrimental to the whole organization. If we invite a team from out of town, it's midnight before they go home. It is very late for the younger ones. A lot of girls are ready to pack it in."[29]

Czerneda and his wife, Julie, pursued the matter. In February 1995 they sent a letter to Cliff Turner, director of the Parks and Recreation Department, protesting the city's refusal to acknowledge the league or treat it fairly. With their letter they forwarded a copy of the handbook that outlines the Ontario government policy on equity in sport. The Czernedas asked if Turner was aware of the policy and, if so, if he had explained to City Hall that it stipulates that girls and women must have fair and full access to recreational facilities. Turner replied that he knew of the policy but had done nothing to implement it:

> I act and react relative to various policies/legislation. To my knowledge this is not legislated. This is a policy position. Having said that, Members of Council are interested in providing services for all ages and both sexes in an equitable manner. As a Department Head, I act on their behalf.[30]

But Turner then writes that of the 74 percent of ice time contracted to youth organizations in the city, 19 percent is allotted to girls' figure skating and hockey. This means that girls receive 14 percent of the town's ice time, a fraction of which goes to female hockey.

Czerneda was angered by Turner's response, but was reluctant to file a human rights complaint. "This is a very close-knit community," he explains, almost apologetically, "and we're afraid there will be some retribution there. They could try to give our sons the worst ice time if we push too hard for the girls. So we're trying to be careful and not make enemies."[31]

Girls' hockey in other regions of Canada has not fared much better. In Saskatchewan, where women and girls now make up 12 percent of the province's registered players, funding for girls' teams has proven to be the most serious obstacle. In Saskatoon, the Youth Sports Subsidiary Program requires team players to reside within city limits to be eligible for city funding. Because newly formed girls' teams have such difficulty filling their rosters with players from one area, some have to function with no funding at all. In 1993–94 the Saskatoon Selects, a Midget girls' team, found itself paying the full costs for rink time, referees and the performance bond — a sum that totalled $10,000. On the other hand, boys who are part of the Saskatoon Minor Hockey Association can easily comply with the residency restrictions. As members of the association, they are reimbursed by the city for approximately 39 percent of their ice costs and have schedules and referees booked automatically. "It is ridiculous the way we have to go about raising money," says the Selects' former coach Sandy Johnson. "Not only do we have to organize bingos, but because the team wasn't comprised just of city players, we didn't qualify for subsidy or practice time. Because of that, we must book our own ice, arrange our own games, and arrange to have ice time cancelled if we go out for a tournament so we don't get charged."[32] Johnson, who has been involved in hockey in Saskatchewan for over a decade, says that approximately 70 percent of girls in the province play on boys' teams. Regina is the exception. There the Queen City Hockey Association has managed to secure decent ice time for its players and ensure a thriving girls' league.

In Prince Edward Island, Susan Dalziel, director of female hockey with the PEI Hockey Association, reports that parents' have been the largest impediment to girls' participation. Dalziel, whose no-nonsense commitment to female hockey has led the game to its current popularity, recounts that once parents abandoned the notion that girls shouldn't be playing hockey, the game flourished in the province. Although local hockey boards made no effort to develop the game, they did not put up roadblocks as boards have done in other provinces. Prince Edward Island also fares well compared with most other provinces in regard to female representation on local boards. The PEI Minor Hockey Association appointed a girls' coordinator in 1977 and a director of female hockey in 1980. The latter appointment was made two years before it even occurred to the CAHA to create a female council.

Ninety-five percent of PEI's female players are members of girls' teams who play other girls' teams under the auspices of the local hockey associations. PEI enjoys the distinction of having the highest number of indoor ice rinks per capita in the world, says Dalziel, with twenty-five rinks for a population of 125,000. The province's girls also profit from the fact that they are seen as the saviours of the game. The number of male hockey players has dropped significantly in the last decade. In order to revitalize the sport, leagues are now encouraging females to form teams.

Another league that is flourishing is the Ontario London Devilettes Girls' Hockey Association. In 1986, its first year of operation, it had thirteen players. The Public Utilities Commission (now the Parks and Recreation Department) cooperated with the association's founders, who worked hard to win the city's support. Although the league was initially given poor ice time, it now shares time equitably with the boys' league. By 1995 more than five hundred girls belonged to the league which now has thirteen competitive teams and twenty-eight house leagues. The league brought home three provincial gold medals and one silver medal in 1995 alone. Its recent success is no doubt related to the improved ice time.

Although Devilettes' President Connie Rice says she still has to contend with parents who accuse the league of "using the boys' ice," the association's size prevents those who oppose it from edging the girls off the ice. The league not only represents the girls' interest in the game, it also sets an example of how women can effectively run a sports association with female-centred goals. More than 50 percent of the association's twenty-five-person executive is female. Parity in gender representation is unheard of in boys' leagues, where women are usually confined to organizing fundraising dances or bake sales. The league's next step, says Rice, is to bolster the number of female coaches, who currently account for less than 20 percent of the coaching staff.

The allocation of ice time not only affects the hours in which women play and practise, it also affects the length of their games. Most women continue to be given three ten-minute stop-time periods compared with men's three twenty-minute stop-time periods. However, since the mid-1980s at least one group of players has been allocated longer playing periods. Members of the Central Ontario Women's Hockey League who are at the Senior AA level now play for two fifteen-minute periods and one twenty-minute period. According to Fran Rider, male organizers have claimed for years that shorter periods were all girls could handle. They have argued that female players do not possess the stamina to last three twenty-minute periods. "If there's a shortage of ice," comments Rider, "people will come up with lots of different reasons to turn women down."[33]

For more than two decades feminist women and men have protested the inequitable allocation of sports facilities and resources to activities aimed at grooming boys for professional careers. In 1981 these dissenting voices united to form the Canadian Association for the Advancement of Women and Sport and Physical Activity (CAAWS), an organization that has since been highly critical of the persisting bias against women and girls in sport.

Although the need for a national organization that would address the issue of gender equity in relation to sports was not formally recognized until CAAWS formed, conferences, workshops and seminars on women and sport had begun to spring up in the early seventies. Leaders in this area included Abby Hoffman, Marion Lay, Bruce Kidd and Penny Werthner, former world-class athletes who remained connected to sport through administrative or academic positions. When CAAWS was formed, its founders defined their mission as "advanc[ing] the position of women by defining, promoting, and supporting a feminist perspective on sport and .... improv[ing] the status of women in sport,"[34] a statement that would prove to be problematic given the diverse and often diverging views of feminism held by members. For CAAWS' first six years, however, the sheer excitement of tackling equity issues with other like-minded people produced a dynamic, if cash-strapped, organization. Members focussed their energy on leadership development, research and especially advocacy. This initial period of productiveness waned by the late 1980s, however. CAAWS became increasingly estranged from the very sports organizations it was trying to influence and more closely aligned with feminist organizations such as the National Action

Committee on the Status of Women (NAC) and the Canadian Research Institute for the Advancement of Women (CRIAW). Rather than educating organizations about how to promote sport for girls and women, CAAWS took on the "bad guy" role of publicly chastising groups for excluding women from promotional materials or failing to fund female programs. Dissension within the organization also contributed to its inability to effect change.

Marion Lay, former manager of the Sport Canada Women's Program and a founding member of CAAWS, attributes the resulting frustration and internal strife partly to the mistaken tactics of its leaders. "We put the sport agenda on the women's movement, rather than put a women's agenda on sports," Lay explains. "We need to do both." Lay comments wryly that by the early 1990s, CAAWS had become "the menstrual hut of Canadian sport. More blood was let there due to infighting and lack of direction than anywhere else."[35]

Nevertheless, Sport Canada hardly helped, despite its official commitment to equity. Its 1986 policy on gender equity provided an excellent discussion of how fairness could be achieved, but it lacked accountability and specific goals, and because of this was in essence a non-agenda. Consequently, sports agencies such as the CAHA have continued to swallow millions of dollars while doing virtually nothing to boost female participation. "It's been shocking how little change has happened. And this newest policy that just came out still won't address sports equity until 1996," says Lay, referring to the Sport Funding Accountability Framework, initiated by Sport Canada. "It will be interesting to see what kind of teeth they'll put into it ten years later. Change has always been left to best intentions."[36]

The Sport Funding Accountability Framework, developed with the input of Ann Peel, chairperson of the Canadian Athletes' Association, provides a precise point system for deciding which sports organizations will receive funding from Sport Canada. Groups that commit resources to women and girls and include women in leadership roles will be awarded points for their efforts. The accountability framework offers the first objective evaluation of who receives money at the federal level. Prior to 1996 Sport Canada raised or cut an organization's funding based on the previous year of the group's budget, the history of the sport and its performance internationally.

At the same time that these policy changes occurred at Sport Canada, CAAWS underwent a major shift in focus. As a result, it no longer acts as a feminist watchdog group for sports organizations: it has now assumed the "good guy" role of educating sports organizations about how to boost the participation of female athletes, coaches and administrators. On the provincial level, however, only Quebec, Ontario, Saskatchewan and British Columbia have designed sports equity policies. Ontario's 1995 equity policy is known as Full and Fair Access for Women and Girls in Sport and Physical Activity and is particularly noteworthy. The handbook that outlines this policy is appropriately entitled *Walking the Talk,* a reference to the need for action, not just discussion. The policy has helped municipal equity groups such as Toronto's Women in Action and London's Females Active in Recreation (FAIR). The policy also brought equity pilot projects in nineteen municipalities to fruition and resulted in these programs being funded to the tune of $230,000.

While *Walking the Talk* is meant to empower women in sport, the process will no doubt be slow. "The problem with policies on women in sports is that they often precede the public's readiness to include women," says Sue Scherer, program consultant at Ontario's Female Athletes Motivating Excellence (FAME). "So many of the committees set up are advisory groups with no 'doers.' And what's to advise? The policies are strategically written so that they almost guarantee no compliance."[37]

Examples of ineffective policies abound. Saskatchewan's provincial amateur sports agency, Sask Sport, touts a policy called Sport for All as its answer to the inequities in sports funding. Here's how it helps girls: this policy stipulates that 35 percent of a sports group's budget must go toward grassroots activities, namely, events that fall below the provincial level of competition. Of this 35 percent, Sask Sport requests that a mere 20 percent — or 7 percent of the overall budget — be earmarked for target groups such as aboriginal people or people with disabilities, seniors or women. According to Dale Kryzanowski of Sask Sport's Regina office, it is up to the individual groups to decide how they wish to allot the 7 percent.[38] Not only are the equity requirements weak, but Sask Sport's methods of assessing whether a program makes a difference lacks accountability. Evaluation is limited to a financial audit and a review of the overall program when the group reapplies for funding. In Saskatchewan, as in many other provinces, the lion's share of its sports budget, 35 percent, is designated for high-performance sports. Male hockey receives a significant portion of this; a small part of it is earmarked for the selection camps for high-calibre female players. "When you ask the provincial sport governing bodies, 'What does this [equity policy] mean?' they say they don't have a clue,"[39] says Pat Jackson, a member of the sports equity group 52% Solution. Jackson claims that the organizations that make up Sask Sport feel that Sport for All imposes rules on them that the associations do not know how to implement. Traditionally, provincial sports organizations have viewed their main role as serving the needs of elite athletes and have not seen any problem in excluding aboriginal people, people with disabilities or women from their programs.

The group 52% Solution (the name refers to the fact that women make up 52 percent of the world's population) is just one of the handful of equity groups that has arisen across the country to help include women and other excluded groups in publicly funded sports. Jackson's group set up its board in June 1994 and has since put out a quarterly newsletter on sports equity issues. Its goal is to act where the province has failed to and to transform Sask Sport into an agency that serves all members of the public. Promotion Plus in British Columbia led the way in 1988 by setting up a network for girls and women in physical activity and sports. Albertans formed In Motion in February 1995. After three years of strategy meetings, the group produced a humorous play about sports inequity called *See Jane Run*, which it used as a launching pad for discussion about gender issues in sport. New Brunswick, which has an equity group called *Alliance des femmes actives*, and Ontario are in the initial stages of forming advocacy groups.

Perhaps not surprisingly, it is the intercollegiate level of sport that may well prove to be the most progressive in terms of gender equity. This is because the growing female student body at Canadian universities is demanding a say about where its tuition dollars go. In 1993 the University of Toronto's Athletic Council set an exciting precedent for how far and how quickly fair distribution of funding can be achieved. A task force identified a $60,000 disparity between funding for men's and women's sports and persuaded the Athletic Council to eliminate the gap by 1996. The move has pumped thousands of dollars into the women's hockey team, a team that was slated for cancellation in 1992 when the university took $1.2 million away from the Department of Athletics and Recreation (DAR). Men's football, a very poorly attended sport, was also slated for extinction. Such a clamour of protest resulted over cutting football, however, that the DAR was forced to reinstate both teams, recouping the lost revenue in increased student service fees. Because students were now required to contribute directly to sports, they began to ask questions about just what they were getting for their money. Since women make up 54 percent of the university's student body, the Office for the Status of Women was particularly interested in how fairly resources were being distributed.[40] When it came to light just how inequitable sports financing was, the Task Force on Gender Equity was created and eventually redressed the imbalance.

Women's hockey benefitted greatly from the reallocation of funds. In 1994 the hockey team, then known as the Lady Blues, scraped by on a yearly budget of less than $11,000 — one-tenth of the men's hockey budget. The women were also allocated second-rate ice time; their practices were scheduled in the unpopular 7:00 PM slot, after the men's team had finished. The team also had to make do with second-rate equipment passed down from the men. As well, the women were absent from the university's annual sports publication, a book that dedicated pages to write-ups and photos of members of the men's teams.

When the equity recommendations were implemented, the situation changed almost overnight. The women's team now shares the coveted 5:00 to 7:00 PM practice slot that was the men's team's for more than sixty years. Furthermore, the women's budget was more than $40,000 for the 1995–96 season, an increase that allowed the team to acquire proper equipment and to travel to more tournaments. "The recognition makes such a difference," says Hilary Korn, a player who was with the team from 1991 to 1995. "People at U of T now know us and how many games we win and lose, so we feel the pressure to win. That's good. We're more like an intercollegiate team, not some recreational league. The calibre is definitely higher."[41] Karen Hughes, a former player who has been head coach of the Lady Blues since 1993, says the whole process also showed up a dangerous apathy on the part of female athletes. "It was a big eye-opening year for us," says Hughes. "We now understand we have to be involved in these issues. It was our own fault that things were so bad. We never participated on committees."[42]

Still, key inequities persist. Publicity, per diems for coaches, and most importantly in these times of government cutbacks, the lack of donations from alumnae remain stumbling-blocks. Women are years behind men in terms of being able to establish networks that can rally round a faltering sport and inject it with vital cash. And although the University of Toronto move represents a critical breakthrough for female university athletes, the reaction of other universities to it hardly inspires hope. "We sent the policy around the country and the reaction was, 'Oh my god, thanks! Now I'm going to have to do one, too!'" says Paul Carson, sports information director for the University of Toronto. "I mean everybody said they liked it, but there were some who said, 'The handwriting's on the wall at my university.'"[43]

Other than the University of Toronto team, the women's hockey team at Concordia University is the only one in Canada that enjoys equitable funding. Concordia has had a women's team since 1975, and since 1985 this team has received its fair share of money from the university's athletic budget. The funding has directly translated into better hockey — and varsity status, which means the team is financially supported by the university. Julie Healy, who is the athletics facilities coordinator and assistant coach, says, "Players see how serious we are about the program, so we get players with high goals. Very few of them don't strive to be on the national team."[44]

But Concordia University, like the University of Toronto, is the exception. The reluctance of other universities to implement equity policies is hardly surprising given the lack of incentives to do so. In Canada, no sports equity legislation exists. The governing body for university sports, the Canadian Intercollegiate Athletic Association (CIAU), has left it up to its forty-five-member schools to offer equal sports opportunities to women and men. Although it has a gender equity policy, the CIAU sponsors nine national men's championships and only seven women's championships. President Liz Hoffman hopes to redress this imbalance by the summer of 1996. But as public funding for both education and sports rapidly evaporates, it is unclear if obtaining equity will translate into more sporting opportunity for university women or cuts to male programs.

For female hockey, in particular, the struggle for financial security will no doubt continue for some years. At thirty-seven Canadian universities, women's hockey remains at club status, receiving little or no university funding. Ontario is the only province that has a league of varsity teams. This league, which is made up of six teams, is part of the Ontario Women's Intercollegiate Athletic Association. If the CIAU decides to add more women's sports to its program, there will be resistance to including women's hockey because the game is not played in official intercollegiate conferences across the country. Liz Hoffman, however, insists that there is tremendous interest in the game but that it lies at the unacknowledged club level, where university women form their own teams and cover their own expenses. "We have this fear that it's too expensive," she says of the CIAU, "but nobody's complaining about how much we spend on men's hockey."

Even in the United States, where female college athletes have had legal recourse to inequity under Title IX legislation, the scales are proving slow to balance. Title IX refers to a portion of a US law that prohibits sex discrimination in all high schools and universities that receive federal funding. Title IX was passed in 1972, and schools can comply with it in any of the following ways: by offering men and women athletic opportunities that are proportionate to the gender ratio of students; by demonstrating that sports opportunities are growing for the underrepresented sex; or by meeting the interests and abilities of the underrepresented sex. When this legislation was enacted in 1972, less than 2 percent of college athletes were female and women received less than half of 1 percent of the sports operating budgets and virtually no scholarships. By 1995 women made up one-third of college athletes, took home one-third of athletic scholarships and received 20 percent of the money allotted for athletic budgets. In February 1992 the Supreme Court ruled that monetary damages could be awarded in Title IX cases. This decision resulted in schools taking equity much more seriously in light of the very real possibility that they might be sued.[45] Nonetheless, some American schools have decided to wage legal battles against Title IX instead of redressing financial inequities.

A less auspicious outcome of Title IX legislation involves the fate of female coaches and women in sports leadership positions. As women's sports programs became properly funded, gained more recognition and, in many cases, merged with men's programs, female coaches and administrators lost their jobs to men. Consequently, there was a sharp decline in the number of women in leadership positions. This is no small point in the US or in Canada. Leadership is the linchpin to equity: without women in key positions, damaging practices in sports organizations will go unchallenged. A number of recent American studies have found that many male athletic directors dismiss the underrepresentation of women in leadership positions. They argue that there is a lack of qualified women, that female coaches are unwilling to travel, that women don't apply for the jobs, and that they are held back by family obligations.[46] In Canada, University of Alberta sociologist Ann Hall studied the gender structure of national sports organizations in 1990 and found that while 60 percent of women reported that discrimination played a major role in the absence of women on their organizations' boards, only about one-third of men cited sexist attitudes as the barrier.[47] Another study of board staff relations in provincial sports organizations was completed in 1994 by Sue Inglis, a University of McMaster professor. Inglis found that the women she surveyed perceived that including them on boards was not a priority and that developing female programs was seen by some male board members as an "unfavourable exercise." Female respondents in the study also reported that they had to work very hard to be listened to and to ensure that their suggestions were not dismissed by male colleagues.[48]

Penny Werthner, a sports psychologist and founding member of CAAWS, has worked to help women move into positions of leadership in sports organizations. In 1992 a group of Werthner's colleagues visited Norway, where they discovered how equity legislation at the government level has transformed the country's workplaces to reflect the needs of women as well as men. "What they learned is that you need a critical mass of women in leadership positions in order to change the culture of an organization," relates Werthner. "They also saw that working with individual women to give them specific skills was essential."[49] Werthner's greatest fear is that with government cutbacks, women and other marginal groups will be squeezed out of the few positions they now hold. When it comes to the crunch, she says, male programs and positions remain in place, while female initiatives get dumped. Werthner cites the reneging of the Canadian Basketball Association on its promise to centralize the female national team in Victoria in 1995 as an example. Head coach Kathy Shields resigned in protest and was swiftly replaced by a male coach. "There are very good women who get passed over constantly because the assumption is they can't take the pressure," says Werthner angrily, "and that the best coach will be a male coach."[50]

Shannon Miller, the coach of the women's national hockey team, agrees. Miller has dedicated most of her adult life to developing her coaching skills and has paid a high price for her commitment to this profession. Before heading up the women's high-performance hockey centre at Calgary's Olympic Oval, Miller worked as a police officer and was constantly encouraged by the force to gain the necessary qualifications for promotion. But she turned down these offers, because she could not put equal amounts of time and energy into both coaching, which she did on a volunteer basis, and her career.

Unlike coaches of the men's national team, Miller is not paid for coaching the women's national team, although her expenses and flights are covered by the CHA. Appointed as an assistant coach in 1994, she received an honorarium of $1,500 for what she estimates added up to about four months of full-time work over a two-year period. Although the CHA initiated a Women's High-Performance Coaching Pool in 1994 to groom five women for national team coaching positions, it has done little else to encourage female coaches.

Putting women in leadership positions will not only help to increase sports opportunities for girls and women, it will also help bring to the fore the problem of harassment, which is rarely acknowledged. Harassment can be as overt as leering, whistling and hostile accusations of lesbianism or as subtle as a coach commenting on the looks, not the performance, of a female player. One former member of the women's national hockey team recalls a male coach praising another team member for her "bedroom eyes."

But coaches are not the only culprits. By all accounts, parents can be the worst offenders. When a girls' team dominates a boys' team in a game, for instance, parents of the boys have been known to encourage their sons to use violent tactics against the girls. Coach Sandy Johnson recalls that her talented Saskatoon Midget team has put up with parents yelling, "Hit her! Smash her! Knock her down!" from the stands. Although the league was no-contact, by the end of the season violence had escalated to such an extent that the referees cut

*Ontario's Karen Hughes with Alberta's Melody Davidson
and Shannon Miller, members of the CHA's first national
team coaching pool for women's hockey.*

games short several times. One outstanding team member was
singled out for abuse by the male team. The injuries she received were so serious that she was unable to participate in the
Canada Winter Games in 1995.

Star player Hayley Wickenheiser has experienced similar
harassment from parents who objected to a girl playing in
their boys' league. Wickenheiser's father remembers parents in
the stands yelling, "Kill her, kill her!" On one occasion the
Wickenheiser family will never forget, the mother of a boy
from the opposing team followed Hayley to her makeshift
dressing room, where she hammered the door with her fists
and screamed, "You little bitch! That's not the way to play
hockey. Get out of here and never come back!" "Would it have
happened had she been a boy?" Wickenheiser's mother, Marilyn, asks. "I would suspect not because that town had a boy

that was pretty equally skilled as her, but there were no vicious attacks on him."[51]

While this outward rancour clearly makes sports arenas a hostile place for girls, more often than not it is the everyday kinds of innuendo and sexist remarks that have kept many girls off the ice. Shirley Cameron, former Team Canada member and twenty-year veteran of the women's game, admits that until the mid-1980s, she hid the fact that she even played hockey. She feared that if she revealed this she would be subject to verbal and physical abuse. "We used to be called that [dykes] every time we stepped on the ice," Cameron says of the Edmonton Chimos, anger resonating in her voice. "It got so only those married with kids would feel safe saying they played hockey."[52] Even at the organizational level, the Chimos have had to deal with pressure to comply to a heterosexist image of how women should appear. In the fall of 1994, the president of the newly formed girls' hockey league in Edmonton requested a "feminine-looking representative"[53] from the Chimos to address its board. These kinds of requests are nothing new. Helen Lenskyj's research reveals that women who participate in sports that have traditionally been the domain of men have been called lesbians for decades. This labelling not only deters females from becoming involved in sports, but prevents many athletes from rejecting unwanted sexual attention from male coaches.[54]

Harassment, inadequate access to ice time, underfunding and the underrepresentation of women on organizational bodies all attest to a sports world that promotes and guards the aspirations of some boys and views the aspirations of girls as a threat. That the resistance to female hockey players is so widespread and, in many cases, so acute, speaks volumes about what is at stake. As has been said countless times before, hockey for Canadians is more than just a game: it is a tradition, an entrenched way of life. Accompanying this tradition

— as glorified and reassuring as it may be — are myths, op-position to change and a "putting on the blinkers" attitude as Pam McConnell so aptly dubs it. Not only have many hock-ey enthusiasts not welcomed the influx of girls and women into the game, many will not even acknowledge that women want to play.

Overcoming such resistance is a daunting task, one that has not been tackled with the unity and force that have been applied to other sectors that exclude women. This is in part due to the perception of sports as a male domain. But it is also due to ignorance of female sports history. Women have, after all, been playing hockey for almost as long as men, and as Alexandrine Gibb wrote in 1938, they have been continually denied ice time. Despite this fact, many female players and or-ganizers share the misguided belief that with gentle prodding and just a little more time promoters of male hockey will open the rinks to women and girls.

*Officials at the 1982 women's national championship.*

This has not been the case. Nor is it likely to be in the near future. Female hockey players must insist on equitable ice time by using one of the most effective means employed so far: human rights complaints. Filing such complaints is uncomfortable at best. In smaller communities in particular this act does not come without retribution, as Chris Cardy of Parry Sound has shown. But it does expose the raw prejudice that lurks behind so many of the excuses that keep girls away from hockey.

This is not to say that other methods of ensuring ice access are not valid. Certainly the efforts of Phyllis Berck and Pam McConnell in the City of Toronto have been extremely worthwhile. So, too, have the networking and educational efforts made by feminist sports administrators and female hockey representatives. But in order for all of these approaches to succeed the "old boys' club," which lies at the core of our hockey culture, must be tackled. This challenge has not been taken up by enough female hockey advocates. Until this changes, opportunities will continue to glide by girls and women.

In the meantime the loss continues to go unacknowledged, even by the most well-meaning chroniclers of hockey history. "The sorrow is that there may also be Wayne Gretzkys of the piano or the paint brush who, because we expose our young to hockey so much more than to the arts, we will never know about,"[55] writes Peter Gzowski in his classic account of hockey, *The Game of Our Lives.* While this is undoubtedly true, Gzowski and others have failed to pen such touching requiems for the lost sporting opportunities of girls with whom, as children, they scrimmaged in their backyard rinks. The fierce drive towards the pro leagues and the intense sense of ownership felt by many advocates of male hockey have all but numbed Canadians to the fact that "the game of our lives" has really been the game of *their* lives, a game from which half the country has been coolly shut out.

## Chapter Seven

# MEDIA, MANON & HOCKEY INC.

*Funny, but he doesn't look jockish.*
*Except for maybe the shiner.*
*Striding through the concrete corridors of the Trois-Rivieres' Le Colisee, Jacques LaPrairie, 19, moves more like a model than a hockey star.*
*"Can you give me a few minutes to go home and fix my hair?" he asks in broken English, adding in French, "I can't let you take my picture like this."*
*Not that there's much wrong with 'this' — five foot six, a lithe 140 pounds, long, dark hair, velvety brown eyes, tawny skin.*
*But underneath it all is solid muscle and determination. The kind of determination that can carry the young goalie as far as he wants to go.** 

IF YOU THINK THERE is something odd about this depiction of Jacques LaPrairie, your reaction is justified. Who would ever describe a male sports star in terms that focus exclusively on his good looks? Yet that is exactly how the real subject of this 1991 *Toronto Star* article — elite hockey player Manon

*Adapted from a 1991 *Toronto Star* article.

Rhéaume — was portrayed.[1] And it is how many female athletes are depicted.

Although the article excerpt may be a particularly overt example of how the media have portrayed female athletes, this kind of description is by no means uncommon. With Rhéaume's name back in place, the article does what many features do to female athletes: it showcases the sexual attractiveness and femininity of the athlete, discussing her physical strength and skills only once her aesthetic appeal has been established. The message conveyed is that the real worth of female athletes lies not in how they perform, but in how they appear.

While the focus on the appearance of female athletes reflects the historical discomfort with celebrating the competitiveness and power of women, it also points to a deeper role that athletics play in our lives. The world of sports has traditionally been male terrain; it has provided not only a setting in which men can prove their masculinity but also a place in which their actions are glorified. The fact that even today girls and women must undertake legal battles to gain access to the sporting opportunities enjoyed by most boys and men indicates the extent to which the female presence in sport is unwelcome.

Yet the focus on the femininity of female athletes is just one of the ways in which their accomplishments are undermined. For the most part, women are simply ignored. The sports media's near exclusive concentration on professional male sports has ensured women's absence on most sports pages and in television and radio broadcasts. With the exception of golf, tennis and figure skating, the vast majority of female sports fall into the larger category of amateur sports — a category that also receives meagre attention. To some extent, this accounts for the lack of reporting on women in sport. But not entirely. Even when the media do turn their attention to amateur sports such as hockey, women still receive far less recognition than do their male counterparts.

Amateur sports organizations are partly to blame for this. Many of the organizations do a poor job of getting word out to the media about their athletes and events; they often lack both the money and the savvy to hire qualified media liaison people. Money, however, isn't always the problem. The Canadian Hockey Association (CHA) has a budget in the millions of dollars, yet has been unable to secure much in the way of media attention and sponsorship for its elite female athletes.

And so it is no coincidence that with the increasing, and increasingly serious, media coverage of women's hockey since the first world championship in 1990 a disproportionate amount of it has focussed on Manon Rhéaume, the first woman to make the pro leagues. The predictable interest in Rhéaume is in part due to her marketable "assets," but it is also because Rhéaume has played on men's teams and within a male sports context — a context that the vast majority of sports reporters and corporate sponsors know and feel comfortable within. Like most women's sports, female hockey is caught in a seemingly inescapable orbit outside the realm of the professional male game: without proper media recognition, corporations will not invest in the athletes; and without the marketing drive of a committed sponsor, the media will not take notice.

The symbiotic relationship between media and sponsorship in hockey first took shape in the early 1930s in Canada. At the time women began to be shut out of sports pages as part of the gradual exclusion of amateur sports from all media coverage. In his excellent history of amateur sports in Canada, *The Struggle for Canadian Sport,* Bruce Kidd chronicles the shift in media coverage from focussing on sports at the community level to focussing on professional teams. Kidd follows the formation of the National Hockey League (NHL), describing how promoters of the professional game in the 1930s left nothing to chance in replacing fans' allegiance to community teams with loyalty to the Toronto Maple Leafs, Montréal Canadiens or American teams. "In Toronto, the Leafs management [offered] reporters pre-written features, statistical information and privileged access to stars and 'scoops' if they filed stories on a daily basis ..." writes Kidd. "In some cases, the entrepreneurs bribed reporters outright."[2] If reporters failed to write what promoters requested, they were often cut off from information sources.

Nowhere was the reshaping of fans' loyalty so powerful as on the radio. Foster Hewitt, the CBC announcer of *Hockey Night in Canada* for more than three decades, is still revered as Canada's most beloved "voice of hockey." What is less well known, however, is that Hewitt was on the payroll of the Maple Leaf Gardens, hired as director of radio — in essence, a paid publicist — in 1927 by the team's owner to call its Saturday night games. Kidd rightly likens the set-up to "turning over the news department to the campaign director of one of the political parties, the music department to RCA records, or farm broadcasts to the Winnipeg Grain Exchange. One narrow, vested interest was given virtually unrestricted opportunity to define the hockey culture for us all."[3] The broadcasts were immensely popular: by 1934 the Stanley Cup semifinals blared from over 70 percent of the one million radios across Canada.[4] Although the program was sponsored initially by General Motors, Imperial Oil came on as sponsor in 1936, keen to gain access to the largely male listenership.

Hewitt's broadcasts did indeed "define hockey culture" and Canada's interest in sports as an exclusive focus on male hockey. This happened at the expense of the many other sports that Hewitt announced over the radio in the early 1920s, including women's basketball, softball and hockey. As *Hockey Night in Canada* grew to dominate sports broadcasting in Canada, women's coverage virtually vanished from newspapers and the airwaves. Writes Kidd:

Despite the large number of men who paid to watch women's games, it was felt that only men's sports would attract a male audience. While girls and women listened to the Hewitt broadcasts, they did not have the spending power or perceived household influence to attract the interest of sponsors such as General Motors and Imperial Oil. As a result, the fundamental production function of the sports-media complex was designed for an all-male universe. It helped keep women's sports off the air.[5]

To this day coverage of women's sports remains scant at best. From 1991 to 1994 the Canadian Association for the Advancement of Women and Sport and Physical Activity (CAAWS) conducted informal surveys of the sports sections of twenty Canadian daily newspapers. The survey involved measuring the inches of space devoted to women's sports stories for one day in 1991, one week in 1992 and two weeks in 1993 and 1994. In 1991 CAAWS found that women received a trifling 2.8 percent of sports coverage nationally. The *Ottawa Citizen* rated the highest at 12 percent, the *Globe and Mail* followed at 5 percent and from there the percentages dropped steadily to the lowest, 0.2 percent in the *Montreal Gazette*. In 1993 the overall national total of space devoted to women's sports in the period studied was 8.8 percent.

When CAAWS released its findings to sports editors, the most common explanation proffered for the low coverage was that reports on professional male football, baseball and hockey games left little room for any amateur sports, not just women's. However, during the 1994 baseball strike and NHL lockout, not only did the coverage of women's sports not improve, it dropped in thirteen out of the twenty dailies to a national average of just 5 percent. The Halifax *Chronicle-Herald* ranked the highest at 18 percent with the St. John's *Evening Telegram* coming a close second at 16 percent. The *Toronto*

*Star,* Canada's largest daily, remained at the bottom of the heap at 1 percent with Quebec's *Le Droit* at 0.6 percent.

Many sports reporters and editors pointed out that the surveys were conducted in the fall, a time when summer amateur sports had just ended and major winter sports such as alpine skiing had not yet begun. Because amateur sports constitute the major sporting outlets for women, not much was going on at the time for female athletes and this was reflected in the papers. Nonetheless, rather than pause to question the enormous emphasis on professional male sports, sports section editors and reporters denied the validity of the survey or attacked CAAWS as a special interest group. Don Sellar, the *Toronto Star*'s ombudsman, was just one of a number of journalists to dismiss the cry from CAAWS for more coverage of female athletes as self-interest. In the *Star,* Sellar quotes the paper's managing editor Lou Clancy also as being unimpressed with the survey. "I don't believe in quantitative research," Clancy told Sellar. "You can't bring a feminist agenda to sports coverage."[6] David Perkins, the editor of the sports section since 1994, also did not take the survey's results seriously. "[The] study was not based on fact. They [CAAWS] admitted themselves that it was not scientific,"[7] Perkins insists. Sheila Robertson, CAAWS's communication consultant, responds that the organization "admitted" nothing. "That annoys me," says Robertson, "because we always said it was not scientific in the sense that we did not hire an academic to do the research. But of course it was valid. We measured the coverage very carefully, [a process that] ... took hours."[8]

The second article reacting to the survey came from Mary Ormsby, the only full-time female sports reporter at the *Star.* "A misleading one-week survey done each of the last three years annually convicts Canadian newspapers of a sex crime: Deliberately ignoring the accomplishments of female athletes," writes Ormsby. "Nothing could be further from the truth. But that matters little when a feminist cause decides that the women-as-victims-of-men angle is the easiest way, not the best way, to build its cause."[9] Ormsby's article is of particular interest because in it she addresses and alas, defends, the prevailing myths of why it is natural that male athletes are reported on more than female athletes. "The No. 1 priority of a newspaper is to make money," Ormsby writes. "To do that, a newspaper responds to matters that interest the community in the hope of selling more papers. This community loves male sports (sorry, it's a fact) and the year-round coverage of those leagues reflects that interest."[10]

The assumption that the media only respond to people's interest, and play no role in creating this interest, is seldom questioned by sports reporters and editors. But as Bruce Kidd has shown in his description of the rise of the NHL, the media have in fact shaped the public's ideas about which teams, athletes and issues are important. "It's a chicken and an egg thing," says Wendy Long, the sole female sports reporter at the *Vancouver Sun*. "We can't cover it unless there's the interest, but if we gave women's hockey the same amount of coverage, we'd be telling people that that's important. I think the media does set the agenda about what's important and just by how we cover things we're sending a message to the public. [For instance,] the Vancouver Canucks play eighty-four games a season and you cannot tell me that each of those eighty-four games is the be-all and the end-all of sports that day."[11]

Furthermore, this obsession with stars, scores, winning teams, and in the case of hockey, brawls, means that more relevant stories go untold — one notorious example being the non-reporting of Alan Eagleson's alleged dubious financial dealings in hockey. Allison Griffiths, co-author of *Net Worth*, a book that covered some of Eagleson's alleged shady financial deals, observes that when a reporter resists the pack mentality by writing stories that are critical of professional male sports, she or he will encounter hostility not only from the sports organizations but also from other reporters. Griffiths, who helped expose the corruption within professional hockey, speaks about the same phenomenon that Kidd describes in sports reporting in the 1930s — namely, that a reporter will be cut off from sources for not parroting the professional sports gospel. "It's who you know and who you can get access to. If you don't know anybody, you're nowhere,"[12] says Griffiths.

The second assertion that Ormsby makes in defending the overwhelming coverage of professional male sports is that "this community loves male sports." Given that sports is the newspaper section that is least read by women, the parameters of the "community" to which Ormsby refers are very narrow indeed. While few studies have been done on readership of sports sections and results of these studies vary, one trend has emerged: fewer women, teenagers and children are reading the sports section than fifteen years ago. According to statistics from the Newspaper Association of America (NAA), the percentage of women who read sports dropped most dramatically. At the organization's convention in 1994, the NAA proposed that one of the best ways to increase female readership was – amazingly enough! – to include more stories on women athletes.[13] In other words the main reason that women are not picking up the sports sections of papers is not because they don't care about sports, but because women's sports activities aren't reflected on those pages.

To assert that the community wants only professional male sports is all the more incomprehensible given declining readership of newspapers. Indeed, newspapers in the 1990s are under siege: the cost of newsprint is rising, advertisers are harder to woo and competition with television is proving to be a losing battle. Yet rather than attempting to appeal to a broader, more inclusive audience, sports sections editors are frantically trying to hold on to the limited readership they already have. David

Langford, the sports editor at the *Globe and Mail,* also views the coverage of professional sports as inescapable. "Of course professional sports is going off the end of the scale," he concedes. "People want more and more and more professional sports, so something has to lose out somewhere along the line."[14] The *Toronto Star*'s sports editor, Perkins, goes even further: "We don't create the demand [for pro sports], we just reflect the demand," he contends. "Getting the coverage to fifty-fifty [male-female] is not a realistic goal because the number-one interest of the readers is the Leafs, then the Raptors and then the Blue Jays. Those are the priority for the readers and resources."[15] Jane O'Hara, sports editor at the *Ottawa Sun* from 1988 to 1993, reports that while she tried to ensure that women in amateur sports received coverage equal to that given to their male counterparts, she made no attempt to curb the dominance of professional male sports at the *Sun,* lest she alienate the male readership.[16]

The next issue that Ormsby tackles in her article criticizing the CAAWS survey is the argument that many women are great fans of male sports, and "there's no need to shovel women-only articles at them. That's sexist."[17] It is true that many women are fans of male sports: about 50 percent of the audiences at professional basketball games are women,[18] as are almost 30 percent of hockey viewers.[19] Yet when there is little else available, what option do sports fans have but to watch male games? To say that it would be sexist to "shovel" women-only stories at readers is an odd assertion indeed given that Ormsby and others find little sexism in the fact that more than 90 percent of sports coverage centres on men.

Ormsby goes on to claim that the "real story is that female athletes are getting better coverage than ever."[20] While she offers no general evidence to back this up, she does rightly point out that the *Star* has made an effort since 1994 to feature women more frequently on the front page of its sports section.

Editor Perkins says that from 1993, the number of days women were featured on the front page of the sports section rose from fifty-four to ninety-six.[21] It is worth pointing out, however, that "featuring" can mean anything from printing a picture with a caption underneath to running an article. It is also worth noting that 1994 was an Olympic year, and consequently one in which amateur athletes on the whole were written about far more often than usual. Furthermore, many Canadian medallists in both the Olympics and the Commonwealth Games are women. Despite the large role that Canadian female athletes play in international amateur events, says Jane O'Hara, "[o]nly when amateur athletes like [Olympians] Myriam Bedard and Sylvie Fréchette do really well do they bump hockey or baseball off the front pages."[22]

The situation is perhaps the worst for young female athletes, who are consistently the media's last priority. From September 1993 to April 1995, the Scarborough Board of Education in Metropolitan Toronto studied the *Toronto Star* and the *Toronto Sun*'s sports sections, tallying the number of articles that each paper devoted to male and female high school sports. The total number of articles on high school sports in the *Star* was 158, only 27 of which were on girls' athletics. The *Sun* ran a total of 98 articles, 9 of which focussed on girls.[23]

Yet despite numbers like these, many sports journalists and editors maligned the CAAWS survey results, and in some cases even gloated over their self-perceived excellence in reporting on female athletes. "Our paper is regularly singled out for our excellent coverage of women's sports, and I know that at any other time of the year you would find us at the top of your survey," responded *Edmonton Journal* editor Wayne Moriarty, whose paper devoted a whopping 5 percent of its sports section to women athletes in 1994. He also told CAAWS, "We are proud of the job we do."[24]

Steve Dryden, editor at the *Hockey News,* also defends his

paper's track record on covering female players. The newspaper is one of the most successful weeklies in Canada, with a circulation of approximately 110,000, with 55 percent of sales occurring in the United States.[25] The *Hockey News* focusses almost exclusively on the NHL and its editors do not profess to cover much amateur hockey. When the paper does report on the amateur game, however, editor Dryden maintains it has tried hard to cover women. This is a puzzling assertion, given the scant sprinkling of articles on female teams and players over the years. Citing four profiles of national team players Geraldine Heaney, Stacy Wilson, Vicky Sunohara and Hayley Wickenheiser, Dryden defends his paper's coverage of the women's game. "We've probably done more than anyone on women's hockey," he says. "I'm not saying we've done a lot at all, but I'm not making any apologies."[26]

There is a prevailing belief among sports journalists and editors that the coverage of women's sports is improving, but today's female athletes may well receive *less* coverage than they did sixty or seventy years ago. In the 1920s and 1930s, Alexandrine Gibb of the *Toronto Star,* Phyllis Griffiths of the *Toronto Telegram,* hockey great Bobbie Rosenfeld of the *Globe* and Myrtle Cook of the *Montreal Star* all wrote daily women's sports columns. Other women who reported on major women's events included Patricia Page of the *Edmonton Journal,* Lillian "Jimmie" Coo of the *Winnipeg Free Press* and Ruth Wilson of the *Vancouver Sun.*[27]

Today no daily column on women's sports is published in a Canadian newspaper and most female sports reporters are the only women in their departments. "My sense is that more women are leaving sports journalism than entering it," says Jane O'Hara, who now teaches newspaper writing in the journalism program at Ryerson University. "There was a blip in the seventies when women were moving into sports, but then a lot of them left [to go to other departments] because they were much more comfortable elsewhere."[28] Even if more women were hired by papers to cover sports, it would be no guarantee that they would even want to write about female athletes. In fact, some say it would be professional suicide to take on women's sports as a regular assignment. As Mary Ormsby puts it, "I won't get on the front page if I cover ringette. You want to cover what's hot."[29] Furthermore, female reporters such as Ormsby resent being pigeonholed as the "girl columnists." In 1991 Ormsby was asked by her editor to write the weekly women's sport column, "At Large," for the sports section. "I was upset and mad and I thought, 'Oh great, you want to do a women's column so who are you going to get? The only woman working in the department. Thanks very much,'"[30] relays Ormsby. After five years of writing the column she says it still rankles but she continues to cover women, often out of guilt. Indeed, in the early 1990s, Ormsby provided some of the best coverage of the women's national hockey team in the country. "If I don't cover [female sports], no one else will,"[31] she surmises.

Although many sports reporters and editors acknowledge the limited perspective on sports that prevails in their papers, they are also quick to point out that a lack of support from female readers makes reporting on women even less rewarding. Ormsby says she rarely gets any feedback from her column. "I'm wondering 'Are you even reading this stuff?'" she says. "[Women] phone about the Leafs well enough." CAAWS's executive director, Marg McGregor, however, contends that women's silence with regards to sports coverage is in itself an expression of protest — that women are simply skipping over sports because there is nothing there for them.[32] Wendy Long of the *Vancouver Sun* doesn't agree. She maintains the silence serves only to assure editors that nothing needs to change. "I constantly have women coming up to me and complaining about the lack of coverage of women's sport, but they're choosing someone who is already committed to the cause and someone who doesn't have the power to make the changes," says Long. "Yet, when I ask them to phone or write a letter to our editor in chief and promotions people, rarely do they take that step."[33] Asked what action women should be taking, Long cites the example of what soccer fans do in Vancouver when they feel the sport isn't in the newspaper enough. "[The soccer fans] jam the phone lines, write letters and generally make life miserable for us," reports Long. "To get them off our backs we make sure we print the scores!"[34] It is a strategy that Diana Duerkop endorsed in a CAAWS newsletter editorial entitled "Only Ourselves to Blame." "Canadian women squandered an opportunity they'll have only once," wrote Duerkop about women's failure to capitalize on the October 1994 labour unrest in professional hockey and baseball by flooding newspapers with story ideas about female athletes. Instead, observed Duerkop, "[women] stood by as newspapers published an interminable supply of stories about minutiae that even dyed-in-the-wool sports nuts found nauseating."[35]

If women — and men — who are interested in women's sports are failing the reporters, so are many of the amateur sports organizations, whose task it is to promote their female programs. The Canadian Hockey Association is no exception. At the core of the CHA's promotion of female hockey is the same "little sister" principle that seems to govern so many of its decisions regarding the development of the female game. Promotion of the women's game simply has not been a priority in the world of male hockey, a reality that is reflected by the constant inability of the CHA to procure decent television, radio and newspaper coverage for national and world championships.

The general disregard for women's hockey at the CHA means that the responsibility for the entire women's program, including media relations, has fallen almost entirely on its sole manager, Glynis Peters, who juggles a host of disparate tasks. Moreover, the gains that have been made in the female game, namely, its inclusion in the larger CHA sponsorship package in 1995 and the national team program leading up to the 1998 Olympics, seem precarious both to national team players and to Peters. Fearing that any critical reporting on female hockey and the national team could jeopardize women's gains within the CHA, Peters has appeared increasingly reluctant to question inequities within the organization. For instance, in February 1996 Peters defended the CHA requirement that the top fifty-four female players in the country pay a fee of $100 to attend a national team evaluation camp. "Sometimes I have to tell players, 'I'm sorry all you do is look over your shoulder and see how things are for the guys,'"[36] she said. Although as amateur sport funding dries up in Canada more elite athletes are having to pay for some of their training expenses, such a fee is not required from members of the men's senior national team, who enjoy a full-time salary.

With regard to the CHA promotion of female hockey, a number of editors and reporters complain that they receive little or poor-quality information about the sport's events. It is a criticism levelled not only at the CHA, but at amateur sports organizations in general. The *Toronto Star* sports editor, David Perkins, says he received "not one piece of advance information from the CHA" about the 1996 women's national hockey championship, and was flabbergasted to learn that the CHA had faxed its press releases not to the *Star*, but to Lois Kalchman, a freelance reporter for the paper, who happened to be away at the time of the event. Consequently, Perkins says, the paper missed covering the story itself, printing instead a short piece from a wire service. The *Hockey News*, too, complains of the CHA's ineffectiveness at notifying the paper about its female events. "For example," says Dryden, "I don't even know who the PR person is for women's hockey."[37] He says he also does not know who holds that position at the Ontario Women's Hockey Association, which represents half the female players in Canada.

While by many accounts the CHA does a poor job of letting the media know about its events, when it does promote the sport, it often makes the classic blunder of billing itself as "the fastest-growing sport" in North America — a claim the CHA has often made regarding the female game. "That's a guaranteed turn-off," says Perkins. "It's just a buzz-word and it's not possible to believe all the twenty-eight sports that claim this each year."[38]

The kind of press releases sent out for the 1996 Pacific Women's Hockey Championship held in Richmond, BC can pretty much guarantee women's hockey will be overlooked. Although these press releases do not necessarily reflect the quality of most CHA releases for women's hockey, it is disturbing that in 1996 such poorly written promotional material is forwarded to the press. The release for the first Team Canada versus Team Japan game reads:

> The second game of the night featured Our National Team playing Team Japan. This being the first ever Championship game played in Richmond our National Women's Team wanted to put on a show and that they did .... The Coaching staff, lead [sic] by Shannon Miller of Calgary had this team very focused going in to this game and not once did they take their opposition lightly, as games can change very quickly. Team Canada out shoot [sic] Team Japan by a large amount of 70 to 8. The skill level is not quite there for our visitors from Japan but they are to be commended as everyone connected with the team were very friendly to everyone and were very pleased to be a part of this major event.

> The next opponent for Team Canada is Team
> China .... To win they must stay focused and have lots
> of discipline to stay in the hunt for the Championship
> Trophy ....

With press releases like this, one can hardly blame the major
newspapers for having failed to print even the perfunctory
bottom-corner articles they ran for the 1996 women's national hockey championships the week before.

Another example of publicity that falls short of its goal
occurred in October 1995 at the Hockey Hall of Fame in
Toronto. In a move supposedly aimed at drawing attention to
a national training camp, the CHA arranged for elite players to
sign autographs at the Hall of Fame. Present to receive the
public were five national team contenders, including sport
celebrity Manon Rhéaume. Rhéaume, who can draw hundreds autograph signings, sat alongside the other players inside the Hall as confused stragglers trickled by. "Oh, I thought
it was the men's national team!" exclaimed one clearly disappointed woman as she entered the side-room in which the
players idled. Her confusion no doubt stemmed from the absence of any signs at the entrance of the Hall and from the lack
of prior publicity, save one token last-minute announcement
in the *Toronto Sun*.

The fact that such an unsuccessful publicity event occurred within the chambers of the Hockey Hall of Fame only
emphasizes the fact that not one women has been inducted
into the Hall. As Bruce Kidd writes: "Halls of Fame play a
strategic role in the public remembering and interpretation of
sports. Through their annual, often well-publicized selections
and inductions, they confer status (and lifetime bragging
rights) upon those selected ...."[39] In 1995, former national
women's team member Heather Ginzel decided to change this
and nominated female hockey veteran Shirley Cameron to the
Hall. Despite Cameron's impeccable credentials — she is a

former national team member and has been part of twenty
consecutive championships as a player and then as coach of
the Chimos — simply filling out the nomination form was a
challenge. "I looked for someone who would blow them out
of the water, but the form is made for men," says Ginzel. "I
had to go through it and doctor it so her whole career could
be placed in it." Furthermore, when Ginzel wrote to the CHA
for a letter of endorsement, she was turned down. What the
CHA proposed instead was that it could strike a committee
that would establish criteria for female players to be nominated to the Hall. Such a committee has not yet been formed, and
Cameron's nomination was rejected by the Hall of Fame.

The lack of proper promotional materials and media coverage of women's sports is not unique to hockey or the print
medium. A study conducted by the Los Angeles Amateur Athletic Foundation in 1990 found that women's sports comprised only 5 percent of televised sports in the US. Most of the
coverage went to gymnastics, figure skating, tennis and golf.
Although women receive better coverage during the
Olympics, male athletes are still followed much more closely
by the media. A Sport Canada study on the CTV coverage of
the 1994 Winter Olympics in Lillehammer revealed that in-
terviewers overwhelmingly chose male athletes, coaches, and
even male persons on the street for comments. Forty-one percent of the events in the Winter Olympics were female and 56
percent male (3 percent were mixed), yet men received 64 percent of the coverage, compared with 26 percent for women
(10 percent was devoted to mixed events). Interestingly, the
telecasting of men's hockey was largely responsible for the imbalance; men's games made up almost half of the coverage of
all the male sports.[40]

For the duration of the 1988 Winter Olympics, Margaret
MacNeill, a professor at the School of Physical and Health Education at the University of Toronto, went behind the scenes

with the CTV domestic television crew in Calgary to study how (male) hockey was produced. In the late 1980s, rating agencies that measured the size of TV audiences for broadcasters usually gave just the total number that could be expected to tune into the Olympics, without breaking the audience down by gender — something that is now done by the rating agencies. What soon became apparent to MacNeill was that the cameramen geared the coverage to men. "[The] television crews assumed the audience-of-address they broadcast to was wholly male. Although many Canadian women are fans of hockey and the growth in participation is booming, women are not assumed to be 'serious' fans of the game according to the crew, yet they have no market research to substantiate these claims," writes MacNeill. "When close-ups of female fans ... were broadcast ... they were constructed as cheerleaders, not fans. The crew's choice of passive, young feminine-appearing women to fill what they called the 'beauty shots,' served to reproduce the notion of hockey as a rugged masculine game."[41] Furthermore, while the European and French Canadian broadcasters chose to leave out much of the violence by switching to commercials, "CTV, on the other hand, broadcast fights in their entirety," reports MacNeill. "CTV considered fighting to be an 'essential' part of the 'news' of the game."[42]

Although women and men follow the Olympics with near equal interest, men watch televised sports more than twice as much as women do in Canada.[43] Indeed, about 70 percent of the viewers of Canada's sports-only network, The Sports Network (TSN), are men, a percentage that matches the proportion of hours allotted to male sports on the network.[44] The circular argument that keeps newspaper editors from giving more print to amateur and women's sports also keeps network heads from broadcasting them. (This is despite evidence from one survey that 70 percent of sports fans would be equally interested in watching men's and women's competitions if they

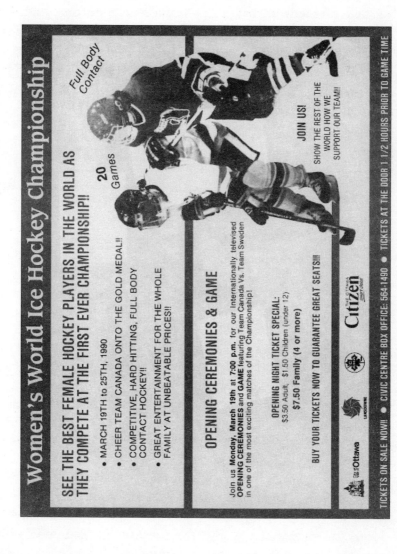

*Poster from the first official world championship assures fans of "hard hitting, full body contact hockey."*

were telecast.[45]) "TSN is seen as male-dominated in terms of audience," says Rick Brace, vice president of broadcasting at TSN. "We get some criticism [for that]." But Brace goes on to say that the network has no immediate plans to broadcast more women's sports because it covers events only according to audience demand.[46]

During the first world hockey championship for women in 1990, TSN broadcast four of the games. However, since then the network has telecast only one other world game: the gold-medal game for the 1994 world championship. Although the commentary improved somewhat in the 1994 game, for both final games the main commentators were men — Michael Landsberg and Howie Meeker in 1990 and Peter Watts in 1994 — whose expertise lay in the men's game, not the women's. In 1990 Landsberg focussed on the pink theme of the event, a promotion tactic the CHA devised, as discussed in Chapter 1. Although he was sincerely enthusiastic about the women's game, Howie Meeker felt the need to frequently re-assure the audience of the "tough-hitting" style of the game.

From a media perspective the 1990 championship was a smashing success — more than 100 print, radio and TV journalists covered the event, which was attended by more than 20,000 people; the television audience averaged 450,000 for the first three televised games and about 1.5 million for the gold-medal game. However, media coverage dropped off precipitously immediately following the event. In 1992, when the championship was held in Finland, TSN opted not to broadcast any of the games, citing a mid-afternoon time slot and little interest from advertisers as two of the reasons for not covering the event. The network also said it considered the cost of the satellite feed — $40,000 — to be too high. "The first year [1990] we covered the Worlds there were a lot of promises from the organizers that didn't come through," explains Brace. "The companies [who the CHA said would buy advertising] didn't come through and we ended up subsidizing the event. We were cautious the second time around."[47] Indeed they were. The caution, however, struck many fans of the female game as excessive, and even the CHA voiced its objection to the absence of coverage in a letter to Brace.[48]

TSN was also cautious the third time around. For the 1994 world championship, which was held in Lake Placid, New York, the network decided to broadcast the final game only. Although this game took place on a Sunday at 3:00 PM EST, TSN did not televise it until 10:30 PM EST, which meant those intent on watching the historical "three-peat" victory for Canada had to stay up until 1:00 AM. With a time slot like that, ratings hardly stood a chance of improving.

In 1995 TSN renewed a second five-year contract with the CHA to broadcast sixteen amateur hockey games yearly. Women's hockey was included in the package this time, although TSN says the CHA made no stipulation in the deal that female games must be broadcast annually. Since 1995, TSN has covered one female game each year — the final game of the national championship. Brace says he does not foresee the coverage increasing for at least the next few years. "The game will have to be considered where men and women are at the same playing field," he says. "The women's game is different ... and the numbers make it harder to sell."[49]

"Selling" is absolutely fundamental to the telecasting of sports. Networks operate as businesses, selling viewers to advertisers. The televising of a sport, and hence the sponsorship of it, are critical to a sport's growth and survival. Yet only very recently has corporate money — and a very small amount of it — come the way of women's hockey. From 1982 to 1996 national championships for senior female hockey players have received corporate funding for a total of five annual events. Shoppers Drug Mart gave $15,000 annually for the championship from 1982 to 1984. Rhonda Taylor (then Leeman),

the development coordinator for the OWHA during that period, says that in return for sponsoring the national championship, Shoppers Drug Mart required a high-profile press
conference; its name on the official championship title, logo
and souvenir items; and television coverage. "I look back now
and laugh at [the deal]," says Taylor. "They wanted everything
under the sun. But we were just so happy and grateful simply
to make the event occur."[50] For the 1982 championship, Taylor says that Shoppers Drug Mart even took it upon itself to
subsidize its own donation with other donations from Scott
Paper Ltd., Planters, Wintario and Air Canada, putting their
names on 25,000 flyers it distributed in its stores. The total
amount donated, including a small sum from Sport Canada,
covered only the costs of ice time, officials and half the players' travel expenses. CBC's *Wide World of Sports* ran selected
highlights from the game, *Hockey Night in Canada* promoted
it during an intermission and CFTO, CBLT and Global reported briefly on the event during their news programs.

After sponsoring national championships for three years,
Shoppers Drug Mart decided against renewing the agreement.
The fanfare of women's hockey as a "new" sport had blown
over and media coverage had quickly dried up. It was not until
ten years later that women's hockey was again to have any private funds channelled into it — this time through the CHA. In
July 1995, the women's national championship and the national team were at last sold as part of a package deal with the
men's national junior team program to Imperial Oil, Air
Canada and, in 1996, the Royal Bank. The CHA negotiated
with Imperial Oil to be the title sponsor for women's hockey,
which means that since 1995 the women's national competition has been called the "Esso Women's National Hockey
Championship."

Although neither the CHA nor Imperial Oil will disclose
the total amount of the sponsorship package, the CHA says it

allocates approximately $50,000 towards the women's national championship and the national team.[51] The money comes to women's hockey in the form of direct financial support for participating teams, advertisements for the national championship and national television coverage. TSN, the "official broadcaster" of the CHA, is also considered a sponsor due to its telecasting of CHA games.

Ron Robison, the new senior-vice president of business for the CHA, negotiated the contract with the sponsors. Robison decided to include the women's program and other products that were considered difficult to sell, such as the tier-two male Junior A championships, as part of the whole amateur package, thus guaranteeing at least some money for these programs. The difficulty in selling female hockey to sponsors, parents and girls lay partly in its "image problem." "The sport has been historically male, aggressive and violent at times, and we have to work on all those to make it a more attractive sell to all girls," he explains. "All we want to do is assure parents through vehicles like corporations that the sport can be safe."[52]

But trying to distance the female game from the NHL is not without its pitfalls, either. What is circumspectly referred to by marketing executives as "the physicality" of the men's game is a factor still regarded as crucial to selling hockey. "The problem is that a lot of people have the perception of [women's hockey] as a poor cousin to the real thing. They see it as a physical sport where a big part of it is banging people into the boards," says John Dunlop, executive vice-president of the St. Clair Group, the CHA's marketing company. "It's a lot easier to sell [a game like] women's tennis where the emphasis is on finesse. It's tougher to see women participating in those physical games. It's not a positive in terms of sales circumstances; it's a hurdle to overcome."[53] The statement that it is "tougher to see" women participate in physical games assumes that the public is not ready to handle aggressive, powerful images of women.

Yet given the paucity and relative newness of such images in both the media and advertisements, it is unlikely that marketing executives or anyone else have a solid grasp of what the public would like to see.

To make matters worse, corporate sponsorship of the women's game has proven to be a more challenging sell due to the recession of the 1990s, according to Dunlop and his colleagues. Corporations will no longer simply attach their name to an event or product as they might have done in the 1980s; they require an integrated packaging, including television, print, product sampling, promotion and rights affiliation. The more stringent requirements of corporate sponsors will particularly affect women's hockey. While the sport's rapid growth is considered a "positive sidebar" by marketers, in terms of public recognition it is a long way away from other amateur hockey properties. Television ratings reflect just how far away it is: eighty-two thousand people watched the final game of the 1996 national championship on TSN. Although this represents an increase of six thousand from the previous year, this number is low in relation to the 146,000 people who watched the male Junior A championship, the Memorial Cup, in 1995.[54] Furthermore, because the TSN audience is largely male, advertisers of women's products are not exactly lining up at the network's door.

Although younger elite players such as Nancy Drolet of Quebec are becoming more vocal about the need to procure sponsorship, most current and former players, parents and fans have been noticeably silent on the issue. This passivity is particularly troubling given the increasing government cutbacks to all amateur sports. In 1995–96 alone, funding to 121 national sports was slashed by 20 percent and dozens of sports have had their funding eliminated altogether. Athletes are being forced to rely more and more on corporate sponsors. Canadian female athletes would do well to take their cue from their American sisters. Members of the US women's soccer team — a team that placed first in the 1991 world championship and third in 1995 — went on strike in September 1995. They refused to attend their training camp or sign contracts until they were assured they would get a bonus sum of money if they won a gold medal, or a silver or bronze medal.

While sponsorship and media coverage are important ways to help the growth of women's hockey, retaining the integrity of the athletes will be increasingly difficult with corporate pressure. Female athletes are still marketed in a way that stresses their sexual attractiveness rather than their abilities. It is hardly surprising that most of the female sports that have garnered sponsorship so far are sports such as tennis, gymnastics, golf and figure skating – sports that often feature women in skimpy outfits. Indeed, some female figure skaters earn even more than their male counterparts.

Needless to say, hockey, as a team sport that emphasizes aggression and toughness, does not capitalize on traditional feminine qualities. That has not kept some sponsors from trying, however. The program for the 1982 Shoppers Drug Mart national hockey championship presented the game this way:

> For years sports were viewed as predominantly male activities, but the recent surge of interest in physical fitness in women's health and beauty plans has prompted a greater awareness of the importance of organized women's sports.
>
> Today many vibrant women experience the excitement and challenge of playing team sports without the once-prevalent "tomboy" image. Terri, a dedicated sports enthusiast, has been playing hockey for years .... [Girls] such as Terri strive for fulfilling social lives, where new friends are often surprised to find that beneath their beauty, poise and femininity, lie enthusiastic and talented hockey players ....

Doug Philpott, the head of Hockey Projects Client Services, who has marketed women's hockey for the St. Clair Group, talked excitedly about the "really good-looking ladies" now playing and how this would help sell the game. "You wouldn't even know that a lot of these ladies played hockey if you had to pick them out of a lineup," he exclaimed in 1996. "And the Finnish team! What a striking team. The women are just gorgeous. They look like runway models."[55] When asked if the attractiveness of players was a factor in marketing male hockey, he laughed: "It's not an issue at all. We even run guys with no teeth."[56]

What lurks just below the surface of the "feminine" marketing angle of female athletes is the attempt to distance women athletes from suspicions of lesbianism. Indeed, as many female hockey players readily acknowledge, the word "feminine" is often a code word for heterosexual. In a society that has defined sport as an activity for boys and men, women who participate in athletics have been regarded as breaking a well-entrenched feminine code of conduct. This view of female athletes is nothing new. Beginning in the 1880s, doctors warned parents and teachers about the "masculinizing effects" of certain sports on girls, claiming athletic involvement would lead to masculine mannerisms, deeper voices and bulky muscles. Sports for girls, the argument went on, would also put in jeopardy their ability to have children and confuse their sexual identity.[57] Labels such as "mannish" were applied to women who took sports seriously. Implicit in this designation was a deep suspicion of female athletes' sexuality. As early as the turn of the century, pressure mounted for women to prove their heterosexuality. By the 1930s sexy or feminine clothing codes were imposed on female athletes by schools, coaches and sports organizations. Short hair was discouraged and women were urged to present their boyfriends to the public. By the 1950s all-girl activities, especially team sports, fell under public scrutiny for fear of the "lesbian threat." Sports such as tennis, golf, bowling and horseback riding were recommended in their place.[58] These themes of concern resound within the field of sports research to this day. "[T]here's never research on the femininity of ballet dancers or female figure skaters or female synchronized swimmers," points out sports sociologist Helen Lenskyj, "but there's a hell of a lot of research about the femininity ... or the lack of ... [it in] basketball players, and sport administrators and softball players. And so it's pretty obvious what's going on."[59]

The effects of homophobia and the attempts by sports organizations to hide the lesbian presence on teams have repercussions beyond the theoretical for both athletes and coaches today. Coaches, for instance, have been fired or passed over because of their sexual orientation. In one public case, the head coach of the Canadian women's volleyball team, Betty Baxter, was suddenly dismissed by the Canadian Volleyball Association in 1982. While no mention was made of her lesbianism when it was explained why she was dismissed, Baxter protested the firing, telling the *Toronto Star* that, "qualifications had nothing to do with it."[60]

Because admitting the presence of lesbians and gays in a particular sport can have such devastating effects on its athletes in terms of sponsorship and media coverage, it is difficult to find athletes who will talk about the issue on the record. Only two former Team Canada members would. "Because we're becoming a higher profile sport, there's even more pressure to project a certain image," says Chimos coach Shirley Cameron. "It's a kind of a joke amongst players: grow your hair long or you won't make the national team. It's a joke because there is that pressure to sell the sport and they may pick players not always just on talent. There's the image part of it — the being married, having kids sort of thing."[61] Another former national team member, Heather Ginzel, puts it this way: "The CHA thinks that the majority of women are straight, and no one will talk about it," says Ginzel. "How does that make you a good person or a bad person or good or bad hockey player? There are unfortunately a lot of people who disagree with [lesbianism]. It's an image thing. 'We don't want a bunch of dykes representing our country.' If they only knew."[62]

The monetary consequences of non-feminine females in sports or allowing open lesbians to represent a sport are palpable. Elite women's teams, no matter how successful they are, have a much harder time procuring sponsorship dollars than women's individual performance sports do. Yet even within individual sports, the negative repercussions for an athlete who does not play up her heterosexuality are powerful in terms of sponsorship. The example of tennis player and "out" lesbian Martina Navratilova gives some indication of just how costly it can be for lesbians *not* to hide their sexuality. In 1992, with fifty-four Grand Slam titles, Navratilova had sponsorship contracts worth $2 million. Heterosexual Steffi Graf, on the other hand, had only eleven Grand Slam titles, yet earned three times that amount.[63] Jennifer Capriati and Gabriela Sabatini, who at the time had never ranked number one, made as much or more than Navratilova.[64]

In addition to pressuring teams to present feminine-looking athletes corporations pressure the sports media to stay away from sports that have traditionally been associated with men. Former basketball player and author Mariah Burton Nelson reports that when she worked at *Women's Sports* magazine in the 1980s, advertisers threatened to withhold ads if the magazine covered bodybuilding, weight lifting, basketball, softball or other "dykey" sports. The magazine soon changed its name to *Women's Sports and Fitness* to downplay female athleticism and included more photos of slim, heterosexually-appealing women in its issues.[65]

A less visible but just as pernicious effect of homophobia within sports is that it keeps girls and women from joining up in the first place. A number of national team players recall that in their teens they stayed away from hockey, despite their interest in the game, because of rumours that many of the players were gay, and their fear of being seen that way by their peers. "Everybody knows and assumes [you are a lesbian], so you have to be confident of who you are," says one national team player, who wished to remain anonymous. "With young kids this could make or break the sport. I know some mothers who wouldn't let daughters play with lesbians ... [even though] they know their daughter loves the game."

Homophobia also has the effect of causing players, both gay and straight, to scrutinize their clothing and behaviour for any hints of masculinity. Many hockey players talk of the need to "clean up" the image of the game by presenting themselves in a "professional manner." At Female Council meetings with the CAHA, the former Nova Scotia representative Lynn Hacket recalls members were very conscious of trying to counteract the stereotype of female players: "We always wore a skirt, a dress or dress-pants. We always looked like females," she says, adding, however, that, "I didn't have a problem with the lesbian presence, but I had a problem with people who told me I didn't look like a hockey player. I realize now they were saying that I didn't look like a lesbian."[66]

Although almost all female hockey players who play at the elite level complain about being questioned by the press about boyfriends or husbands in what they see as transparent attempts to determine their sexuality, some say lesbian-baiting among players can be just as strong. Melody Davidson, coach and female hockey advocate in Alberta, maintains that some of the baiting comes from the players themselves. "A lot of things that are created are created from within," she says. "Players always sitting around questioning who's gay and who's not. People always assume I'm gay. At times when I first started, it was guilty until proven innocent."[67]

In a female sports world that generously rewards tradition-al feminine qualities and that punishes traditional masculine characteristics, it is no wonder that lesbian athletes are not lin-ing up to reveal their sexual orientation. Yet until this changes, homophobia will remain a powerful tool to intimidate all women in sport. The so-called lesbian issue is, in fact, a gen-der equity issue. When corporations refuse to sponsor "mascu-line" female sports, when the media fail to properly report on them and when sports organizations encourage women to hide their sexual identity, all female athletes are affected. What ho-mophobia does in the long run is assure that money and media attention continue to go almost exclusively to men's sports and to straight-appearing male athletes. This is not to say that ho-mophobia within male sports is any less forceful — indeed, sports have traditionally provided men with an arena in which to *prove* their masculinity and heterosexuality. The pressure for gay male athletes to hide their sexuality is, therefore, perhaps even more powerful within the realm of men's sports. As Brian Pronger, a lecturer on sports and ethics at the University of Toronto, observes: "In our culture, male homosexuality is a vi-olation of masculinity, a denigration of the mythic power of men, an ironic subversion that significant numbers of men pursue with great enthusiasm. Because it gnaws at masculinity, it weakens the gender order."[68]

While the strong tendency among sponsors and media to emphasize the attractiveness and femininity of female athletes is disturbing, in general this kind of portrayal is decreasing. Editors and journalists alike are becoming more aware that fo-cussing on the appearance rather than the abilities of players is no longer acceptable. "I think that the media generally have improved over the last ten years," says Marg McGregor of CAAWS, "[and] that we are seeing more stories of the women's hockey team and [other female athletes].... But we're still a long way away from where I think we should be."[69]

Glynis Peters of the CHA also thinks journalists are doing a better job at reporting on women. "The quality of coverage has improved dramatically," she says. "It used to focus on the sensational angle of women actually playing the game, when the first woman would play in the NHL and how they first started to play. Now the media is in general more educated and willing to take women's hockey at face value."[70] In the early 1990s, reporters began to be more aware of the traditionally overlooked subject of female sports, but they showed their ignorance of history in the frequency with which female athletes were hailed as "pioneers" in the press. Many reporters had only recently discovered the calibre of certain female sports, writing about them as if they were something entirely new, rather than something entirely new only to the reporter. In the case of hockey, the discovery of the women's game was particularly amusing given that girls and women had been playing it for more than a hundred years. Amusing too — though tiresome — was the apparent fascination on the part of some reporters with the fact that girls and women even *want* to play hockey. As one reporter acknowledged in a story on Team USA member Cammi Granato, "The burning question [for reporters] is how they [athletes] compete in their chosen sports. For women hockey players, it is still, 'Why?'"[71]

When the novelty-approach reporters were not asking, "Why?" they were scrambling to understand the game within the only context they know: men's hockey. Even today, female players continually lament being compared to men. Indeed, the number of references to national team players Angela James, Geraldine Heaney, France St. Louis and Hayley Wickenheiser as "the Wayne Gretzkys of female hockey" again reflects reporters' ignorance of the female game rather than their attempt to compliment a player.

"It's great to get coverage, but not when it assumes all girls want to play with boys and like boys," says Glynis Peters. "If the media would only phone somebody who knows about the sport when they go to cover it and not just assume that hockey's hockey and use the same points of reference that they use with male hockey and just apply it to girls."[72] Sue Scherer, a former Team Canada player, agrees. She says that journalists have frequently missed the point. "When journalists wrote about me when I was younger, they would say I love sports, which I do. But then the articles would go on with some reference to growing up with boys being responsible for my success. My success isn't due to my brothers. It's due to a lot of hard work and having the guts to do it,"[73] she says.

Nobody in women's hockey better typifies the various ways the media and sponsors have framed female players than Manon Rhéaume, the most famous female hockey player in the world. Rhéaume, a Québécoise from Trois-Rivières, was the first women in North America to sign a contract with a men's professional team and to play a game in a professional league. Several months after earning a place as the number-three goalie for the Trois-Rivières Draveurs of the Quebec major junior league — the highest level of hockey below the NHL — Rhéaume played with the team in a regular-season game in November 1991. Less than a year later, she was asked to try out for the NHL Tampa Bay Lightning by owner Phil Esposito, and played her first period of professional hockey in an exhibition game in September 1992. Soon after, Rhéaume signed a three-year contract with the Atlanta Knights, a minor league team affiliated with the Lightning. In December 1992 she became the first woman to play in a regular-season game in men's pro hockey and in April played her first full game. Since then Rhéaume has played on a number of professional and semi-professional hockey teams, most recently for the Charlotte Checkers of North Carolina.

*Commercial portrayals of Manon Rhéaume (top);
celebrating Team Canada's third gold medal.*

With her entry into the pro leagues, Rhéaume found herself suddenly catapulted into stardom. Never before had a female hockey player received so much press attention — or fan adoration. As Rhéaume skated onto the ice wild crowds chanted, "We want the chick! We want the chick!" Within weeks of her first major junior game, Rhéaume received the much-reported offer from *Playboy* to pose nude for $40,000, a proposal she declined. Soon after the exhibition game with the Lightning, Rhéaume ranked fourth in a survey of Quebec's favourite athletes and thirteenth in a December 1992 *USA Today* popularity survey of athletes — ahead of Mario Lemieux. She was also heralded by *Time* magazine as the seventh wonder of the sports world that year. By the end of her first year in the pro leagues, she had attracted the attention of CNN, ESPN, *The Today Show, Good Morning America, Entertainment Tonight* and had even appeared on *Late Night with David Letterman.*

Hundreds of articles have been written on Rhéaume. Many have focussed on what they assumed was the "gimmick" element of her participation in the pro leagues, dismissing her as nothing more than a cheap ploy to sell tickets. Other reporters have vacillated between depicting Rhéaume as a gimmick and hailing her as a great benefactor of women's hockey. "Women's hockey has landed a celebrity who has provided the game with an unbelievable opportunity for promotion,"[74] wrote Mary Ormsby in 1992. Exactly a year later, Ormsby's take was different: "This latest girl-goalie promotion smacks of the same masterful media manipulation so beautifully orchestrated by Phil Esposito last fall. He didn't sell hockey to Floridans ... but sold an attractive female goalie instead."[75]

Many other articles zeroed in on her physical appearance, completely side-stepping her performance as an athlete. Two of the most glaringly sexist features on Rhéaume were published in the *Toronto Star.* In one, columnist Rosie DiManno described Rhéaume as "a comely nubile with hazel eyes, a glowing complexion, and a decidedly feminine grace. There is no hint of testosterone in her nature."[76]

Constant mention of the offers from *Playboy*, and later *Penthouse*, to pose nude also surfaced in articles on the player, once again drawing attention away from Rhéaume as an athlete and onto her image as a sex object. The use of this angle to cover her reveals a great discomfort on the part of the media at the prospect of a woman succeeding in a traditionally male sport. Rhéaume soon found herself in the position of having to defend her choice and field endless asinine questions about whether or not she broke a fingernail while in net, or spit on the bench like most hockey players, or how her boyfriend handled her hockey career.[77] In her book, *Manon: Alone in Front of the Net*, even she feels obliged to reassure her fans of her femininity. In one passage she writes:

> I don't exactly eat nails for breakfast, but I can bench-press a few pounds and I do a few hundred sit-ups a week. I have no plans to compete for the Miss Muscles title — far from it. I work out to improve my cardio-vascular system and my muscular endurance. I don't want big muscles, just what I need to be able to stay in the shape a good goalie needs to be in. I try to keep a feminine figure and I have no desire to "bulk up" with extra weight. [78]

Yet even those reporters who claimed to endorse Rhéaume the athlete did so entirely within the context of the male sports world. Not only did many expose their ignorance of the female game by referring to her as the best female goaltender in the world, which she was not, but they also lauded her for successfully fitting into the men's jock culture, as if this were an accomplishment of the highest order. In a profile on Rhéaume in *Saturday Night* magazine, journalist Brian Preston relays a conversation about hockey between Rhéaume and another reporter, and concludes, "You can't help but like her. She's twenty-two, and even in a second language knows how to banter with men."[79] As sports columnist Michael Farber observes, "The subliminal message of Rhéaume's triumph is unsettling: To be successful, women have to be validated in a man's world. In men's teams. In men's terms."[80]

Of course, what is missing from 90 percent of the press stories on Rhéaume is context. The real reason Rhéaume jumped at the chance to play in the pro leagues was neither to champion the cause of female hockey players nor to become rich and famous: she did it simply because it was the chance of a lifetime to receive professional training and ice time she would never have received playing on a women's team. As the *Globe and Mail* columnist Mary Jollimore writes, "How many male hockey players with such limited experience were invited to the Tampa Bay training camp or that of any other NHL team? None. But consider this. It's not exactly Rhéaume's fault she's had limited experience .... Because she's a woman she hasn't had the same opportunity as her male counterparts."[81]

Rhéaume herself partly addresses the opportunity gap in her book, recounting the harassment and resistance to her participation in hockey she withstood growing up. Rhéaume was fortunate in having a very supportive father who actively ensured she was given the same chance as her brothers. "Every time I attended a hockey camp, Pierre [her father] insisted that the coach test me under the same conditions as the other goaltenders," Rhéaume recounts. "He made sure that the duties were shared half-and-half with the other goalie. In this way, no one could say, 'Yes, but she was in net against a weaker team ....' He didn't want to leave any room for doubt."[82] Pierre, however, could assure equal treatment of his daughter only up until a point. When Rhéaume reached the Midget level age at sixteen, pressure intensified for her to leave the game. Although a scout for a Midget AAA team put her on his draft list, when he discovered she was a girl, he scratched out her name. The only team that agreed to let her play was a Midget CC team — one step above what Rhéaume refers to as a "fun league."[83] After a year on the team, Rhéaume quit hockey. She picked it up a year later when she briefly played for the female Quebec team of Jofa-Titan. Attending games and practices, however, involved long hours of commuting and late-night time slots. The chance to play on a men's team, therefore, was a dream come true: not only was she coached by professionals, supplied with the best equipment and the recipient of excellent ice time, but she was also well paid and amply rewarded through sponsors, poster sales, autograph signings and speaking engagements. The fact that she rarely played in games was a minor irritation in light of the exceptional practice time she has had, and what she would have had to put up with had she switched to women's hockey.

Whether journalists hone in on the attractiveness of Rhéaume or focus on the publicity aspect of her rise, articles about her invariably trumpet the player as "making history," "breaking the gender barrier," as a sport "pioneer" or the inevitable "ice-breaker." The implication in all of these labels is that it is only a matter of time before other women rush through the gap in men's professional hockey she has created. Yet as players and supporters of the female game know all too well, Rhéaume is the exception both in terms of her heterosexual appeal and the position she plays. For goaltenders, physical strength and size are less important than they are for other players and gender differences are fairly minimal. This explains why the only other women to play on men's semi-pro teams have been goalies. As sports sociologist Nancy Theberge writes,

> It is significant that in the media constructions of Rhéaume's experience, little attention is given to an aspect of her biography that people in the sport understand to be central to her story. The result of this inattention is that Rhéaume is constructed as the female

athletic version of "everyman," when in reality by virtue of the position she plays, she is in fact rather unique.[84]

The irony that the most famous female hockey player came to public awareness by playing with men is not lost on female players. While many journalists and admirers of Rhéaume insist that she has done much for the women's game, others contend that Rhéaume has brought recognition to herself alone — albeit reluctantly — and not to the women's game. Interested in how Rhéaume was perceived outside the standard male realm, Theberge interviewed two groups of female hockey players, one of girls between fourteen and seventeen years old and the other of elite players between sixteen and thirty-four. Theberge reports that most of the younger players found Rhéaume to be a positive force, commenting that she brought publicity to sport and proved that women can play hockey. As one young American player (not in Theberge's study) wrote in *Newsday*, in defence of Rhéaume,

> A girl has to earn the respect that male players give each other automatically. When the goaltender is female, there's always a guy on the other team who winds up and fires a screamer at her head to prove he is too much of a man to be playing around with girls .... Manon Rhéaume [and other semi-pro female goaltenders] encourage the hundreds of girls who are working hard outside the spotlight. Thriving throughout the stages of boys' hockey, they have proven their skill and ability again and again.[85]

While this young player describes what many like her may feel about Rhéaume, the older players Theberge interviewed maintain that the emphasis on a woman's success in men's hockey has detracted from the appreciation and awareness of women's hockey. Theberge reports that none of the women expressed resentment towards Rhéaume personally and few denied that they would take the chance to play in the pro leagues if offered it. Yet many elite female players do resent the fact that Rhéaume was not the best female goalie in North America when she was selected for the pro leagues. "At first it bothered me because, [I felt like,] 'Who are you? I don't know anything about you,'" says national team member Angela James. "And I know a lot more people who should be in there ahead of her like [goalies] Cathy [Phillips] or Kelly Dyer."[86] Former national team goaltender Phillips, no longer able to compete after a tumour was removed from her brain in 1990, goes even further. "She hurt women's hockey in my eyes," says Phillips. "I would have thought she would have been fantastic ... [and] a lot of people who don't even know women play hockey would think she was the best. Unfortunately, there are a lot of female goaltenders who are better than she is to this day, although Manon has improved dramatically."[87] Twenty-year female hockey veteran Shirley Cameron concurs: "There are so many women who go through female leagues and then she plays one game and gets all the exposure in the world. It's a real sore spot for many female players."[88]

The resentment players such as Cameron express towards the media for celebrating one female player in a male league while ignoring the many others who have played for years on female teams in understandable. Despite the efforts of the game's promoters, women's hockey is still measured against the male game, and in the eyes of the media and sponsors, has not fared well in the comparison. Sport has rapidly been taken over by the entertainment businesses — indeed, at the professional level it is now impossible to distinguish where show business ends and sport begins. Given the priorities of corporations and the dominant culture of professional male sports, the female game has stood almost no chance of being appreciated for its own merits and achievements. The "masculine" image of the game and the general ignorance of its history and players have left little room for promotional manoeuvring.

Yet until fans, supporters and the athletes themselves join forces and demand the same appreciation for women's accomplishments — both in terms of sponsorship and media coverage — the situation is unlikely to change. Female hockey players have been silent far too long about their treatment in the media, and grateful for far too little in terms of funding. Collective action is essential. Those who want to see women's hockey in the media need to start phoning broadcasters, writing newspapers, lobbying corporations and the CHA themselves for more support. It is time to challenge the reign of professional male sports, especially given the inequities that persist within the sports world, the continued glorification of men's prowess and the undermining of women's. Only if women join forces off ice will their power on ice at last be celebrated.

*Fans of the women's game cheer on Team Canada*
*at the 1994 world championship.*

*Chapter Eight*

# TEAM CANADA: NEGLECTED HEROES

THE MCCALLION WORLD CUP sits in the North American zone of the Hockey Hall of Fame in Toronto, a noble but abandoned symbol of the birth of women's elite international hockey. It resembles a short Stanley Cup, and weighs about thirty-five pounds. The inscription on the cup reads "McCallion World Cup/Donated by the Ontario Women's Hockey Association." Hazel McCallion is the mayor of Mississauga and a staunch supporter of female hockey. She played in the Gaspé, Quebec, in the late 1930s, and joined the Montreal Women's Hockey League in 1942, where she is known as the first woman ever paid to play hockey: she received five dollars a game.

A more telling keepsake from the first world tournament is a battered hockey stick, signed by all the members of the Hamilton Golden Hawks, the team that represented Canada in the first world tournament in 1987. The stick symbolizes both the harsh struggle women have endured simply to play Canada's national sport, and the indomitable spirit that kept them going when the odds were against them. Along with the McCallion World Cup, it stands as one of the few public reminders of the tournament that jump-started women's hockey on the road to world competition and ultimately to the

Olympics. Just as important, the first world tournament ushered in Team Canada, a long-awaited breed of heroes for the women's game.

The idea of a women's world championship took root in 1985, when Fran Rider, then president of the Ontario Women's Hockey Association (OWHA), invited teams from Europe, North America and Asia to participate in Brampton's Dominion Ladies Hockey Tournament, the oldest and largest women's hockey tournament in the world. Two European countries, West Germany and Holland, joined two American teams to play the host Canadian teams from Ontario and Quebec. This modest undertaking prompted the first discussions with representatives of the International Ice Hockey Federation (IIHF), the governing body for amateur hockey internationally, about the possibility of a world championship in 1987.

Rider made valuable contacts in the 1985 tournament and spent the next two years writing to hockey officials as far away as China and Australia to invite them to compete in a world championship. The Canadian Amateur Hockey Association (CAHA), which was responsible for the formation of Canada's national women's team, resisted Rider's initiative claiming that it was too soon for international competition in women's hockey. There were already too many issues to address at the national level, the CAHA argued, such as the development of coaching, refereeing and minor hockey — issues that were still being ignored as far as the women's hockey community was concerned.

The CAHA had only begun to contemplate the idea of women's hockey in the late 1970s, and was still unaware of the distinctive characteristics of the female game, such as the emphasis on finesse and the absence of bodychecking. But for female players and those who were committed to advancing the game, the time for patient waiting was over. Women's hockey needed more than one national championship, it needed world competition, a catalyst that would not only boost the profile of women's hockey at many levels (including within the CAHA) but that would finally showcase the stars of the game, introducing these elite athletes to players and hockey fans across the country. As well, a world championship would reward the most talented players with the thrill of international competition and the chance to represent their country — to compete for Canada, as male players had been doing since 1951. A national team match-up could also garner new fans and enthusiastic volunteers and, in the perfect scenario, generous sponsors and supportive media. For fans, organizers and parents, the event would give credibility to a game that many people thought women should not even be playing.

For the OWHA, the time had come to take matters into its own hands. After much lobbying, including a letter of support sent from Brent Ladds, president of the Ontario Hockey Association (one of the provincial governing hockey organizations), the CAHA finally consented to the international competition on the condition that it be called a "world tournament," as opposed to a "sanctioned world championship." This endorsement, in the CAHA's view, implied no obligation on its part to supply funds or administrative support, which it declined to do even though it had already set a financial precedent with male hockey when it launched the first men's world junior tournament in 1974. For the men's event the CAHA had paid the airfare and domestic expenses for all the teams in order to ensure participation, and persuaded the IIHF to launch a world junior championship. The IIHF also refused to sanction this first women's competition or provide financial assistance. Instead, it simply said it would encourage its members to attend. Nonetheless, the IIHF used the world tournament to judge both the calibre of women's hockey and to assess the potential for an "official" world championship, which it would consider sanctioning in the future.

Because of the lack of financial and administrative support from the CAHA, a team of rookie volunteers from the OWHA ended up staging this first world competition. Hazel McCallion headed the committee as honorary chairperson and lassoed several corporate sponsors. The Ontario and federal governments issued grants totalling $25,000. The budget for the tournament climbed to $250,000 but without national or international assistance the OWHA fell short by $60,000. To reduce expenses, each team — including Canada — had to foot the bill for its own accommodation and travel. The British and Australian teams were forced to drop out, as were a number of key players from other teams when their hockey federations refused to finance them and they were unable to raise enough private money to cover expenses. Even the games suffered from the financial constraints: they were limited to three fifteen-minute periods to reduce ice time costs.

The Hamilton Golden Hawks, winners of the national championship that year, won the "Team Canada" designation more or less by default, since the OWHA had neither the authority nor the funds to organize a selection camp to choose a real national team. However the tournament rules did allow the Golden Hawks to make themselves look more "national" by bolstering the lineup with players from other teams across the country. Two of those selected were Shirley Cameron, a thirty-five-year-old veteran forward from the Edmonton Chimos, and France St. Louis, the leading scorer from the Montreal Carletons, also an experienced player. Ontario's powerful scoring ace Angela James had been recruited by the Golden Hawks for the national championship earlier in the year but for this tournament she returned to her club, the Mississauga Warriors, which acted as the host Ontario team. Sweden, Japan, Holland, Switzerland and the US managed to pull together teams that agreed to pay their own expenses. China, Britain, Norway, Australia and West Germany sent observers.

Unlike the other countries, West Germany did not absent itself from the tournament for financial reasons. The tournament rule prohibiting bodychecking was the stumbling-block that prevented its participation. The country refused to send its team, claiming hockey without bodychecking was not "normal hockey."[1] Although Ontario had been playing with bodychecking up until that time, the rule was changed at the national championship in 1986 because of the vast disparity in ages and skills of players. Several provinces, including Quebec and British Columbia, had eliminated it from all divisions. Top senior female players were not paid to play in women's hockey and therefore could not risk injuries that might result in unpaid time away from work. Astute OWHA officials decided to disallow bodychecking in the tournament because of the immense differences in skating and checking skills, especially between Canada and the European countries. No one wanted broken bones to be the legacy of this first world event. Despite the controversy and budget problems, this was a world event, and official or not, the players were ecstatic. For parents, friends and supporters of the women's game, it marked the long overdue recognition of a game that was close to one hundred years old. For high-flying twenty-three-year-old forward Angela James, considered one of the best female hockey players in Canada, this world tournament was the first chance to see just how good she could be.

For James, the youngest of five children raised by a single mother, these opportunities did not come often. James's family stands in stark contrast to society's conventional model. Defying the social norms of the day, James's white mother, Donna Barato, bore three white and two mixed-race children, each child with a different absentee father. Leo James, Angela's black father, spent much of his time at his nightclub in Mississauga. Although James grew up with two brothers and two sisters in her family, according to James, thanks to her father, she also has "other brothers and sisters all over the place."[2]

Barato was a loving mother, fiercely determined to raise her children on her own. She even found time to "adopt" a troubled friend of Angela's for several years. Mother and daughter share a deep affection. Protective and passionately loyal, James declares her mother is the key person in her life. "My mom is my influence for everything. She's been there for me all my life," says James. "She went to as many national [championships] as possible. She still goes to all my league games. If I don't pick her up she gets mad."[3] Her mother's support was critical for a mixed-race child growing up in a tough neighbourhood. When James was six years old, Barato found her daughter vigorously scrubbing her arm in the tub one night. James explained, "I'm trying to get the dirt off. They told me I was dirty." "Who?" asked her mother. "The kids at school," answered Angela.[4]

James remembers a happy family life. Being the youngest, she was spoiled and somewhat undisciplined; her involvement in sports was the one thing in her life that provided her with structure and discipline. "Sport was my way of getting out of a ghetto really, getting out of Ontario Housing," says James. "I grew up in the parks. There was nothing to do, there weren't outings," remembers James. "Every day in the wintertime you went to the outdoor arena and you played hockey. If you didn't do that you weren't in with the crowd and you had no friends. That's also what I loved to do. [The arena] was right next to my school so I could always see it. You ran home, got your skates and went down there."[5]

Donna Barato settles into the couch of her four bedroom townhouse in North Toronto (she, a friend and Angela are co-owners of the dwelling.) She lights a cigarette in a jam-packed living room while a five-year-old sits watching TV on the floor. She shares the house with a family of four and the son of another friend, who lives in the basement. Just turned sixty,

Barato complains good-naturedly about working two jobs at her age. Plump and easy-going, she points with pride to a collage of photos of "my Angela" atop a glass bookcase; she brags about her daughter walking at nine months and about her natural athletic ability in track, basketball, and volleyball. But hockey was Angela's passion. When she was nine she had her appendix removed, and although normal recuperation time was six weeks, James didn't want to miss the playoffs, and to her doctor's amazement was back on the ice in two and a half weeks.

When she was seven, after several years of playing street hockey and shinny on outdoor rinks with neighbourhood kids, James joined a boys' hockey team. Before long she had won the

*Angela James, age 8, receiving high scorer and MVP trophy at Flemingdon Park Boys' House League Hockey banquet, North York, Ontario, 1973.*

high-scorer award, much to the annoyance of some teammates and a few parents. "The boys weren't too excited about that. They loved it when we won the games, but not when they didn't win the awards."[6] In a fine example of the gender politics of sport, the boys' league refused to allow James to return the next year, insisting that she play on a girl's team.

Female hockey welcomed James with open arms. By age fifteen she had advanced to Senior A hockey, the highest level for female players at that time. She went from being a scrawny fifteen-year-old to a 160 lb.(72.5 kg) freight train that few people could stop. Fuelled with an outsider's desire to prove herself and the drive of a teenager competing against senior players, James became known for both her scoring skills and her intimidating physical presence. Some players were afraid to step on the ice against her and over the years, she sent more than a few people to the hospital. While playing in the Central Ontario Women's Hockey League, she won the high scoring award in 1987 and would go on to dominate the league winning the award for the next seven years.

James also overpowered many of the players in the Ontario College Athletic Association (OCAA) league from 1982 until 1985, capturing all-star-defence and high-scoring honours three years in a row. Part of James's sports history is enshrined in a glass case at Ontario's Seneca College of Applied Arts and Technology where her number 8 hockey sweater hangs on the wall. The college retired James's sweater in 1984 and 1985, when she broke five Ontario College Athletic Association records.

Relaxed and joking in a black T-shirt and jeans, James leans back in her chair in her office at Seneca College where she coordinates intramural athletics. She is as informal as her nickname, AJ. Despite the devilish twinkle in her eye, she grows instantly serious when she speaks of those who have given her guidance, and points to former Seneca coach Lee

Trempe as an especially vital influence. "She was able to discipline me," James recalls. "I didn't have a father figure in my life. She was just doing her job, but at that time she was probably a figure that I needed in my life more than she realized." In 1985 Coach Trempe railed against the lowly status of women's hockey and the lack of opportunity for stars like James. "You won't find a better player anywhere in women's hockey," says Trempe. "If she were a man there would be no stopping her, but she'll never find competition good enough for her."[7]

Two years later, thanks to the OWHA, James at last got a chance to test herself against other world-calibre athletes. She and her teammates at the first world tournament faced six other teams in a round-robin format. The winners of the two semifinals played in the gold medal final. In the first round Team Canada easily swept the three European teams, overpowering Switzerland 10–0, Sweden 8–2 and Holland 19–0. Japan was thrashed 11–0 by the larger and swifter Canadians. Even James's Team Ontario fared no better, falling 5–0 to Team Canada.

The first real competition came from the US, which played a tight, defensive game and managed to severely limit Team Canada's scoring punch until late in the game. Canada's Margot Verlaan, known among her peers as the best read-and-react player in women's hockey, had injured her knee earlier in the tournament. Refusing to let a bad knee stop her when a moment she had long waited for was so close, she pleaded with Coach Dave McMaster to let her play with a knee brace. "I used to tell my mom I wanted to play internationally and she told me I couldn't do it in hockey. She told me I would have to go into gymnastics. But here I am," she later told a reporter triumphantly.[8] Verlaan scored the winning goal in Canada's 2–1 victory over the US. The stage was set for an all-Canadian final when Team Ontario beat Team US 5–2 in the semifinal match.

The all-Canadian gold-medal game was a fierce contest. A disciplined Team Canada patiently built its lead, scoring one goal in the first period and another in the second. As the minutes of the final period ticked away, Team Canada popped in two more goals, finally wearing down Team Ontario's offensive might, to win 4–0. One of the key players of the tournament, goaltender Cathy Phillips, earned the shutout by making sensational stops, including a diving save on a breakaway by her friend Angela James. Phillips was named best goaltender, thanks to her acrobatic moves and lightning reflexes.

Almost a hundred years after women first took to the ice, Team Canada proudly claimed its first gold medal. This marked its debut in the history-making world competition. Media attention was paltry however, with many of the sportswriters unable to get over their astonishment that women could actually play the game at all. But the OWHA was determined to keep the momentum going. After the tournament it asked each country to file a report with the IIHF. After discussions with its members, the IIHF would decide whether to sanction an official world championship. The Ontario association continued to lobby the IIHF in the face of both national and international apathy. The march towards the ultimate goal, the Olympics, had begun.

Glynis Peters, current manager of women's hockey for the CHA, readily acknowledges the importance of the OWHA contribution. "I realize how enormous it was for the OWHA to do [the 1987 world tournament] single-handedly ... with limited financial [and] administrative resources that were purely volunteer. It was a phenomenal accomplishment because it was the last time that only women and the men involved in women's hockey organized an event of such scope."[9]

Despite the work that went into the tournament, some members of the CAHA simply treated it as a non-event. They were embarrassed that a provincial association had led the international drive for women's hockey, and hence preferred to downplay the event. "There was no admission by the CAHA that 1987 existed," said *Toronto Star* reporter Lois Kalchman. "It's not that there was resistance to it, it just didn't exist. At the press conference for the first world championship in 1990, I sat down with France St. Louis and I said to France, 'Well, isn't it wonderful you've been in the 1987 world tournament and the 1990 world championship.' She said, 'We're not supposed to talk about 1987.'" [10]

If the CAHA had conflicting views regarding the 1987 tournament, it could no longer turn a blind eye, in the following two years, to the world-wide momentum building for women's hockey. In April 1989, the IIHF's president, Gunther Sabetski, hosted the first Women's European Championship in West Germany. The OWHA's Fran Rider was invited by Sabetski to attend the event to discuss a future sanctioned world championship. The IIHF proposed that the top five teams from the European championship, along with Canada, the US and an Asian team would play in two pools for the first official world championship which was planned for 1990. The only significant rule changes from the 1987 tournament consisted of lengthening the games to three twenty-minute stop-time periods and permitting bodychecking. The latter allowance was due to considerable pressure from the European countries, despite vehement objections from the CAHA, who now understood the skills gap between Europe and North American teams and did not want unnecessary injuries to mar the sanctioned event. At further meetings with the IIHF, the CAHA offered to host the championship in part because Canada was an acknowledged leader in hockey, but also because few other countries had expressed any serious interest in hosting the event. Moreover, the CAHA realized that it was time to take a leadership role in women's hockey internationally or risk losing credibility within the IIHF; and they were also embarrassed by the possibility of the OWHA taking control of this aspect of the game.

Not surprisingly, the CAHA's involvement in the 1990 championship revealed its conspicuous ignorance of the female game. This became all too evident in the way it bungled the selection of the first national team. The CAHA announced the first fourteen players to make the team at a press conference at the Hot Stove Lounge in Maple Leaf Gardens, on January 18, 1990. Dave McMaster, a long-time advocate of women's hockey and coach for thirteen years for the University of Toronto Lady Blues, was chosen head coach, along with assistant coaches Lucie Valois (Female Council representative from Quebec) and Rick Polutnik (technical director for the Alberta Amateur Hockey Association).

Unbelievably, after dominating women's hockey for almost ten years, Angela James did not make the list of the first fourteen national team players. It seemed impossible. Coach McMaster told James that she didn't have a good training camp, but because of her reputation, they would surely take a second look at her at another camp just before the world championship. "My skills didn't change in the next few weeks. I thought it was bullshit," recalled James angrily. "It's my sport and I wasn't going to kiss ass." James's attitude may have played a part in her failure to make the first cut. She was a street-smart kid with a fierce loyalty to her sport, but she had no experience with CAHA politics and no interest in hiding her frustration about the unorthodox selection process. Privately, however, James was devastated. Her mother says it was the first time she ever saw Angela cry.

The CAHA named five more players to the team in mid-February. One month later, the final roster was announced in a press release. Although speculation about the unusually drawn-out selection process ran high, no official reason was proffered. Rumours circulated that some of the final five, including Angela James, were selected late to punish them for their "bad attitude." Players such as James, Stacy Wilson and Geraldine Heaney, who would become the backbone of future national teams, endured this humiliating and disorganized selection process.

Part of the problem with the selection procedure lay in the CAHA's lack of interest in women's hockey. Prior to the discussions for the 1990 championship, the CAHA expressed no interest in considering elite world competition for women's hockey. Nationally, it had mustered only enough energy and funds to organize one national championship in 1982. Elite female hockey was an incomprehensible leap of the imagination for the male hockey world; indeed it was a leap for most of society. Consequently, no scouting records or coaching pool existed and decisions regarding player selection involved more politics than playmaking skills. The CAHA chose team members based on a six-day selection camp with feedback from coaches and evaluators, many of whom were unfamiliar with the players. Although skilled in their own right, some players with high-profile brothers were chosen for their added appeal to the media, who were familiar only with the men's game.

The CAHA's ignorance regarding women's hockey also translated into a lack of confidence in promoting a women's world championship. Never having seen most of these talented women play, the CAHA made novelty the central selling point of the championship. Silly gimmicks took over; the CAHA director of operations, Pat Reid, told one reporter that most potential spectators would be attracted by the tournament's curiosity value. "We don't want to make this out to be something like mud wrestling," he said, "but let's face it, the novelty factor will be important." [11]

As previously mentioned, in its quest for novelty the CAHA even went so far as outfit the players in pink. Apparently oblivious to the sexist stereotyping, Reid justified the pink uniforms with white pants as a way of adding "appeal" to the game. He seemed to regard women's hockey as more of a fashion show than a sport. "This is the first time that women's hockey is going to get national exposure," Reid told the press, "and I think people are going to think this is a lot more attractive."[12]

Had Reid asked Fran Rider, then director of the Female Council for the CAHA and the woman who had spearheaded the first world tournament less than three years earlier, he might have rethought his choice of uniform colour. "If they were manufactured in pink because the players are women, we find that offensive," Rider stated, summing up tersely what many women's hockey advocates felt.[13] Although Reid's pink decision did generate copy, it was hardly the sort that brought the kind of respect or attention for female athletes that players and fans desired.

Some reporters took their cue from the CAHA and happily focussed on the sex appeal aspect. Others were highly critical of the colour choice and wrote about it. "Is Canada's pink and white national women's hockey team in town for the world championship a dazzling statement of cool high fashion for the future or an example of a degrading stereotype of the past?" wrote Earl McRae of the *Ottawa Citizen*. "Personally, I love pink and wear it, but I am left with one, nagging question: Would Canada's national men's team be happy to wear hot pink and white?"[14] The *Ottawa Sun*'s sports editor Jane O'Hara was more to the point in her headline, which read: "Sorry Girls, Pink Stinks."[15]

Walter Bush, the president of USA Hockey and chairman of the IIHF women's committee, explained that Tackla, the Finnish company that made the pink-and-white uniforms paid the IIHF $250,000 for the rights to outfit the eight teams at this first world championship. Ironically, had Tackla paid minimal attention to the growing popularity of the sport, its participation in the event would have proven far more profitable.

Tackla brought only $23,000 worth of products to Ottawa to sell during the course of the championship. They sold out in one night. If the pink uniforms weren't bad enough, the CAHA added to the buffoonery by offering one hundred "beauty makeovers" as part of the draw prizes to promote the semifinal game between Canada and Finland. As for the players, they remained understandably reticent about the promotional schemes. This was the first official world championship and no player was going to protest the decision of a sponsor or the CAHA if she planned to continue playing the game at that level. In the privacy of the team's dressing room, Angela James described the attitudes towards the uniforms. "The pink jerseys were a bit of a gimmick. The girls said if that's what it's going to take to get the fans out, fine. We'll show them on the ice."[16]

Despite the previous lack of recognition, the 1990 world championship garnered international attention for the first time. New fans, the media and even the CAHA were surprised to witness skilled and intelligent hockey played superbly. The gold-medal game held the same excitement as a Stanley Cup for the fans and players. Team Canada rallied from a 2–0 deficit to thwart Team USA 5–2. France St. Louis, her voice still raspy from a stick to the throat earlier in the tournament, topped off her comeback with two goals and two assists in two games. Angela James was named to the all-star team along with Dawn McGuire, who was also chosen Most Valuable Player of the gold-medal game. Canada's goalie, Cathy Phillips, was voted the tournament's MVP. Captain Sue Scherer summed up the importance of the championship for female hockey: "We wanted to give young girls playing hockey something to strive for and I think we did just that."[17]

Player registration and national team awareness soared after the 1990 world championship. Team Canada set the standard for elite female hockey. Players for the next world event now had to be conditioned like never before — hockey-smart with exceptional defensive and offensive skills. Bob Nicholson, the new director of operations for the CAHA indicated that the time had come to give the women's national team equal treatment with the men's junior national team, which meant equipping it for competiton with a similar support squad, including a sports psychologist, the usual motivational T-shirts and off-ice team sweaters. He also outfitted the 1992 team in red and white, the regular national team colours.

For the 1992 world championship, gifted players started to emerge from several provinces. Representation on the national team from Quebec doubled from four to eight players — an indication that both the national and provincial hockey associations had improved their selection process. Newcomers such as eighteen-year-old Nancy Drolet and twenty-six-year-old Danielle Goyette would both figure prominently in the scoring and add more firepower to this already imposing squad. Quebec forwards France St. Louis and France Montour, and defence Diane Michaud also returned. Back again from 1990 for Ontario were Angela James, Margot Verlaan, Heather Ginzel, Sue Scherer, Geraldine Heaney, Laura Schuler and Dawn McGuire. Andria Hunter, a Canadian attending the University of New Hampshire; Karen Nystrom, the lanky speedster from Scarborough, Ontario; and Natalie Rivard, a defensive workhorse from Ottawa, were new to the team. New Brunswick's hard-working defensive forward, Stacy Wilson, and Alberta's crafty defence Judy Diduck, both 1990 national team veterans, completed the 1992 roster.[18] Goaltender Marie-Claude Roy returned to the roster. Relatively new to women's hockey but making headlines everywhere was Team Canada's newest goaltender, Manon Rhéaume from Lac Beauport, Quebec, famous for being the first woman to play seventeen minutes on a Quebec major Junior A male hockey team. The CAHA's selection of Rhéaume to the Team Canada roster remained controversial. She was not experienced with the women's game nor was she one of its leading goaltenders. Many observers in the women's hockey community maintained that Rhéaume's selection to the national team had more to do with her media profile than her goaltending skills. Two new assistant coaches joined Team Canada: Pierre Charette, a coach with a girls' high school hockey team in Laval, Quebec; and Shannon Miller, a police officer from Calgary. Head coach Rick Polutnik, who had been the assistant coach from the 1990 championship, emphasized "speed, speed and more speed" in practices.[19] On the larger international rink, velocity was crucial in forcing the competition to make quick and (it was hoped) rash decisions.

Canada's competition was also determined to improve its standings and the results were evident in Tampere, Finland, in 1992. (The IIHF decided to hold biennial world championships to allow countries more time to develop their women's hockey program.) In two years the talent had improved dramatically on every team and the scores reflected the increased emphasis on defence. In 1990 Canada had outscored the competition 68–8. In 1992 that number dropped by almost half to 38–3.

For the 1992 event, the IIHF had decided to ban bodychecking in the world championship since the disparity in skills among most of the European and Asian teams had not changed. Fearing complaints or lawsuits from parents, the IIHF also wished to avoid repeating the excessive number of injuries in the 1990 world championship. Despite the absence of bodychecking and the improvement in their opponents' skills, Canada overwhelmed the other teams in every category. Team Canada swamped China and Denmark, the two new entries in their A Group. China, the brash Asian entry, fell 8–0. New to the championship, China complained that no one had informed them that bodychecking was not permitted. And even though Denmark was one of the top five European teams,

Canada overpowered the Danes 10-0. Team Canada fired seventy-three shots on beleaguered goalie Leni Rasmussen, while Canada's Manon Rhéaume faced a mere four shots.

It soon became apparent that Canada's only real competition remained the US and Finland, with Sweden closing in quickly. Sweden lost to Canada only 6–1 versus a fourteen-goal gap in 1990. The other countries languished well below these top four. In Group B, Finland was the only real competition for the American team. The US overpowered Norway 9–1, embarrassed Switzerland 17–0 but only managed to outscore the fleet-footed Finns by two goals winning 5–3. Canada's three top lines overwhelmed the weary Finns in the semifinal, beating them 6–2. In the gold-medal game, Team Canada thrashed the US 8–0 with a faster, more aggressive players whose forechecking and speed overpowered the Americans. The Canadian goal-scorers included familiar names such as Angela James, who scored two goals, along with Margot Verlaan and newcomer Andria Hunter, who had one goal apiece. Three goals from Sherbrooke's Nancy Drolet helped to launch her as one of Quebec's talented new players. Danielle Goyette from St. Foy, Quebec, who weighed in as Canada's scoring leader for the tournament, also added a goal.

Canadian players dominated the all-star team once again. Manon Rhéaume joined veterans Angela James and Geraldine Heaney along with the US's Ellen Weinberg on defence, and scoring whiz Cammi Granato on right wing. Canada's newest national squad was now undefeated in two world championships. A euphoric national team arrived back in Canada with its second gold medal, exhilarated by its second successful world competition and the rising status of women's hockey in other countries.

Despite Canada's second gold medal, media interest in the world championship was low. With less than a handful of reporters covering the games, the press room was conspicuously quiet. The CAHA, which sent their communications manager to the men's world junior championship, did not bother to do so for the women's world event; instead they foisted the media relations job on the already overburdened national team manager, Glynis Peters. Moreover, some of the press complained about Peters's inexperience and unwillingness to allow sufficient access to Team Canada. Nor did the CAHA apparently deem the championship important enough to secure television coverage. TSN did not broadcast any games, citing lack of advertising money and costs for the transatlantic feed as their reason for not doing so. What media attention there was mainly surrounded Manon Rhéaume. The word was out in hockey circles that Rhéaume was invited to appear in *Playboy*. European papers picked up the story and dwelled on it tediously, displaying only lukewarm interest in the other athletes.

The most significant event of the 1992 world championship, however, occurred off the ice. Representatives from the International Olympic Committee (IOC) attended the games to assess women's hockey for inclusion in the Olympics. The CAHA, OWHA and IIHF lobbied for Olympic acceptance at cocktail parties and in improvised huddles in the stands. Letters of support were drafted by the CAHA and OWHA, who urged the IOC to establish women's hockey as an Olympic sport in 1994 in time for the Olympics in Norway. In the summer of 1992, the CAHA announced that women's hockey had been accepted into the Olympics — but not in time for 1994. Norway, apparently, would not cover the additional expense of adding the sport. The Japanese Olympic Committee (JOC) agreed to launch women's hockey, however, at the 1998 Olympics in Nagano, Japan after months of negotiations with IIHF representatives, with input from the CAHA.

Team Canada's participation in the 1998 Olympics will mean more than just long overdue recognition. "The Olympics have an aura," said the OWHA's Fran Rider. "It's something special, it's credible ...."[20] The impact will be felt at all levels of women's hockey. For provincial hockey organizations, it is a chance to build on the momentum of women's hockey's rising status, which will attract new players and coaches along with government funding that is increasingly geared towards Olympic sports. It is also an opportunity for the thousands of girls and women across the country for whom hockey is a passion to train with new hope. At last women will join their male counterparts at the ultimate amateur competition, the Olympics.

But for now Team Canada's immediate challenge was "going for the three-peat," the catchphrase describing its goal for the 1994 world championship in Lake Placid, New York. Only once before had three consecutive gold medals been won by a Canadian national team. (Canada's men's senior national team won the world championship three times from 1951 to 1953.) The CAHA chose as head coach the preppy, thirty-six-year-old Les Lawton, an eleven-year veteran with the Concordia Stingers in Montreal. Lawton had already proven himself: the Stingers had won several league championships and Concordia was known for its dedicated varsity program, which attracted female players from across Canada and the US. For the first time ever, both assistant coaches for Team Canada were female: Shannon Miller, an assistant coach in the 1992 world championship and for Team Alberta at the Canada Winter Games in 1991; and Melody Davidson, from Castor, Alberta, a recreation director involved in women's hockey schools.

The competition to make the team was unprecedented. "It felt like I was trying out for the first time," said two-time world champion Geraldine Heaney of Weston, Ontario. "The level of play was much higher and more evenly spread out this year. Some of the younger players were fantastic, and I'm looking forward to playing with Hayley [Wickenheiser]. She's awesome."[21] Fifteen-year-old Wickenheiser, from Calgary, Alberta, surprised everyone with her intelligence and maturity both on and off the ice. As Coach Lawton surmised, "Hayley might already be better than any player we've seen in the game. She's really skilled, has strength and speed and is very bright. There are others like her coming up and ready to make a statement. That's why the future is so good for women's hockey."[22]

The composition of the national team was changing. Two-time veterans France St. Louis, Geraldine Heaney, Angela James, Stacy Wilson, Judy Diduck and Margot Page all won places on Team Canada. Seven players represented Quebec, including 1992 returnees Nancy Drolet, Danielle Goyette, Nathalie Picard and Manon Rhéaume. Another eight new players joined this high-velocity roster. But it took time for the blend of veterans and youngsters to gel. In an exhibition game the week before the world championship, Finland defeated a disorganized and tentative Canadian team 6–3. Worried fans began to wonder if the Canadians could overcome their initial jitters and thwart their most consistent rival, the US, in their final exhibition game before Lake Placid.

During the game, the US team attempted to outmuscle the Canadian team and slow them down against the boards and in the corners, a foreshadowing of its strategy for the world championship. But the tactic failed. Canada squeaked out a 3–2 victory in a ragged game with twenty-six minutes of penalties. Backstopping Canada, Rhéaume recorded twenty-five saves and was voted MVP of the game. Wickenheiser scored the winning goal and contributed an assist.

Much of the media attention continued to focus on Rhéaume. Although she arrived at camp vastly improved — trim and muscled after two years of training in the semi-pro ranks — her celebrity status once again gave her an added advantage in the selection process. For the newly launched Canada–US Challenge Cup game played at the Ottawa Civic Centre, the pre-game radio and television promotion focussed almost exclusively on the goalie. Still lacking confidence in the drawing-power of women's hockey, the CAHA and sponsors clung to Rhéaume's celebrity status, viewing it as a surefire way to attract spectators. Although young male and female fans clamoured to see Rhéaume, they also lined up for autographs from the rest of Team Canada, excited more by their on-ice skills than the media-made interest.

With the Olympics only four years away, the pressure was on all the teams to step up their play. In 1994 Canada, Finland and the US once again set the standards for play. Canada rolled through its A Group, starting with a 7–1 win over the Chinese, who had dramatically improved their passing and skating skills but persisted in extra shoving and hooking to compensate for lack of experience. An ankle injury Wickenheiser received during practice kept her off the ice for all but five minutes of the China game. (She returned later in the tournament to play against Finland and the US, but was ineffective because of the injury.) The two Scandinavian countries fell prey to Canada next: Norway bowed out 12–0 and Sweden 8–2. The determined Finns lost in the semifinal 4–1. In Group B the US subdued Switzerland 6–0 and Germany 16–0. The US team's biggest test was against the fleety Finns, but they salvaged a 2–1 win. In the semifinal the US toyed with China easily winning 14–3.

The final showdown of the championship pitted the highly favoured Canadians against the hometeam United States for the third time. Karen Kay, assistant coach in 1990 and now in her second year as head coach at University of New Hampshire, guided Team US. Its talented line-up included oversized goaltender Kelly Dyer, the three-time national team veteran who played for the West Palm Beach Blaze in the men's semi-pro Sunshine Hockey League. Dyer, who towered over her teammates and the competition at 5 ft. 10 in. (179 cm) and 172 lbs. (78 kg), was joined in the US line-up by Cammi

*Team Canada celebrating their world
championship gold medal in Lake Placid.*

Granato and Karyn Bye, all-star forwards from the 1992
championship.

After being thrashed 8–0 by Canada in the 1992 gold
medal game, the US was hungry for revenge. Fans anticipated
a fierce match and they were not disappointed. The US led
1–0 at the end of first period. Then Danielle Goyette popped
the first goal for Canada on a power play at the beginning of
the second period. But it was Angela James who charged up
the Canadians. In a magnificent solo effort, she jetted down
the left wing, faked a slapshot against the defence, then
swooped in and flipped a shot over the goalie. A few minutes
later she scored again, and by the end of the second period
Canada led 3–2.

In the third period, another power play goal by Danielle
Goyette and markers by captain France St. Louis and Stacy

Wilson dashed the spirits of the young US team. Canada won 6–3 in a heart-stopping game that was still undecided until midway through the third period. The US had blown it by taking bad penalties. It was the second-most penalized team in the tournament, picking up eight out of the ten penalties in the final. "The penalties hurt. They killed our momentum," confirmed US forward Karyn Bye.[23] Whatever the reasons for the US loss, in 1994 Team Canada made hockey history by becoming only the second Canadian team ever to win three consecutive world championships. (In 1995 Canada's male junior national team won a third consecutive gold medal in the world championship in Alberta.)

Once again, Canada dominated the all-star team. Canadian stars included Danielle Goyette who had been top scorer for Team Canada for the second time; goaltender Manon Rhéaume, and Therese Brisson on defence. Twenty-year-old Finnish sensation Riikka Nieminen and two US players, forward Karyn Bye and defence Kelly O'Leary, completed the all-star roster. Geraldine Heaney earned best defence honours and Angela James was chosen as MVP for the final game. Nieminen was named top forward with four goals and eleven assists in five games and Finland took home the bronze medal for the third time. China moved up to fourth place, even though it had a mere 250 registered players from which to select its team.

It wasn't until 1994 that the CAHA finally sent Phil Legault, its manager of communications, to the women's world championship to ease the burden on national team manager, Glynis Peters, who had juggled both the communications' and manager's job in 1992. But the CAHA still failed to aggressively champion its most successful and promotable product in the women's game. TSN broadcast the history-making "three-peat" game, but fell back on the predictable: an interview with Manon Rhéaume and another historical look at women's hockey. Moreover, Peter Watts, the TSN announcer for the final game, was clearly bored by this lesser assignment, making numerous mistakes with players' names, and rarely allowing colour commentator and former national-team player, Sue Scherer, to express an opinion. Watts was even overheard grumbling earlier in the tournament that if the Finnish team made it to the final, he wouldn't bother learning those difficult names: instead, he would just call the players by their number.

But Olympic status has conferred some benefits on Team Canada: in 1994 the CHA announced the formation of a coaching pool for the women's national team. Six coaching trainees, five women and one man (who dropped out in 1995), would attend additional training courses and scout players at provincial and national championships. The coaching pool began to fill the need for elite female coaches, essential role models in the development of women's hockey. Shannon Miller, two-time head coach, with five years' experience with the national team, now mentors both male and female coaches for women's hockey. Miller has been overwhelmed by the requests for advice. "I can't believe the number of phone calls I get at home at night, from all over Canada. For the 1995 Canada Winter Games I had coaches from three provinces calling me for advice." The fact that these coaches are constantly scouting players, at provincial and national championships across the country, forces aspiring young players to gear up under the additional scrutiny. It is also apparent that Olympic status dramatically affects how female hockey coaches and players are treated. "It affects the mentality of the men who are involved in the game," explains Miller. "Before they could ignore women's hockey, now they can't. It's real and we could win gold. The men are taking the game a lot more seriously."[24]

Olympic status has meant that sponsors are slowly discovering Canada's "other" national team. As mentioned in Chapter 7, in 1994 the CHA announced that Imperial Oil would be a new sponsor for its women's national team, part of the CHA's new premier sponsor package. The Royal Bank and Air Canada are also part of the premier sponsor contract with the CHA and between them doled out $25,000 for the Pacific Rim tournament in 1996. Unfortunately neither the CHA nor the sponsors will indicate the total amount of money which actually goes towards Canada's female national team.

The inclusion of women's hockey in the Olympics also prompted the IIHF to add international competitions. In April 1995 the IIHF launched the Pacific Rim championship to offer China and Japan a chance to sharpen their skills prior to the Olympics. For Team Canada this meant two extra national team selection and evaluation camps in October 1995 and 1996, as well as additional international competition.

In preparation for the 1995 Pacific Rim championship, the CHA implemented two significant changes. For the first time it chose an all-female coaching staff, with Shannon Miller acting as head coach and newcomers Julie Healy, assistant coach of the Concordia Stingers, and Danièle Sauvageau, a police officer and head coach with Ferland–Quatre Glaces in Montreal. Both assistant coaches are part of the Quebec senior all-star program. The CHA also chose a developmental team composed of sixteen rookie players, bolstered by previous national team veterans such as goalie Leslie Reddon, Judy Diduck, Stacy Wilson, Danielle Goyette, Marianne Grnak, Cassie Campbell, and sixteen-year-old Hayley Wickenheiser. The most imposing player on the Canadian team, now 5 ft. 9 in. (174 cm) and 170 lbs. (75 kg.), Wickenheiser challenged allcomers with her in-your-face hockey, playing on the first line with scoring ace Goyette and playmaker Wilson.

The outcome of the first two games was predictable: Canada humbled China 9–1 and Japan 11–0. In game three, against the US, Canada's defence faltered, unable to contain the bigger, more experienced Americans. Team USA outskated the rookie Canadians, beating them 5–2. In the semifinal the unthinkable almost happened: the aggressive and brash Team China fought to a 2–2 tie after three periods. Canada managed to squeak by China 3–2 in a shootout, with goaltender Leslie Reddon thwarting the nervous Chinese forwards who were shooting in their first overtime. The gold-medal game against Team USA spoke volumes about Canada's gritty determination and character. With players injured from the China game — Goyette and Grnak were in neck braces and Wilson's legs and shoulders were black and blue from the excessive slashing and hooking — coach Miller stoked up the Canadian defensive game with aggressive forechecking and tight backchecking. The score was tied 1–1 after three periods with goals by Wickenheiser and Team USA's Karyn Bye, although the US outshot Canada 36–23. Canada calmed down in the deciding shootout and was rewarded with a win when several US players choked and shot over the net. Wickenheiser departed the tournament several pounds heavier, thanks to three awards for her contribution to the team, including the MVP award in the final game.

The fact that a team of sixteen rookies with two new assistant coaches had defeated the US team in a tournament that most observers expected the Canadians to lose was yet another instance of Team Canada's determination to prove its mettle. "It had a lot to do with motivation — to play for their country and national pride," says coach Miller. "We stressed making history, playing and winning in the first Pacific Rim championship. The team played over their heads and were willing to pay any price for their country."[25]

The CHA again selected Shannon Miller as head coach for the 1996 Pacific Rim tournament. Miller, the head coach of the new Olympic Oval High Performance Female Hockey program in Calgary, Alberta, has become a key role model for players and coaches. She possesses superb technical expertise and facility for motivating players. Two new assistant coaches — Karen Hughes, with the University of Toronto Lady Blues, and Melody Davidson, head coach for Team Alberta in the 1995 Canada Winter Games — completed the coaching staff. In announcing the new team, Miller pointed out the need for the development of elite players to move forward. "For the past two years, we've been evaluating and initiating players at an introductory level," maintains Miller. "We're now going to take these players to the next level of preparation for international games."[26]

Team Canada 1996 represented the culmination of the gradual evolution of the women's high-performance program since its rather chaotic beginning in 1990. With the new coaching pool, the CHA was finally able to scout both future and existing female players. The results were evident. This team was a formidable blend of veterans, including three-time gold medalists Angela James, Judy Diduck, Stacy Wilson, Geraldine Heaney, thirty-seven-year-old France St. Louis and Quebec scoring aces Danielle Goyette and Nancy Drolet. The mix also consisted of new, young players from both the 1994 and 1995 teams, including seven rookies and the number-one-rated player in the country, Hayley Wickenheiser. Danielle Dube, now Canada's highest ranked goaltender, and Manon Rhéaume shared the net duties.

The Pacific Women's Hockey Championship (the name was changed in 1996) offered an opportunity to assess Canada's team against its most formidable opponent, the US. It was also a glimpse of the state of hockey in Asia. Japan's small and inexperienced players — the average height is 5 ft. 2 in. (157 cm) — had little chance of winning against any of the teams. Canada routed Japan 12–0 in its first game. The Chinese remained a stubborn, tough team, who were able to confound the Canadians with their defensive box, thwarting the Canadian scoring threat. Once again, Team Canada barely managed to win, beating China 1–0, after being frustrated by the exhaustive goaltending of China's Hong Guo.

## · TEAM CANADA: NEGLECTED HEROES ·

The US, with its youthful energy and bolstered defence, also tested the Canadians. The first game against the US in this tournament was marked by end-to-end rushes. But Canada's depth eventually wore down the US, which was using only two lines. The final score was 3–2 for Canada. Canada now faced Japan in the semifinal, an easy win by a score of 19–0. The gold medal contest between Canada and the US was more of the same. The game was scoreless until five minutes into the third period when the US popped its first goal. Canada's speedsters took over: Nancy Drolet fired two goals and Cassie Campbell blistered a slapshot. Wickenheiser scored into the open net in the last five minutes of play. Goaltender Danielle Dube made thirty saves and was named MVP of the game. The local media warmed to this first international event in BC but TSN did not televise the final game which Team Canada coach Shannon Miller called "the best hockey ever played by the two best teams ever on ice."[27]

This national team is the first stage of the five-year development plan for Team Canada, which began in the fall of 1995. The next task will be the selection of the head coach for Canada's first Olympic women's hockey team by August 1996. It is most likely that this person will be Shannon Miller. In the fall of 1996 Team Canada will play in a ten-day warm-up tour in Ontario and Quebec against the two top teams, Finland and the US. At a selection camp in January 1997, the CHA will choose the pre-Olympic team to play in the qualifying world championship in Kitchener, Ontario, in April 1997.

The last selection camp for players hoping to win a spot on Canada's first Olympic team will be in August 1997. Once chosen, the team will likely relocate to Calgary in October to train together for four to six weeks, then go back home until January 1998, when they will convene for another training session, which will continue until just prior to the Olympic Games in February. For the hockey players, this Olympic schedule is close to athlete heaven: the players will be on the ice every day, attending strategy sessions and working with coaches. Facilities and all expenses will be paid by the CHA. And for the first time, members of the national team will address high school students, hold clinics and attend public-relations events — things the men's national team has been doing for years.

Watching the CHA play catch-up with the women's high-performance program is both gratifying and frustrating. Elite hockey is an important catalyst that has pushed the development of the women's game farther and faster. But even Team Canada sits at the end of the bench when it comes to financial and marketing support from the CHA. While player evaluation and coaching development has improved dramatically, elite female players are still only beginning to benefit from the advantages and privileges male players have enjoyed for years.

The sheer number of elite male teams and the range of competitions is staggering. The CHA Program of Excellence (POE), begun in 1982, is an example of a very successful system committed to developing the highest calibre of male players for Canada's national junior team. The POE boasts a database of statistics on all elite male hockey players in Canada, starting at age sixteen. The CHA employs a full-time scout to tour the country and report on players. The POE consists of a three-stage plan involving the development of elite male players starting at age sixteen. At the first stage the players try out for the five regional under-17 Canadian national teams that face off against Russia, the Czech Republic, Sweden, Finland and the United States. Canada hosts this World Hockey Challenge, which is held every two years. In alternate years there is either a Hockey Festival or the Canada Winter Games to pit the five regional Canadian teams against one another. The next stage consists of an annual four-country under-18 championship, in addition to the Air Canada–sponsored under-18 Pacific Cup.

The third stage involves selection and training camps for the national junior team and its participation in the annual world championship. Keeping this revolving door of tournaments spinning takes commitment and cash, both of which are in secure supply for the men's national teams.

To develop Canada's senior male team Hockey Canada, a second national hockey organization, was launched with government funds and sponsorship in 1964. Hockey Canada's responsibilities included the Canada Cup tournaments, and the organization employed a full-time head coach, assistant coach and general manager for Team Canada. By 1993–94 the men's tour consisted of sixty-five games in Europe and Canada. In 1994 Hockey Canada merged with the CAHA under the new moniker the Canadian Hockey Association (CHA). The senior men's team will no longer represent Canada in the Olympics since the NHL, IIHF and IOC have agreed to NHL "dream teams," starting in 1998.

Elite male players do very well, revelling in the perks of competition as early as age sixteen. Yet to hear those involved with the men's national team tell it, they are barely scraping by. "We operate on a shoestring budget," Canada's coach Tom Renney lamented in 1994. "Our total budget is less than $500,000 and from that we have to give twenty-two guys contracts, equipment and supplies, travel costs. It all adds up. Only a small percentage of our budget comes from the government, but since the merger with the CAHA the government is playing a more direct role so we've been affected by the cuts."[28]

Female national team players are not paid a salary and will not be training year-round prior to the Olympics. "Certainly the women are not going to train on a full-time basis like the men's team," says manager Glynis Peters. "It would drive them nuts. For one thing, you'd be asking people to give up friends, family, jobs. We think we can build a plan that gets them to the Olympics with the best team and still keep some balance in their lives.[29] The CHA seems unaware that many of the players, including Manon Rhéaume, are planning to leave jobs and pay to train full-time at the new women's hockey high-performance program at the Olympic Oval in Calgary. Many of these women have to pay just to play the game. New Brunswick's Stacy Wilson not only loses her teaching salary when she attends a camp or tournament, she must also pay the substitute teacher who replaces her.[30]

For the first time the women's national team will receive "carding" as Olympic athletes, which entitles them to Sport Canada funding to train. In the fall of 1995, thirty female hockey players were carded to receive money for two years. This infusion of funds allows the athletes to pay at least for such things as new skates and even memberships to sports clubs. For example, Team Canada member Angela James cannot afford to quit her job, but with her carded status she can now get advice from a personal trainer on how to supplement her regimen.

The difference between men and women's teams lies almost entirely on the CHA's financial commitment. In 1994–95 the CHA budget showed government revenue for Canada's national teams is listed at $625,500. Although CHA officials will not divulge how much of that goes to the women's team, the women's national team expenses were listed as a meagre $25,210. This compares to $1,833,885 allocated for the men's senior and junior national teams and the national under-17 and under-18 programs. The CHA might argue that the junior and senior men's teams pay their way with gate receipts totalling $1,784,000 from play in the heavily promoted world championships and tournaments, where prize money is offered.[31] But given the same marketing and administrative support male hockey receives, it is conceivable that Canada's female national team could also pay for themselves.

Advancement of Canada's female national team should mean sharing more of the sponsorship opportunities, staff, and federal government funds allocated to the CHA. In a climate resistant to female sport, championing the relentlessly successful Team Canada is one easy strategy for advancing women's hockey. Yet the team's success is often perceived as a threat to the men's game because female hockey is seen as competing with male hockey for crucial components such as ice time, volunteers, government funds and sponsorship. Indeed, the remarkable success of the female game and the increase in participation are at times viewed as an annoying distraction to male hockey. Women's hockey emphasizes finesse and agility, and is devoid of the fighting and violence so prevalent in male hockey; this is a formula that spells family entertainment. For parents and fans who dislike the goon mentality promoted in the media, women's hockey is a refreshing alternative. Yet, practically speaking, the CHA and its provincial counterparts have a case of conflicting interests. If they aggressively promote Team Canada, they are diluting male hockey resources by encouraging female players. Women's hockey is cutting into the opportunities for male players, whose membership fees and sponsorships have been paying the CHA staff salaries for years. CAHA President Murray Costello expressed this fear in the wake of the 1990 women's world championship. "The biggest concern I have for the CAHA is how we're going to share already scarce ice time between girls and boys, especially in small-town Canada," he said. "We're not sure what we're creating here." [32] That the organization should be creating equal opportunity for girls seems to elude him. But by neglecting Team Canada the CHA is ignoring a hugely successful hockey property that is not only likely to win one of Canada's gold medals but can boost registration and line the CHA's coffers.

Despite the neglect, the women's national team remains a beacon of hope in the barren hockey landscape of little-known female heroes. And its performance has not gone unnoticed among female sports advocates. "The women's national ice hockey team which made history in 1994 by winning a third consecutive medal in world championship play, had an impact far beyond the ice surface," declared the selection committee for the Breakthrough Award presented by the Canadian Association for the Advancement of Women and Sport (CAAWS) to Team Canada in 1995. "Their style of play and outstanding success have captured public attention and raised the level of competition to international standards." The players' dedication also helped to win them the award, which recognizes individuals and organizations whose accomplishments have pushed the limits and enhanced the participation of girls and women in sport and activity. "Many [of the women] played for years before a national championship existed and long before a world championship was ever conceived. Time off from work without pay, missed promotions, delayed schooling, hours of travel to practice were common sacrifices," said CAAWS chair Bobbie Steen of Vancouver.[33] Karen Wallace, volunteer director of the Female Council at the CHA noted with some amusement that after the third national team gold medal, she no longer had to watch half the CHA membership leave before she read her female hockey report at the annual meeting.

The significance of Team Canada for women's hockey is profound. As Shannon Miller puts it: "You could credit the survival of women's hockey to the national team. Players will go to another sport if there is no place to advance. The national team program is like a carrot and just as big as the NHL for women's hockey."[34] For individual players, the importance of both hockey and Team Canada is palpable. In the hallway of Angela James's townhouse in North Toronto hangs a large framed colour photo of the 1990 women's world champions. With the proliferation of mugs, pucks, trophies and plaques, her home is more hockey shrine than residence. "My whole life is hockey," says James. "I live and breathe it. I never thought much about it until I got older, but people say 'Is that all you do is hockey?' I step back and say 'Yes. I coach, I referee and I play. That's my life and I don't think I would ever change it for anything else.'"[35]

Athletes like James play a fundamental role in the lives of young female players. In a drawer James keeps a poem dedicated to her by fourteen-year-old Jennifer Neil. For Neil, a grade eight student from an elementary school in Kitchener and a mixed-race child like James, AJ is an idol. Ever since Neil first witnessed James at a national team camp she's been enthralled with AJ. "My four friends and I were sitting in the stands talking about who is the best player. I said number 8, she's really good, I wish I could be like that," recounts Neil. "Then something clicked in me and I wanted to set a goal for myself. The way she skated, her shot. She's awesome. She looks so confident and comfortable out there. Even though it's tough it didn't get to her. Nothing will stop her."[36]

*Jennifer Neil and Angela James at Canada's national team selection camp, Kitchener, Ontario, January 1994.*

After the game Neil asked James for her autograph. "I was so nervous I couldn't breathe. [It was] like meeting Doug Gilmour [of the Toronto Maple Leafs]." Early in 1994 Neil had planned to quit girls' hockey because the calibre was so low where she plays. She changed her mind after meeting James. "I decided to stay in hockey and went to AJ's and Margot's [Page] school that summer [1994] and improved a lot," she recalls. "I really let her know I never would have [stayed with hockey] without her encouragement. I got a real confidence boost from her." Hockey is now once again a significant part of Neil's life. In 1996 she played on two junior teams.

The inspiration Neil received from James is testimony to the importance of visible female sports heroes. Not only do women such as James deserve admiration for their athletic feats, but girls such as Neil deserve role models. Indeed, as Neil herself makes evident, their presence can make all the difference in the world.

*Chapter Nine*

# THE ROAD TO NAGANO

*I am ten years old and have been playing hockey for five years. I am quite a good player and was just chosen as one of the top ten female hockey players in Mississauga. While I was at the Olympics [1988] I saw six hockey games. I did not see any women's hockey teams. When I get older, I want to be able to compete in hockey with other countries from all over the world. I want the chance to stand on a podium and know I am one of the reasons they are playing 'O Canada.' Will I have that chance? If not, could you please let me know why? I will try to understand. Also, if the answer is no, is there anything you can do to change that. I don't want to give up my dreams.*

(Excerpted from Samantha Holmes's letter to Prime Minister Brian Mulroney, 15 March 1988.)

THE SNOWY PEAKS OF THE Japanese Alps overlook Nagano, the site of the 1998 Winter Olympics. In this tourist area famous for the beauty of its mountains, forests and lakes the first women's Olympic hockey teams will step onto the ice and into sports history. Yet the story of how they reached that moment — how they arrived at the pinnacle of amateur sport — will be known to only a small number of devoted hockey fans. A new class of hockey is emerging and each player is vividly aware that the success of women's hockey at these Olympics could be their passport to a future expansion of the game.

The decision by the International Olympic Committee (IOC) to accept women's hockey as an Olympic sport was due to a combination of factors, the first of which was timing. In the late 1980s the IOC began to express interest in adding more Winter Olympic events. As of 1988 there were only 46 winter events compared with the 260 in the Summer Games. A second factor in the decision was continued pressure from women's sports associations, and from individuals, for equitable female participation in the Games. There were also several committed and visionary members of the International Ice Hockey Federation (IIHF), the international governing body for hockey, who were determined to build on the growing popularity of women's hockey, and they aggressively lobbied the IOC and hockey federations for Olympic participation. The fact that the IIHF was flush with additional revenue from a new television contract for the men's world championship only helped the cause. Gord Renwick, the IIHF vice-president of marketing from 1982 to 1994, and a sixteen-year veteran of international hockey, was keen to activate an Olympic plan that included women's hockey while the money was still available. "The money was there so we could make it happen," says Renwick. "If we had to cut [men's hockey] programs, we would never get approval. Once you get on the road to the Olympics you can get IOC funding and government support."[1]

The IIHF is the sole voice for women's hockey internationally. Founded in 1908 and based in Switzerland, it is a small organization with an international volunteer board representing fifty-four member countries. The Federation provides administrative, financial and technical support for twenty-six annual tournaments, which include the men's senior, men's junior, and women's world championships. Despite its broad mandate the IIHF is not known for its marketing or management expertise.

On the contrary, critics have accused it of poor organization and a somewhat crippling lack of imagination. As one source, who did not wish to be identified, explained, "They don't have any real plan. They just go from meeting to meeting."

For most member countries men's hockey is the priority. Indeed, women's hockey is often viewed as an anomaly and many IIHF members fail to comprehend why women even want to play the game. By 1992 about twenty-five countries offered women's hockey, and most of their national teams were not formed until the late 1980s and early 1990s, although in several countries women had been playing the game for four or five decades — despite the lack of societal approval or federation recognition. But women's hockey in many other countries is still regarded with some hostility or, at best, considered a curiosity. Organizers of male hockey resent the competition for federation money and precious ice time, especially in cash-poor countries such as Russia. It is important to remember that in most countries women's hockey is a young sport. Outside North America it is only about ten to fifteen years old. As Jan-Äke Edvinsson, IIHF general secretary, puts it, "Except in Canada where [hockey] is a religion, it is not [as popular] in other parts of the world."[2]

Until the late 1980s the IIHF was oblivious to the women's game. The Ontario Women's Hockey Association (OWHA) prodded it into action when it hosted the first world tournament in 1987. For Edvinsson, this tournament was critical because it spawned two official IIHF women's championships: the European in 1989 and the World in 1990. The IIHF was quick to incorporate the women's game into its organization: it wanted to prevent a separate international women's hockey federation from forming, as had happened in field hockey. By 1991, after two world tournaments and two European championships, women's hockey was still struggling with the universal problems of recognition and funding. In addition lack of ice time made it almost impossible to improve the calibre of the game. Without federation funding it was impossible to hold events that could attract media attention and sponsorship. Given its inferior status and poor financial condition, it's not surprising that to this day the calibre of women's hockey varies dramatically from country to country.

Gord Renwick, Canada's IIHF representative, pushed hard for Olympic status, recognizing it as an essential catalyst which would drive the game forwards at many levels. Although support for women's hockey within the IIHF was limited, Renwick and several IIHF colleagues aggressively lobbied both the IOC and member organizations for two years. Renwick, with help from Murray Costello, the CHA president, led the drive for Olympic status; the only support came from Norway.

In April 1992 two IOC representatives were dispatched to the world championship in Finland. Surprised and impressed by the female players' speed, playmaking and intensity, the IOC announced in July 1992 that women's hockey would become a new Olympic sport. The IIHF then pushed for the game's inclusion in the 1994 Lillehammer Olympics. The Norwegian Olympic Committee (NOC) refused to accept women's hockey, however, citing lack of facilities and funds: the committee claimed it would need US$1 million to build the necessary arenas. Despite offers by the IIHF and the Norwegian Ice Hockey Federation to pay for all accommodation and transportation of teams, the NOC did not relent. The decision was a painful blow to many of the older players, who realized they had probably lost their last chance of playing in the Olympics.

In preparation for the 1998 games, Renwick opened negotiations with the Japanese Ice Hockey Federation and the Japan Olympic Committee, hoping to have women's hockey included in the 1998 Olympics. This was not an easy task. As the host country, Japan would receive an automatic entry into the Games, but the Japanese have not been successful in the game: their national women's team has qualified for only one world championship since 1990. "There was a lot of resistance to women's hockey in Japan. The organizers didn't want to pay to host another sport and besides that, the Japanese don't have a strong women's hockey program," recalls Glynis Peters, manager of women's hockey at the CHA. "Now they will have to finance an entirely new sports operation to bring their team up to Olympic standards in a few years. They were really reluctant to commit to that."[3] A crucial part of the negotiations regarding Olympic inclusion therefore involved assistance from the CHA to create an exchange program that would send Canadian coaches to Japan and Japanese players to Canada. The Nagano Committee also insisted that the IIHF should pay for food and accommodation for five of the six teams in the Olympics. In the end Renwick's hard work paid off. On November 17, 1992, the IOC announced that women's hockey was accepted for the 1998 Olympics.

With the Olympic imprimatur women's hockey carried new status. The impact of this status reverberated throughout both national and international sports organizations. The IIHF set aside about Cdn$1.5 million to fund competitions from 1995 to 1998, including the Olympics, in order to elevate the level of play internationally.[4] The first world event to be instituted was a badly needed Pacific Rim Women's Hockey Championship to be held in 1995, 1996, and then every two years after the Olympics. This meant that the two active Asian teams, China and Japan, which had lacked serious competition, would now face the two top teams, Canada and the United States, at least twice before the qualifying world championship in 1997.

The IIHF also decided to hold consecutive European championships in 1995 and 1996. This European competition serves as a qualifying tournament for the biennial world championship in which the top five European teams compete against Canada, the United States and the winner of the Asian Cup (China or Japan). In 1989 ten teams registered in the A Pool for the European championship, but to minimize expenses the IIHF only allowed eight teams to participate, and in 1991 a B Pool, consisting of six teams, was added. Two years later, the B Pool increased to eight teams, reflecting the quest for Olympic status. The Olympics has also motivated countries to create their own international competitions. Hungary, for instance, established a tournament with Switzerland, Norway, Germany and Denmark. In 1995 even Italy, a weak hockey country, launched a new tournament, inviting Switzerland, Germany and France. China announced its new five-nation tournament to be held in January 1996.

While the IIHF had expanded the number of competitions in preparation for Nagano, it still needed to address matters affecting the future of the game. Bodychecking has proved to be a contentious issue worldwide. In competition at the national level in China and some European countries bodychecking is permitted, but has not been sanctioned by the European championship rules. Despite the European ban, at the first world championship in 1990 the IIHF insisted on bodychecking, pandering to the prevailing notion that real hockey must include tough physical play. This insistence on bodychecking, combined with the vast difference in skills between the Europeans and the North Americans, resulted in injuries: several players had to be hospitalized. Consequently, bodychecking was disallowed at the world championship in 1992, and the policy is not likely to change prior to the Olympics.

In Japan, the US and Canada, women have played hockey since the mid-1980s without bodychecking. The Canadians and Americans had good reasons for removing bodychecking: most female players had not had any experience in minor hockey and had never learned how to bodycheck properly. As well, in the 1970s and 1980s a fifteen-year-old might find herself playing against a twenty-five-year-old, because there was no minor or junior hockey for girls in many communities. As a result, the skills and ages of the players have varied dramatically, resulting in too many injuries.

Although bodychecking has been banned in IIHF events, body contact is still very much a part of the game. This has caused confusion among players, coaches and referees since the point at which body contact becomes bodychecking has never been precisely defined. The IIHF bodychecking rule states that a penalty will be given for "any overt or intentional contact that is designed to apply physical force to a player." The key words are "intentional and overt," which would seem to mean physical force applied against a player whether or not she has the puck. The confusion occurs because referees tend to call more bodychecking penalties in the less important early games of world tournaments than in the semifinals or the final, leaving players and fans uncertain about the exact status of bodychecking. The only attempt at clarification made by the IIHF was a video produced in Canada in 1995 that purports to show the difference between bodychecking and incidental body contact.

The general feeling among many players is that the reinstatement of bodychecking would make their game more like men's hockey, and thus it would gain in respect and credibility. Many women also genuinely like the physical rush they get after a solid hit. Yet there is also a widely shared fear that women's hockey could degenerate to the same level as male hockey, in which bodychecking is used to compensate for lack of skating and passing skills, favouring larger and stronger players, forcing smaller players from the game. After the 1994 world championship Germany, whose players were less skilled, was one of the countries pressuring the IIHF to reinstate bodychecking. Germany ranked sixth in the tournament and was the second-most-penalized team, with fifty-eight penalty minutes after just four games. It is possible that body-checking could return to the women's game when the discrepancy in skill levels lessens, says former IIHF rules committee chairman, Gord Renwick. If bodychecking returns to the game internationally it means young girls will have to be taught how to bodycheck from an early age. In order for this to happen, however, most countries would require better and more consistent competition, improved coaching and more ice time.

In the meantime, the US, the silver-medalist in the last three world championships, is bursting with first-rate, highly motivated players who pose the greatest threat to the Canadian team. With almost 18,000 registered club players and an estimated 10,000 girls and women playing on male teams the US has a solid base of talent to produce a contender for an Olympic gold medal.[5] Despite the relatively large numbers, since the first world championship in 1990, the US team has only managed to maintain their ranking as number two in the world. To the surprise of American fans, Team USA even lost to Canada's rookie national team at the Pacific Rim Tournament in 1995 and again in 1996. Moreover, countries such as Finland, Russia and to a lesser extent China are hot-housing (practising together eight to ten months a year) their teams and could well topple the US at the 1998 Olympics.

Some of the blame for the precarious situation of the US team lies with USA Hockey, the country's national hockey organization. In 1989 USA Hockey launched the national team program. Development camps were set up for two age categories: one brought together eighty players aged fifteen to seventeen, and the other, senior, camp had forty players over eighteen. The selection and training of coaches to run the camps was haphazard and inconsistent. National scouting and evaluation, even in 1994, was still erratic. Players have complained about team selection decisions being left to the last minute, and scanty advance information about upcoming events. Team USA, although a definite contender for an Olympic gold medal, has not been a priority for USA Hockey. The female team appeared at its first Olympic Festival in 1993 but was absent in 1995, even though expenses for this event are paid by the US Olympic Committee. Art Berglund, national team director, explained that financial constraints had made it impossible for the women's team to participate (although there was enough money available for four regional men's teams to attend).

In 1995, after four losses to Canada in world women's hockey events, the US realized it had to bolster its national team program. USA Hockey coaching director Val Belmonte was dispatched to the 1995 European championships to scout the competition. That summer, USA Hockey held open tryouts in four states. To cultivate younger players, an annual week-long camp for under-17 players was launched at Lake Placid; it will run annually until 1998. USA Hockey also arranged an under-18 tournament with Russia and a Quebec all-star team, to be held in March 1995 and 1996.

Despite these advances observers of female hockey are concerned with the coaching situation in women's hockey. No initiatives to mentor female coaches exist. "We feel that women coaches are being pushed aside in favour of male hockey coaches since the men's national team haven't won a medal since 1980," notes Lynn Olson, former section director for women's hockey.[6] Since the NHL controls hockey in the Olympics, the only chance for an amateur coach to participate in the Olympics is with the women's team. As of 1995 twenty-four coaches (mostly male) expressed interest in the women's team. In June 1996, USA Hockey announced Ben Smith, coach of men's hockey at Northeastern University, as head coach of the women's Olympic team.

The management of Team USA has been less than satisfactory, but the team does include some outstanding players. Two

*Team Canada's captain France St. Louis (left)*
*fighting for the puck against Cammi Granato, Team USA.*

players who have set the standards for Team USA are Cammi
Granato and Karyn Bye. Granato, a five-time national-team
star was voted most valuable forward in the 1994 world championship, with twelve points in five games. Twenty-six years
old in 1998 she packs speed, accuracy and smarts into her lean
5 ft. 7 in. (170 cm), 140 lb. (65 kg) frame. Beginning at the
age of five Granato played hockey with boys until she was a junior in high school; she was usually the youngest player on the

ice and the only girl. "Guys would take runs at me even if I didn't have the puck," Granato remembers. "[On one occasion] my coach told me that the other team were told to hit number 21 as hard as they could the first period, so we switched jerseys."[7] At Providence College Granato won two Lady Friars Awards, one as the all-time leading point scorer, with 245 points, and the other as all-time leading goal scorer, with 135 goals. She was also named Eastern Collegiate Athletic Conference (ECAC) player of the year for 1990, 1991 and 1992. "There is no more deadly offensive threat in the league than Cammi," says Margaret Degidio-Murphy, coach at Brown University. "She is a force, a very cool character under pressure."[8]

Teammate Karyn Bye's approach to the game is just as committed. A T-shirt she often wears sums up her devotion to the game: "Hockey is life, the rest is just the details." As Bye explains, "If there was no hockey, it would be like waking up and not having air to breathe."[9] A member of the national team in 1992 and again in 1994, this 5 ft. 8 in. (174 cm), 165 lbs. (71 kg) woman is a strapping forward with a blistering slapshot. After an outstanding college career with the University of New Hampshire Wildcats, she joined Montreal's Concordia University in 1994 and led her team in scoring with 86 points, including 43 goals in 40 games that same year.

Both Granato and Bye played with boys as they were growing up because minor hockey didn't exist for girls in the US. National championships were initiated in 1975, but twenty years later, there were only ten states participating. Michigan, Massachusetts and Minnesota have the strongest programs for girls and women, but many of the participants have never had the chance to play minor hockey, or played only with boys. In 1994–95 there were just under 500 teams registered with USA Hockey, plus another 150 college, high school and prep school teams. The popularity of female hockey shot up after the 1990 world championship: registration went from 5,533 players in 1990–91 to 17,537 in 1994–95. In addition, an estimated 10,000 girls play on boys' teams. Despite the extraordinary growth, the female game still accounts for less than 10 percent of the 400,000 registered players.[10]

Management of the women's game is weak. USA Hockey, which was founded in 1951, lists four executive directors among their staff of forty-five, but as of spring 1996 there was no manager appointed specifically to oversee women's hockey, although it did mention that it would try to hire someone before the Olympics. Volunteer regional directors work with staff to coordinate the women's game. USA Hockey held two international women's hockey tournaments. When it hosted the 1994 world championship in Lake Placid promotion was dismal, and included a full-colour program that featured male players on the cover.

Although USA Hockey made amends for its faux pas in 1995 and produced a glossy colour shot of two female hockey players on the Pacific Rim program, it was the same lacklustre attitude towards female hockey that forced the national teams from Canada, the US, China and Japan to play their first Pacific Rim championship on a small practice rink rather than a regulation international rink. The arena seated only about 1,700 people — more evidence of USA Hockey's lack of confidence in the women's game. Promotion, once again, was abysmal. For example, a huge banner that should have emblazoned the championship's name across the exterior of the rink was strung haphazardly over the bleachers at one end of the arena.

USA Hockey, like many other hockey federations, would benefit from a good sports equity policy. As mentioned previously, Title IX has been the legal vehicle for sports equity in the US since 1972. The law applies to federally funded schools and universities and is aimed at prohibiting discrimination on the basis of gender: in plain words, it requires US schools to give male and female athletes the same opportunities. The law has several components: if women make up half of the student body, then fully half of the varsity athletic sports budget must be allocated to women's sports, or the school must otherwise demonstrate that it is meeting the level of interest of female athletes or is expanding women's programs. Schools had until 1978 to comply with Title IX, and by that year women's teams accounted for 33 percent of the nation's college athletes. "Unfortunately, that's where we have remained for the last fifteen years," says Donna Lopiano, executive director of the Women's Sports Foundation. "Thousands of cases have been filed related to gender equity and the court has consistently upheld Title IX."[11] "Males over fifty years old are our toughest opponent," says Lynn Olson, Minnesota's women's hockey representative and a former USA Hockey section director.[12]

Title IX has had some impact on women's hockey, most recently in the state of Minnesota. In 1994 hockey became a varsity sport for the first time in state high schools and later that year the government instituted ice-time legislation to redress the inequities for girls, stipulating that in 1994–95 15 percent of all rink ice time must be allocated for girls, rising to 30 percent in 1995–96 and 50 percent by 1996–97.

Since the new policy, girls' hockey registration has almost doubled in Minnesota, jumping from 119 female youth teams in 1994–95 to 200 in 1995–96. In the fall of 1995 Minnesota introduced varsity hockey in its state university. Lynn Olson, the state hockey representative and a former USA Hockey section director, maintains that college hockey will increase dramatically in the next five years because of Title IX. Even if schools do not add women's hockey voluntarily, some schools may do so through fear of lawsuits. Women are still fighting for equal rights and the same old excuses abound. "'We cannot afford to convert our programs'" say athletic directors, but they can still afford ninety boys on a football team," says Lynn Olson.[13]

Scholarship allocation is another area of glaring inequity in college women's hockey. In 1989 only three colleges offered scholarships for women. By contrast, men collected an average of eighteen scholarships per college per year. The men's game has developed accordingly, with fifty-one colleges and universities playing Division I hockey, thirteen Division II and fifty-nine Division III. Many universities in the 1970s made token concessions to women by allowing community teams to carry the varsity banner, but there was still no money for travel, equipment, coaches, trainers or practice time. In 1994 twenty-three universities and colleges still had only club teams.

The exception to this pattern is the Eastern United States, which has led the country in women's college hockey. Since 1976 six Ivy League schools have competed annually for the Eastern College League championship. The first Eastern College Athletic Championship (ECAC) was held in 1984. The ECAC was the first conference to sponsor an intercollegiate women's hockey league nine years later. During the 1994–95 season the league expanded to include fifteen varsity teams, with the top eight teams advancing to post-season play.

The number of lawsuits based on Title IX has been increasing since 1990, but change is slow to come. In 1994 the National Collegiate Athletic Association (NCAA) set up an equity task force and deemed women's hockey an "emerging sport." The NCAA claims that this new status gives the association a way of demonstrating the level of interest of players and schools. According to Donna Noonan, director of championships for the NCAA, if forty institutions sponsor women's hockey as a varsity sport for two years, then legislation can be drafted to establish an NCAA championship; once the legislation was in place, schools could obtain additional funding. This is not an unrealistic projection since, as of 1994–95, forty universities did have teams, sixteen of which had varsity status. However, the results so far have been negligible. It is Title IX that is really driving the surge in varsity women's hockey.

Colleges have always been an important training ground for national team players. In 1994 half the members of the national team sprang from the US university and college circuit. If it were not for the NCAA rule, allowing players only four years of college eligibility, the numbers would be even higher. As it is, after college female players have nowhere to play. The community leagues offer inferior competition, and as of 1995 only a dozen Senior A teams existed in the US. (In Canada the rules allow post-grad students to play on the varsity team, and a growing number of US national team members have moved to Canada to play hockey at a more competitive level.)

In the meantime USA Hockey, the supposed guardian and promoter of American women's hockey, continues to scramble forward in its attempt to catch up to Canada and Finland. The goal would appear to be well within reach, given the desire and talent of the players, but the competitive gap is quickly narrowing between North America and the rest of the world. Team USA runs a risk of falling far behind countries that are wholly committed to devoting time and money to the female game.

Although many European teams are progressing rapidly, the calibre of women's hockey in Europe and Asia remains generally below the North American standard, except in Finland, Sweden and (more recently) China and Russia. One difficulty is that most European countries have only a very small pool of female players (Finland's registration is the equivalent of that for the province of Alberta). In addition Scandinavian and some European players learned to skate in the mid-1980s playing a different game called "rink bandy," which is like field hockey on ice. As of the 1996 European championship, the top five teams are Sweden, Russia, Finland, Norway and

Switzerland. In a surprise turn of events Sweden took home the gold medal (its first). Russia, the new entry in Pool A, won silver and Finland with five players missing won the bronze medal. Norway and Switzerland ranked fourth and fifth. Coming last place, Germany is now relegated to the B Pool. These European champs, along with the winner of the biennial Asian Cup and the Canadian and US teams, will face off in the Olympic-qualifying world championship in Canada in 1997. The best five teams from that event will then go on to the Olympics.

The 1996 silver medal for Russia was shining proof of just how far this nation has come. While Russia is considered a hockey mecca, Russian women are relatively new to hockey, years behind most of their European neighbours. Moreover, women's hockey in Russia has some of the elements of a Cold-War spy novel: their star player has defected, political upheaval threatens their funding and infighting plagues the Russian Ice Hockey Federation (RIHF).

Russian women today play hockey in a very difficult climate compared to that enjoyed by men who competed in the glory days of the Red Army teams. The exodus of top male players to the NHL, dilapidated rinks, financial instability and political unrest have left hockey in Russia in chaos. Aside from the Central Army Penguins (a team owned by the Pittsburgh Penguins, which has a merchandising agreement with the Walt Disney Company), most hockey games are poorly attended. Many teams charge US$1.50 per game, and attract at most two or three thousand fans — sometimes as few as two hundred. With the average worker in Russia earning approximately US$300 annually, attending hockey games has become a luxury. In addition to all their other troubles players have had to contend with antiquated equipment. Indeed, in 1992 female teams were still coping with twenty-year-old hockey skates and shin guards made of rolled-up newspaper.

Given the financial and political obstacles in Russia, the future of women's hockey rests squarely on the shoulders of the national team. In the event of the Russian national team's qualifying for the world championship in 1997, the RIHF has promised more money: not only to train for the Olympics but also to develop women's hockey in the future, beyond the national team. The players and coaching staff have kept their part of the bargain, rising from obscurity to second place in Europe in the 1996 European championship. Given the team's recent success, it will be interesting to see whether the RIHF will keep its promise to channel funds into grassroots women's hockey after the Olympics.

Olympic status has had some concrete benefits for the Russian game already. Leonid Mikhno, president of the Troika sport club in St. Petersburg and vice-president of the northwest region of the RIHF, created the Women's Ice Hockey Association of Russia (WIHAR) in 1992. In June of that year, WIHAR held its first event, the White Nights tournament, in St. Petersburg, which was put together with the assistance of the New Jersey–based A&L Management, an event organizer for Russian hockey teams. Desperately needing better competition, Russia invited both Canada and the US to attend. Two US club teams arrived and handily defeated the inexperienced squad from Russia and the two entries from Latvia and the Ukraine.

Despite the defeat, the players' enthusiasm prompted the WIHAR to assemble more women's hockey teams. By the end of 1992 there were five teams competing in Russia, one in Siberia, two in Moscow (these were rink bandy teams who also played in hockey tournaments), one in St. Petersburg and one in the central city of Saratov (this team only lasted one year). In January 1993, once again with the help of A&L Management, the WIHAR hosted the Unified Open Tournament for all-star teams from Russia, Latvia, Ukraine, Germany and the

US. Five Latvian and five Ukrainian players from the tournament formed the basis for a new Unified Team, the precursor of the Russian national team.

Although the president of the RIHF acknowledged the women's hockey association, neither financial nor administrative support was forthcoming to the fledgling organization. In order to develop players for a national team the WIHAR desperately needed money to host tournaments and travel to competitions against the more experienced North American teams.

The Russian women's struggle to join the international hockey community despite financial hardship did not go unnoticed in North America. In a gesture of international goodwill, it was the women's hockey community that came to the rescue. In 1993 the Russell Women's Ice Hockey Association, located outside Ottawa, Ontario, agreed to host the first International Friendship tournament, an event designed to aid the Russian teams. The Ottawa group arranged transportation and accommodation for the Russian team (in association with A&L Management). Russia's new Unified Team spent three weeks in the US and Canada, facing off against Senior A and B teams. A&L Management sold Russian T-shirts and hockey jerseys at each game to help pay for the trip. In April 1994 the Boston Women's Ice Hockey Fund, a new not-for-profit organization dedicated to promoting women's hockey, raised US$7,000 to help pay for the Russian national team's second North American tour; they also equipped the team with fourteen pairs of skates.

By spring 1994 women's hockey at last had caught the attention of the Russian Federation. That year the new president of the RIHF decided to create a women's division in Moscow, with a committee to oversee women's hockey and promptly told the WIHAR it was simply no longer needed. The Russian Federation then turned its attention to the Olympics. It chose thirty of the best players from Russian teams and brought them to Moscow to live and train at a sports school. The team will stay together for three years and practise two to three hours a day, eleven months a year. Some are paid (unconfirmed reports suggest US$100 per month) and some are given lodging. In many cases these women, some of whom are girls as young as fifteen, have to travel huge distances, leaving behind their families and friends. Few Russian mothers can afford to visit their daughters in Moscow and many are unhappy that their daughters are involved in what is widely regarded as an unsuitable sport for women.

Life on the national team is difficult. The new coach Valentin Egorov (whose credentials include coaching a Russian Army team), screams at his players and sometimes holds three on-ice practices daily, each lasting two hours. If players don't play well, he docks their pay. The approach has had a demoralizing effect on team members. After watching several

*Russian national team, US exhibition tour,*
*Marlboro, Massschusetts, March 1995.*

games, one Canadian coach remarked, "There was no emotion on the [Russian] bench and no team spirit." [14] Despite the punitive approach, in 1995 the Russian national team won the B Pool in its first European championship, allowing Russia to move to the A Pool in 1996, where its second-place finish was a remarkable feat for a country that only four years earlier had only five women's teams.

Centre Ekaterina Pashkevitch, an MVP in two European and one world bandy championships, is the pulse of the national team. Towering over her teammates at 5 ft. 10 in. (178 cm) and 190 lbs. (86 kg), this twenty-one-year-old accounted for most of the national team's goals from 1994 to 1996. Pashkevitch took to the ice at age three, playing pond hockey with boys. By age seven, she was recruited by a boy's school coach and played in boys' hockey until she was a teenager. She also played professional rink bandy for eight years with her hometown Moscow club. There, in the early 1990s, she became one of the very few paid female athletes in Russia, earning US$50 a month. As a freshman at the prestigious sports institute in Moscow in 1993, Pashkevitch realized she needed stronger competition to improve her hockey skills. After travelling to North America with the national team, she moved to Boston, Massachusetts, in 1994 with the help of Julia Ashmun, director of the Women's Ice Hockey Fund. In August of 1995 she secured a job as head coach of the Massachusetts Institute of Technology club team. In 1996 she made the all-star team and was also voted top scorer in the European championship.

Although Russia beat Finland in the 1996 European championship, Finland is still considered by both Canada and the US as the most formidable team in Europe. The country has won four of the last five European championships and placed third in the 1990, 1992 and 1994 world championships. Finland is the best example of a country that has pumped up its national team program. In the fall of 1994 the

Finnish Ice Hockey Association (FIHA) finalized its Olympic plan: in order to surpass their North American rivals, the national team coaching staff now works with thirty-five to forty athletes, meeting six times a year to test physical and psychological fitness, practise dry-land training and work on team building. Interspersed with these training sessions were practice competitions against Russia, Sweden and the US to prepare the young Finnish squad (as of 1995 all players were under twenty-three years old) for the qualifying European championships in March 1996. Their commitment is paying off. After watching the Finns score four goals in seven minutes in their first game at the 1995 European championship, sweeping by every team in the A Pool, Val Belmonte, director of USA Hockey Coaching Program, heaped praise on the offensive dynamos. "Their tempo and intensity is very high," he raved. Belmonte rated the Finns number one, the team with the best chance of beating Canada. "They are training like world-class athletes. Now they are better than the US," reports Belmonte.[15]

Female hockey players laced up their hockey skates for the first time in 1970 in Southern Finland, the hockey heart of the country. By 1983 ten teams participated in its first national championship. Registration rose after the first world championship in 1990, increasing from about five hundred players to sixteen hundred in just four years. In 1994 FIHA established a league for girls aged fifteen and under. Although total registration has improved, by 1995–96 it still totalled less than two thousand. Female hockey teams continue to cope with poor access to both facilities and federation financing. Games are limited to fifteen-minute periods, except in the top senior league.

The Finnish women play swift, free-wheeling hockey. The lightning-fast centre Riikka Nieminen personifies the Finnish spirit. An all-round athlete Nieminen has won national championships in bandy, rink bandy, hockey and baseball. The US scouting report on this small but wiry speedster noted, "She has a very quick start, drives to the net and reads the ice very well. She's mean, with a competitive fire."[16] Having joined the national team in 1989 at the age of sixteen, Nieminen made the world championship all-star team in 1992 and 1994. (She missed the 1996 European championship due to knee surgery.) Since minor hockey did not exist for girls her hockey experience began at age seven with a boys' team.

But Nieminen's success has its disadvantages, the most annoying of which is a "fan from hell," who has followed her to two world championships, two European championships and all her local competitions since 1991. He writes letters, leaves phone messages and at one point even issued a jealous threat when he saw her with a male friend at a hockey gathering. In Lake Placid in 1994 he wore a Nieminen hockey shirt to all the Finnish games.

Another outstanding Finnish player Toronto fans may remember is number 17, Sari Krooks. Krooks played with the Senior AA Toronto Aeros from 1989 to 1992. She has been one of the top five scorers in Finnish hockey and a member of its national team since 1989. Krooks can literally skate circles around many players and is known for her intensive dry-land conditioning program. After giving birth to her first baby in 1993, she was back on the ice in just three weeks. Krooks now lives in Ottawa and plays hockey with a local Senior A team, the highest level for female players in the Ottawa area. In an attempt to maintain her skills, in 1995–96 Krooks commuted five hours to Toronto on the weekends to play once again for the Aeros. She suffered a broken leg late in 1995 and was unable to play for Finland in the 1996 European championship. She is expected to play for Finland in 1997.

The success of the Finnish national team is not surprising since hockey is Finland's national sport, followed by soccer and rink bandy. Men, however, still dominate the ice, with women

*Sari Krooks, one of Finland's national speedsters
at 1994 world championship.*

accounting for less than 5 percent of the 43,000 registered players. In 1995 each player on the men's national team was paid US$20,000 when it won the world championship. So far the women have received no reward. In the amateur world of women's hockey, that kind of bonus would enable many players to train full-time for the Olympics. It remains to be seen if Finland will express a similar financial commitment to female hockey.

Finland's southern neighbour, Sweden, launched its first official women's hockey league in 1981 in Stockholm. Two years later, the Swedish Ice Hockey Association (SIHA) established a separate ladies' committee but dissolved it within only two years, opting instead to lump women's hockey in with other male hockey committees. Federation support for the female game is notably absent among several key members of the SIHA. The chairman of the SIHA commented in 1993 that although women's hockey is in the Olympics, it is not a sport for women. Instead, he suggested that women should ride horses. Ironically, rather than discouraging women from playing, his sexist remarks generated outrage in the media giving a boost to the women's game. Despite anachronistic views such as these, financial incentives keep SIHA interested in the women's game. The Swedish government aims to reach a 40 percent participation level for women in all sports and it provides funds to sports associations that encourage female participation.

The number of female players in Sweden is rising, but the universal problem of access to ice time has not been solved. Women's games have been cut from three to two twenty-minute periods, to limit ice time. Short practices for the senior elite teams are held only two or three times a week. By 1994–95, only 1,152 players were registered, with thirty-two teams competing in the national championship. The SIHA has taken some steps towards remedying this, however: that same year it launched a hockey program for seven- to fourteen-year-old girls in Stockholm. (Girls aged six and under play with boys.) To encourage more girls to play, Sweden removed body-checking from the women's game in 1994, joining a growing number of countries which are adopting the IIHF rule.

Nacka is one of the most successful senior teams in Swedish hockey. They enjoyed an unprecedented winning streak between February 1982 and March 1987, losing only one game, and triumphed at the national championship for five consecutive years. The team also produced thirteen of the players on the 1987 world championship team. Despite this crop of talent the Swedish national team only managed to place fifth at the 1994 world championship. Disappointed with this showing, Sweden attended two extra tournaments against Russia, Finland and Norway in 1995 and 1996 and added training camps each year prior to the European championship in March. These efforts paid off: Sweden placed first in the 1996 European championship.

Norway is the third Scandinavian country with women's hockey but has not enjoyed the same success as its neighbours. This small country of four million people proclaims soccer as its top sport, and its twenty ice rinks in the country are primarily devoted to boys' and men's hockey. The first female teams were formed in 1987. The national championship followed two years later, but in 1994 registration seemed to have peaked at around four hundred players. In spite of these disadvantages Norway still managed to place fourth in the 1996 European championship.

The Norwegian women's game owes its advancement largely to the efforts of one man. Herman Foss, the former managing director of the Norwegian Ice Hockey Federation and member of the IIHF women's committee, has led a one-man campaign to promote the sport. In 1988 he launched the annual Nordic Cup tournament, inviting Denmark, Germany and Switzerland to participate. In 1993, frustrated by the lack of interest from both his colleagues and the public in women's hockey, Foss hired former US national team member Ellen Weinberg to spend three months assisting coaches of the

Norwegian national team and promoting the game. Weinberg visited communities, introducing national team players and holding clinics. The press picked up the story, because Weinberg was a foreigner and part of the highly rated US national team.

Switzerland, another small country, has had to contend with a very conservative and unsupportive attitude towards female hockey. "Hockey in Switzerland is prehistoric," complains the former assistant coach of the national team, Kim Urich. "There has been no change since 1990."[17] As a result, the sport has grown slowly: player registration as of 1994–95 totalled only 616, compared with 25,423 boys and men.

In most countries, individual members of the national women's hockey teams must "pay to play," and in spite of Switzerland's wealth, the Swiss team is no exception. Even in 1995 each player had to cover the cost of her own air fare to the European championship, the annual Christmas Cup tournament, and the five selection camps — expenses that added up to US$1,000. According to the soft-spoken national team manager and player Barbara Müller, some Swiss hockey fans have suggested that since "the men's national team get a lot of money and they don't place, let the men pay, maybe they will play better."[18]

The first Swiss women's team took to the ice in 1980, but it took four years for women's hockey to be recognized by the Swiss Ice Hockey Federation. In 1986 the first official national championship and Ochsner Cup (an international tournament hosted by Switzerland) welcomed Canada and Sweden. The top Swiss Senior A division is permitted to carry two foreign players. This provision both hinders and helps women's hockey in Switzerland. Foreign players are usually stronger and often play too large a role in national championship. In the opinion of some observers, they allow the Swiss players to be lazy. But according to Barbara Müller, foreign players can attract sponsors and if properly coached motivate players to work harder. Müller reports that the Canadian players are heroes to many girls in Switzerland. Foreign coaches, too, can play a critical role in improving teams. In 1995 France Montour, a member of Canada's 1992 national team, co-coached the Swiss national team to a bronze medal in the A Pool in the European championships — its best effort yet. Amid stiffer competition in 1996, Switzerland managed to salvage a fifth-place finish, the final team to qualify for the 1997 world championship.

In Germany, although women's hockey sprang into action in 1974, only eight teams competed in the first "ladies" national hockey championship, which was held a decade later. Introducing younger age categories has helped develop minor and junior hockey, and consequently the registration in 1994–95 jumped to over two thousand players, including more than five hundred who play on boys' teams. But hockey is still not considered acceptable for girls and women by most Germans, and as result, the game is growing only (approximately) 10 percent a year. The senior women's leagues, however, do play three twenty-minute periods per game — somewhat of a luxury, compared with most other countries.

The German national team has been in existence since 1988 but it has never been strong. In the 1994 world championship it fell to last place. Hoping to develop younger players for the Olympics, the German Ice Hockey Federation added forty more players to its national team selection camp and arranged an under-20 tournament, along with development camps in all provinces. Despite the effort, Germany placed last in the 1996 European championship, failing to qualify for the 1997 world championship, and thus losing its chance to go to the Olympics.

Eight countries compete in the B Pool of the European championship. The ranking for 1996 was as follows: Denmark,

Latvia, Czech Republic, Slovakia, France, Netherlands, Kazakhstan, and Great Britain (Austria and Italy have not so far joined the B Pool). Most of the B Pool nations have very few players; Latvia, for example, has only about forty participants. Many of these countries are relative newcomers to the women's game, most of them starting in the late 1980s or early 1990s.

Opportunities to compete are also meagre in Asia. In alternate years, China and Japan play off in the Asian Cup to qualify for the world championship. Since 1992 China has consistently overwhelmed Japan in the competition to attend these championships. Asian countries were finally awarded an international competition, apart from the world championship, with the launching in 1995 of the Pacific Rim tournament. Exact information on women's hockey in China is not widely available because access to interpreters is limited and these interpreters offer only basic details, some of which

*Members of the Chinese national team*
*at the 1994 world championship, Lake Placid.*

are more public relations than information. What is known, however, is that women's hockey in China plays a different role than it does in European countries. The Chinese see women's hockey (as they do most sports) as a means to improve their country's image internationally. Since the men's team languishes in the D Pool, China is counting on women's hockey to elevate its international profile. Consequently, the Chinese women's national team enjoys relatively strong state support. The rate of improvement is impressive given the small number of players (only about three hundred), the paucity of facilities and China's brief history with the game.

The heart of women's hockey in China is Harbin, a city of three million and the capital of the country's most northerly province, Heilongjiang. Here winter lasts for six months with temperatures as low as minus 38°C. Harbin is an industrial city, but it is also renowned as a winter sports resort because of its ice skating, ice yachting and hockey. Harbin is also home to the Chinese women's national team. Eight of the eleven women's teams practise in the area's three rinks (only nine ice rinks exist in the whole country). Hockey is played only here and in only two of China's thirty provinces. Competition, both nationally and internationally, is limited by the huge distances involved. Only six teams meet at the national championship, which began in 1987.

Like some European teams, the Chinese play with bodychecking. China has become increasingly dependent on its physical play, so much so that it has developed an international reputation for excessive slashing and holding. Nonetheless, this young national team seems wildly determined to succeed. A number of players possess good individual skills, and the team's passing and hockey sense improves markedly with every competition. Spectators are in for an uncommon experience watching these Chinese women with their scarlet uniforms, flying shoulder-length black hair, and constant yelling on the ice. Two players of note have been number 20, Hong Guo, the bold and aggressive goaltender, and number 3, Lui Hongmei, a forward who placed fifth among scoring leaders in the 1994 world championship.

In spite of the dearth of arenas and the limited opportunities to compete internationally, China's national team is surging ahead of some of the more experienced European teams. Its national team was only put together in November 1991, yet China roared into contention, easily defeating the Japanese in the Asian Cup tournament to qualify for the 1992 world championship. China placed fifth in 1992 and moved up to fourth place in the 1994 world championship. At the 1995 Pacific Rim championship, China even came close to beating Canada in a bruising semifinal game, finally bowing to the Canadians in a shootout by a score of 2–1. In the 1996 Pacific tournament, China was just as rough, leading the four team tournament in penalties. Colleen Coyne, a US player, suffered a broken arm as a result of a Chinese slash in the semifinal. Canada was barely able to escape with another victory, this time beating the Chinese 1–0. It was a wake-up call to the world: "China will be twice the threat in 1997," maintains Canada's national team coach, Shannon Miller.[19]

One of the main reasons the Chinese team has been so successful is the players' participation in sports schools. Elementary and secondary students who show promise are sent to one of the 2,400 physical culture and sports schools on a part- or full-time basis. Furthermore, the national team practise together two and a half hours each day, Monday to Friday. China is a country desperate for recognition in the world community, especially given its reputation for human rights violations: sports, therefore, play a critical role in its attempts to improve its tarnished international image.

Despite the national team's growing success, registration for women's hockey in China, in contrast to many European countries, has not increased since 1988. But opportunities for Chinese women to play are increasing nonetheless. In 1990 women's hockey was included in the National Winter Games, an event held every four years. Moreover, when women's hockey was added to the Asian Winter Games (also held every four years) in 1996 in Harbin, China handily defeated Kazakhstan 13–0 and Japan 9–3. The most intriguing development of all, however, is the new Winter Sports Commission started in 1994, an agency that plans to develop ice sports in heavily populated Southern China. The plans are no doubt due partly to China's success in both short-track speed skating and figure skating.

Canada is also playing a role in developing grassroots hockey in China. Since lack of ice rinks is a major obstacle to the development of hockey, the Pacific Entertainment Group Inc. (PEG) from Toronto, has launched a unique venture. The company's goal is to construct eight rinks in two cities in Southern China. PEG's contract also includes teaching ice skating and hockey, employing programs from the CHA and the Canadian Figure Skating Association.[20]

Jack Grover, president of PEG, envisions his company as the "Wal Mart of ice skating" in China, putting three to four hundred people on a rink at one time. Two rinks, one Olympic-sized, with 2,500 seats, and the other, a smaller one, will open in Shanghai in the fall of 1997. At the rinks, public skating will cost US$3, and include a helmet, skates and a lesson. Once the arena is built, skating will also become part of the school program. For US$1, school children will be able to take a lesson and rent a helmet and skates. Furthermore, PEG anticipates 50,000 school kids each year will hit the ice as part of an eight-week "learn to skate" course.

The demographics of this endeavour are staggering. More than 250,000 children attend school within walking distance of the rink. More than 15 million people live in Shanghai, and a total of 225 million people in four surrounding provinces. The opening ceremonies for the first rink will be televised and will feature hockey teams with ten-year-old boys and girls. These children will spend a month in Canada learning to play hockey. Approximately 240 million Chinese own television sets, so millions will likely be watching hockey in southern China for the first time. PEG projects that 100,000 to 200,000 people will be playing hockey within five years.[21] The rink will stay open year round (even through the blistering-hot summers), twenty-four hours a day, seven days a week, to accommodate those looking for a diversion and respite from the heat. As part of its promotion, PEG even taught the sixty-year-old Chinese ambassador to Canada, his fifty-seven-year-old wife and twenty embassy staff to skate.

China's Asian counterpart, Japan, has not benefitted from anywhere near as much state support to improve the women's game. According to Canadian Rick Polutnik, the assistant coach of the Japanese national team in 1995, "Japan is like Canada was fifteen years ago. There are four or five good players on a few teams but no strong league."[22] In fact no regular games take place; there is only one monthly tournament and the national championship. Some teams compete in as few as five games a season.

Women's hockey in Japan dates back to 1973, when six teams began competing: two in Tokyo, three in Hokkaido, and one in Honshu. In 1978 five teams organized the first national championship. Three years later, the Japan Ice Hockey Federation hosted the first official women's national championship. By 1995 sixteen teams were competing in the national championship and registration had swelled to sixty-six teams. In Japan's northernmost island, Hokkaido, hockey and speed skating are part of the physical education program in elementary school. By 1995 Hokkaido boasted nineteen teams and is now famous as the "mecca of skating events" in Japan. Of the almost fifteen hundred players in the country, Hokkaido accounts for a third. Thirteen of the twenty-one players on the 1995 national team sprang from the Peregrines, a Hokkaido-based team. Mr. Tsutomu Kawabushi, the team's manager is a former national team player and coach, and generously covered two-thirds of the female national team's expenses at the Pacific Rim championship in 1995.

As is the case for women's hockey around the world, the ages of players on the senior teams can range from thirteen to thirty owing to the lack of female minor hockey. Girls twelve and under are obliged to play with the boys. In the past inexperienced coaches held practices consisting of mainly skating, with little or no emphasis on passing or playmaking skills, but today this is no longer the case. Women play three twenty-minute stop-time periods, with two-hour practices twice a week. Most players are highly motivated and after every practice, as the culture dictates, they thank their coach and apologize for making bad passes or mistakes.

In order to be a serious contender at the 1998 Olympics, Japan is counting on assistance from Canada. In 1985 Japan sent its first female hockey team to play in Canada and two years later an all-star team came to Canada to play in the world tournament. Furthermore, Rick Polutnik, a former coach with the Canadian women's national team, has been advising the Japanese national team since 1993 and joined the team as assistant coach at the Pacific Rim tournament in 1995. Japan lost every game, but one week after the tournament both the confidence and the skills of the team had improved dramatically. Japan defeated Polutnik's Senior AAA team (ranked fourth in their league in Calgary, Alberta). "They were feeling sorry for themselves after San Jose," explains Polutnik. "I told them I didn't want to be embarrassed by having them lose to my team. They played like a Canadian team, handling the puck and winning in the corners."[23] Part of the reason for Japan's losses in world events is the size and age of the national team. The players are small and young with little upper body strength; many of them fear gaining weight for aesthetic reasons. They munch salads before a game while the other teams wolf down pasta and breads. Regardless of the obstacles facing the Japanese team, Japan's status as Olympic host country puts its women's team in a unique position. It appears it can only benefit from the overwhelming exposure to women's hockey in 1998.

The Olympics are the next benchmark in the women's game, but will these first Games be like the first world championship: much fanfare, then oblivion? Will only the national teams reap the benefits from the Olympics, with no money for grassroots development? And who will champion the women's game at the IIHF? No one can predict the results because the women's game is changing too quickly and lacks consistent leadership. The road to Nagano is the second stretch in the drive for international development of women's hockey. Hockey federations and sports bodies in many countries have already discovered the huge range of talented and ambitious women who love hockey. These female players deserve the chance to play with the same respect, attention and funding given to their brothers.

Finally, Samantha Holmes, the young girl who wrote to Canada's prime minister about the women's game, will get her wish to watch women's hockey in the Olympics. She is one of the new generation of young players who will be inspired to dream of finding their place at the future Olympic Games. These games will be etched in their psyches forever, and friends of women's hockey have every reason to hope that the Olympic teams will also become part of a groundswell of leadership needed to advance the current gains in women's hockey. But at the very least, for two weeks female players will be warmed by the Olympic flame, no longer outsiders in the chilly political climate of international hockey.

*Chapter Ten*

# FUTURE CONSIDERATIONS

*She races down the ice in the six-plex arena where her team trains several times a week. Just fifteen years old, she is the nemesis of every goalie in her girls' high school hockey league. This year, the precocious speedster will likely take home the MVP award in the national Midget championship before testing her skills at the selection camp for the Canadian women's junior team. Touted as the next Hayley Wickenheiser, this talented forward and her parents have already mapped out the options for her hockey career. After high school, she plans to accept a hockey scholarship at a prestigious American university. She may be seen on the sports network, as part of the weekly coverage of women's hockey. Soon she may join the well-established women's professional hockey league, which is run by a dynamic all-female marketing firm.*

WHILE THOSE WHO ARE passionate about women's hockey would like to see the above scenario as an important element of the game's future, it remains an idealist's view. Many complex obstacles hinder girls and women who simply want to play hockey. Ice time is still scarce for female players; harassment ranging from teasing to on-ice intimidation continues to drive girls from the game; media coverage, although improving in quality, falls far short of the copious amount devoted to male players; and while sponsorship money now trickles towards the female game, the flood of funds is still channelled towards men and boys.

The inclusion of women's hockey in the Olympics has provided the greatest impetus for the female game. However, in most countries the development of the game has been limited to the national teams; at the grassroots level, the sport has been largely ignored. China and Russia, the emerging forces in the game, have put most of their resources into producing competitive national teams. In Europe, the number of registered players is increasing in the countries with the most skilled women's teams but minor hockey and coaching programs are still virtually non-existent in these countries. And even though the profile of the women's game has improved, it is uncertain exactly what kind of recognition the players will receive at the Olympics. Many insiders expect that the women's hockey debut will be swept aside by the promotional whirlwind that will surround the men's "dream teams," which will feature National Hockey League players in the Olympics for the first time in 1998.

Nonetheless, it would be remiss not to recognize the gains that have been made in women's hockey. The 1990s have seen women's hockey catapult from oblivion into the limelight of Olympic acceptance. Even before the debut of women's hockey at the Olympics, the Games' effects will have reverberated throughout the world. From Latvia to China, athletes and coaches are flocking to the game, with an intensity and self-esteem never before experienced. Players are sweating through skills camps and penny-pinching to attend extra tournaments. In some cases, they drive for hours just to play an extra game — anything to hone their skills for the ultimate competition awaiting them in 1998.

# · FUTURE CONSIDERATIONS ·

Olympic acceptance has generated gains, particularly in Canada. Following the first official world championship in 1990, female hockey was at last included in the Canada Winter Games and many provincial counterparts, swinging open the doors of sporting opportunity to Canadian girls under the age of eighteen. Hockey schools for female players, many run by national team members, have also sprung up in almost every province. Soon women's hockey may be included as a Canadian Interuniversity Athletic Union sport. In the US recognition of this kind has proven to be a dynamic catalyst for the success of women's sports such as basketball.

The progress of the female game is in part due to a larger societal shift in attitude. The effects of changing views regarding women in sport are manifested in the actions of "hockey parents," particularly "hockey dads," who still dominate the volunteer hockey associations across the country. Fathers, who have long looked out for the sporting interests of their sons, are now playing an increasingly critical role in the hockey lives of their daughters.

In Eastern Canada, Quebec has sent a strong message to other provinces about the value of properly supporting elite female athletes with its successful and well-funded provincial all-star program. The province's new Chrysler Cup championship for girls under the age of sixteen and the addition of women's hockey to the Quebec Winter Games in 1996 will attract even more players to the game at the grassroots level. Women such as Danièle Sauvageau and Julie Healy, also members of the national team coaching pool, make up a key group of women who are committed to building on Quebec's formidable history and passion for hockey. In addition, the Quebec Ice Hockey Federation has shown foresight in establishing training programs for female coaches. It is one of the few provincial associations to welcome women's control of a primary element of the game.

Women's hockey in Ontario, driven by the relatively stalwart Ontario Women's Hockey Association, continues to reap the benefits of the tenacity and resolve the organization showed in the 1980s. It remains the most powerful presence in Canadian women's hockey, both in terms of its number of players and its historical contribution to the game. But the OWHA's house must now be put in order. As interest in the game continues to swell, strong management and a vocal stance on equity and sponsorship are imperative. It is time for the organization to shed its hesitancy and reclaim the vision that so distinguished it in the past. The 1997 world championship, which will be held in Kitchener, Ontario, provides the perfect opportunity for the OWHA to aggressively market the sport.

While Ontario's direction remains uncertain, Alberta is rising in prominence. National team coach Melody Davidson is just one of a growing number of women who have lent a backbone of longevity and commitment to the female game. Many of the women assuming coaching and leadership positions have been part of the Edmonton Chimos dynasty, a pioneering team in the West. But it is the new women's high-performance hockey program, established in the Calgary Olympic Oval and run by national team coach Shannon Miller, that sets Alberta apart from its prairie neighbours and the rest of the country. The elite training program not only attempts to redress the lack of serious training opportunities for the best players both in Canada and internationally, but it also represents an investment in the future of the game. It is an investment that even the Canadian Hockey Association has lacked the mettle to make. Players from as far away as Australia come here to train full-time with national-calibre coaches and to take advantage of the state-of-the-art-sport facilities. Prior to the Olympics national team athletes, including Manon Rhéaume, will likely flock to Calgary to participate in this program in order to prepare themselves for the pre-Games selection camp.

Rhéaume's interest in training with Miller is just one sign that the game now holds more promise for women than ever before. While Rhéaume is still largely immersed in men's hockey, her interests are gradually shifting towards the female game. When Rhéaume was asked to participate in a men's roller-hockey beach tournament in California in the fall of 1995, she went a step further. She pulled together a women's team of elite ice hockey players from Canada and the US and insisted they take part. Plans for 1996 include a four-team women's beach roller-hockey league.

Those who have been watching Rhéaume's increasing interest in the female game say it is likely she will play an important role in women's ice hockey after the Olympics. At a Team Canada selection camp in the fall of 1995, Rhéaume said, "I have a lot of plans to help women's hockey. Perhaps a professional women's team. You could start with, say, five teams. But to put something together you need the right people and money there."[1] If Rhéaume decides to use her financial resources and her connections with the media to pull together a savvy marketing team to promote the female game, it may be only a matter of a few years before a professional league exists for women.

In the meantime, organizations outside the traditional hockey domain also continue to push for more equity for women in the game. In Canada, provincial sports equity groups are lobbying for a fairer allocation of government funds for ice time. In addition, they are trying to change policies regarding ice-time allocation. These groups also provide role models in a sports landscape that is devoid of female faces. In the US, the Women's Ice Hockey Fund of Boston, Massachusetts, is a recent example of a group that is committed to advancing women's hockey internationally. This organization raised money to assist a fledgling and poorly funded Russian team to come to North America.

Also outside the mainstream hockey channels is a World Wide Web site that allows Internet users to access information about women's hockey. Andria Hunter created this site in October 1994. Hunter is a Master's student in computer science at the University of Toronto and a former national team player. The site's home page features women's hockey listings for general, university and international hockey, a player profile page, and tips about shooting and skating.[2] In 1995, approximately *20,000* people accessed this home page. It is proving to be both a vital source of information for newcomers to hockey and a forum through which women can network for better access to the game.

While all of these elements combine to drive women's hockey forward, the pulse of the game beats in the players. It is the players who deserve most of the credit for the survival and growth of women's hockey, especially those players who raced down the ice in obscurity before the 1990 world championship. Although their stories are vastly different, one common theme runs throughout their lives. The success of these players stems not only from their commitment but also from someone else — a mother, father, coach or friend — taking their athletic ability seriously and encouraging them to persevere despite all adversities.

New Brunswick's Stacy Wilson has overcome the isolation of the Atlantic region to become a vital part of the national team. Although Wilson has been denied the calibre of competition her colleagues in other regions enjoy, she has immersed herself wholly in the small hockey community in her province. Taking sustenance from a family and a community that have celebrated her accomplishments as their own, Wilson has returned that devotion to both teammates and the young players whom she coaches, and who hold her in such high regard.

France St. Louis, steeped in a culture of hockey mania, is now a provincial sports hero for thousands of young players in

Quebec. St. Louis is the oldest player on Team Canada and has demonstrated just how long a player can stay in her prime if she is willing to focus her life on the game. The words she often speaks to her high school teams reverberate throughout her entire approach to her training: "Play like you practise. If you don't do anything during practice, you won't accomplish anything during the games."[3] It is words like these and St. Louis' contagious vitality that spark the drive in players around her. As former teammate Therese Brisson put it, "France makes you want to buy into it."[4]

Angela James has also lent her own verve to the female game. The brazen kid from Ontario Housing has become not only a highly respected national team athlete but an example of what can happen when a handful of key people — in James's case, her mother and several coaches — value raw athletic talent in a young girl. James is a success story in the best sense: without losing the defiant spark that has been so essential to her moves on ice, she has matured into a leader in the game and her community, nurturing the ability of girls like herself whose talents and dreams might otherwise go ignored.

Cathy Phillips, too, continues to foster a game she can no longer even play. Following her dramatic performance at the 1990 world championship, Phillips had to undergo surgery to have a brain tumour removed. Since then she has refused to give up coaching and evaluating players, all the while struggling with poor balance, blurred vision and short-term memory loss. Despite her handicaps, of all the players who took part in the 1990 world championship, it is Phillips who can recall moves from the final game of that championship with startling exactness. Not only does she remember who assisted on what goal, she recollects on what side of the net the puck went in.

National team coach Shannon Miller has also devoted significant years of her life to increasing the opportunities and improving the level of training for both younger and more

experienced players. A jam-packed schedule of coaching, men-
toring, study and travel seems only to feed her ambition.
Perched in the stands of arenas across the country, Miller has become a powerful symbol of female leadership. With her devotion to the game and the women who play it, Miller is passing
on the invaluable lesson she learned from her father, who, as she
put it, "made me feel like there wasn't anything I couldn't do." [5]

Hayley Wickenheiser is just one of the girls and women
who has benefitted from Miller's dedication. The tiny eleven-
year-old who watched the 1990 world championship with
such awe has matured into a potent, self-possessed player —
and one of the highest ranked ones — in Canada. Wickenheiser, like many of her older teammates, has come into her
own by making sacrifices and by rising above the injustices
that have kept opportunities away from her. But unlike her
older teammates, Wickenheiser is now reaping the rewards of
the hard-won advances of the women before her. While her
athletic options are in no way as numerous as they would be
for a boy with the same extraordinary talent, they are more
promising than ever before. Whether or not those options
continue to grow will depend largely upon Wickenheiser and
her generation of players and coaches. For they are the ones
who will carry the game into the next millennium. They are
the women who may at last have the opportunity to shape —
and make — their own hockey history.

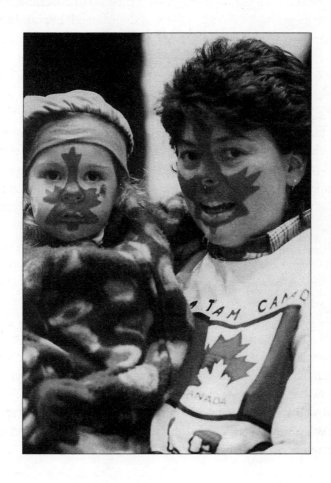

# NOTES

## CHAPTER 1

1. Cathy Phillips, speech at Hockey Hall of Fame, Toronto, August 1994.
2. Cathy Phillips, interview with Megan Williams, 6 February 1996.
3. Cathy Phillips, interview with Elizabeth Etue, 4 October 1994.
4. Cathy Phillips, interview with Megan Williams, 6 February 1996.
5. Angela James, interview with Megan Williams, 19 July 1995.
6. Rick Polutnik, interview with Megan Williams, 17 July 1995.
7. Sue Scherer, interview with Megan Williams, 8 August 1995.
8. Hayley Wickenheiser, interview with Megan Williams, 15 May 1995.
9. Ibid.
10. Mary Ormsby, "Canada Savors Golden Moment," *Toronto Star,* 26 March 1990.
11. *Winnipeg Sun,* "Golden Canucks" by *Canadian Press,* 26 March 1990.
12. James Davidson, "Limelight Dazes Delighted Players at Women's Event," *Globe and Mail,* 24 March 1990.

## CHAPTER 2

1. Alan Adams, interview with Elizabeth Etue, 19 October 1995.
2. Richard Gruneau and David Whitson, *Hockey Night in Canada: Sport, Identities and Cultural Politics* (Toronto: Garamond Press, 1993), 98.
3. Ibid., 104.
4. Ibid., 259.
5. Julie Stevens, "Development of Women's Hockey: An Explanation of Structure and Change within the Canadian Hockey System" (Master's thesis, Queens' University, 1992), 12.
6. Ibid., 60.
7. Angus Reid National Poll, 1993.
8. Bruce Kidd, *The Struggle for Canadian Sport* (Toronto: University of Toronto Press, 1996), 103.
9. Julie Stevens, "Development of Women's Hockey," 12.
10. Brian McFarlane, *Proud Past, Bright Future: One Hundred Years of Canadian Women's Hockey* (Toronto: Stoddart, 1994), 62, 56.
11. Helen Lenskyj, *Out of Bounds: Women, Sport and Sexuality* (Toronto: The Women's Press, 1986), 71.

# · NOTES ·

12. Ibid., 83.

13. Mary Keyes, et al., *A Concise History of Sport in Canada* (Toronto: Oxford University Press, 1989), 234.

14. Julie Stevens, "Development of Women's Hockey," 6.

15. Agnes Jacks, "Mr. and Mrs. Sam Jacks," *The Ringette Review*, January 1994, 4.

16. Aniko Varpalotai, "Girls' Sports and Role Models: Implications for Educators," *CAPHER Journal* (Winter 1991): 28.

17. Ringette Canada, letter to Elizabeth Etue, 17 March 1995.

18. Helen Lenskyj, interview with Elizabeth Etue and Megan Williams, January 1993.

19. Elizabeth A. Garfield, "The Wilson Report: Moms, Dads, Daughters and Sports" (survey conducted for the Women's Sports Foundation by Diagnostic Research, Los Angeles, in 1988).

20. Ringette Canada, letter to Elizabeth Etue, 17 March 1995.

21. John MacKinnon, "Diduck Stars in Juggling Act," *Ottawa Citizen*, 18 March 1990.

22. Gruneau and Whitson, *Hockey Night in Canada*, 191.

23. Ibid., 195.

24. Lois Kalchman, *Toronto Star*, 29 May 1982.

25. Glynis Peters, interview with Megan Williams and Elizabeth Etue, 8 January 1993.

26. Canadian Hockey Association, Special Insert, *Coach Level Participant's Manual, A.1.0 Female Hockey*, 1995.

27. Alan Adams, interview with Elizabeth Etue, 19 October 1995.

28. Glynis Peters, interview with Megan Williams and Elizabeth Etue, 8 January 1993.

29. Julie Stevens, "Development of Women's Hockey," 115.

30. Frank Libera, interview with Elizabeth Etue, April 1994.

31. Janet Brooks, "Powerful in Pink," *Champion* magazine, July 1990, 46. Costello is cited in Brooks's article.

32. Jennifer Brenning, interview with Elizabeth Etue, 23 November 1995.

33. Jennifer Brenning, interview with Elizabeth Etue, 13 March 1996.

34. Phil Legault, interview with Elizabeth Etue, 9 February 1995.

35. Glynis Peters, interview with Elizabeth Etue, 11 April 1995.

36. Larry Skinner, interview with Elizabeth Etue, 14 April 1994.

37. Glynis Peters, interview with Megan Williams and Elizabeth Etue, 8 January 1993.

## CHAPTER 3

1. Brian McFarlane, *Proud Past, Bright Future: One Hundred Years of Canadian Women's Hockey* (Toronto: Stoddart, 1994), 17.

2. Julie Stevens, "Development of Women's Hockey in Canada: An Explanation of Structure and Change within the Canadian Hockey System" (Master's thesis, Queens' University, 1992), 5.

3. Bruce Kidd, *The Struggle for Canadian Sport* (Toronto: University of Toronto Press, 1996), 102.

4. Ibid., 103.

5. Helen Gurney, *A Century to Remember: The Story of Women's Sports* (Toronto: University of Toronto Women's T-Holders' Association, 1994), 11.

6. Brian McFarlane, *Proud Past, Bright Future*, 58.

7. Julie Stevens, "Female Hockey and the Educational System: A Precious Partnership," OFSAA Bulletin, March 1993, 15.

8. Helen Gurney, *A Century to Remember*, 82.

9. Fran Rider, interview with Elizabeth Etue, 17 July 1992.

10. *Ontario Women's Hockey Association News*, April-May 1981, 12.

11. Julie Stevens, "Development of Women's Hockey in Canada," 64.

12. Bev Mallory, interview with Elizabeth Etue, 16 November 1994.

13. Fran Rider, interview with Elizabeth Etue, 17 July 1992.

14. John MacKinnon, "Gerry's Goal Was Classic," *Ottawa Citizen*, 25 April 1992.

15. Sheila Forshaw, interview with Elizabeth Etue, 28 July 1995.

16. Julie Stevens, "Development of Women's Hockey in Canada," 75.

17. Julie Stevens, "Female Hockey and the Educational System,"16.

18. Bruce Tennant, Tournament Coordinator, Canadian Tire Girls' High School Hockey Classic, interview with Elizabeth Etue, 2 August 1995.

19. Helen Lenskyj, interview with Megan Williams, 11 May 1993.

20. Lorrie Mickelson, interview with Elizabeth Etue, 8 August 1995.

21. Fran Rider, interview with Elizabeth Etue, 22 March 1992.

22. Fran Rider, interview with Elizabeth Etue, 10 April 1992.

23. Fran Rider, interview with Elizabeth Etue, 18 March 1996.

24. Ken Dufton, interview with Elizabeth Etue, 19 January 1992.

25. Ibid.

26. Cathy Lehman, interview with Elizabeth Etue, 3 August 1995.

27. Kathleen Bevan, interview with Elizabeth Etue, 20 August 1995.

28. Georgina Raynor, interview with Elizabeth Etue, 24 July 1995.

29. Fran Rider, interview with Elizabeth Etue, 22 March 1996.

30. Julie Stevens, "Development of Women's Hockey in Canada," 72.

31. Joan McCagg, interview with Elizabeth Etue, 21 August 1995.

## CHAPTER 4

1. Shirley Cameron, interview with Megan Williams, 18 March 1995.
2. Cindy Simon, interview with Megan Williams, 12 October 1995.
3. Shirley Cameron, interview with Megan Williams, 18 March 1995.
4. Ibid.
5. Brenda Zeman, *Eighty-eight Years of Puck-Chasing in Saskatchewan* (Regina: The Saskatchewan Sports Hall of Fame, 1983).
6. Cindy Simon, interview with Megan Williams, 12 October 1995.
7. Sandy Rice, interview with Megan Williams, 14 October 1995.
8. Lila Quinton, interview with Megan Williams, 5 October 1995.
9. Sandy Johnson, interview with Megan Williams, 21 June 1995.
10. Shirley Cameron, interview with Megan Williams, 18 March 1995.
11. Hayley Wickenheiser, interview with Megan Williams, 15 May 1995.
12. Shannon Miller, interview with Megan Williams, 11 February 1996.
13. Heather Ginzel, interview with Megan Williams, 17 July 1995.
14. Shannon Miller, interview with Megan Williams, 11 February 1996.
15. Ibid.
16. Shannon Miller, interview with Megan Williams, 16 May 1995.
17. Hayley Wickenheiser, interview with Megan Williams, 15 May 1995.
18. Shannon Miller, interview with Megan Williams, 11 February 1996.
19. Ibid.
20. Shannon Miller, interview with Megan Williams, 16 May 1995.
21. Tom Wickenheiser, interview with Megan Williams, 19 March 1995.
22. Ibid.
23. Ibid.
24. Hayley Wickenheiser, journal entry, 8 September 1994.
25. Shannon Miller, interview with Megan Williams, 11 February 1996.
26. Melody Davidson, interview with Megan Williams, 22 February 1996.
27. Lila Quinton, interview with Megan Williams, 5 October 1996.
28. Sandy Johnson, interview with Megan Williams, 15 October 1995.
29. Cathy Allen, interview with Megan Williams, 5 March 1996.
30. Bev Drobot, interview with Megan Williams, 4 March 1996.
31. Jim Leary, interview with Megan Williams, 4 March 1996.
32. Laura Robinson, "Women's Hockey Night in Rankin Inlet," *Toronto Star*, 11 March 1991.
33. Karen Wallace, interview with Megan Williams, 8 October 1995.
34. Bill Ennos, interview with Megan Williams, 6 March 1996.
35. Karen Wallace, interview with Megan Williams, 8 October 1995.

36. Johnny Misley, interview with Megan Williams, 5 March 1996.
37. Ibid.

**CHAPTER 5**

1. France St. Louis, interview with Megan Williams, 3 December 1995.
2. Therese Brisson, interview with Megan Williams, 15 January 1996.
3. Ibid.
4. France St. Louis, interview with Megan Williams, 3 December 1995.
5. Shannon Miller, interview with Megan Williams, 16 May 1995.
6. Shannon Miller, interview with Megan Williams, 11 February 1996.
7. Lucie Valois, letter to Megan Williams, 6 March 1996.
8. France Lajoie, interview with Megan Williams, 19 October 1995.
9. Ibid.
10. Recounted by Michelle Belanger in an interview with Megan Williams, November 1995.
11. Stacy Wilson, journal entry from March 1994.
12. Kay McQuaid, interview with Megan Williams, 9 April 1996.
13. Kay McQuaid, interview with Megan Williams, 14 November 1995.
14. Kay McQuaid, letter to Megan Williams, 27 November 1995.
15. Susan Dalziel, interview with Megan Williams, 4 November 1995.
16. Lynn Hacket, interview with Megan Williams, 9 November 1995.
17. Brenda Ryan, interview with Megan Williams, 7 November 1995.
18. Gary Smiley, interview with Megan Williams, 3 November 1995.
19. Ibid.

**CHAPTER 6**

1. Ann Hall et al., *Sport in Canadian Society* (Toronto: McClelland and Stewart, 1991), 201.
2. B. D. McPherson and L. Davidson, *Minor Hockey in Ontario* (Toronto: Ministry of Culture and Recreation, 1980).
3. Nancy Theberge, interview with Megan Williams, 15 June 1995.
4. McPherson and Davidson, *Minor Hockey in Ontario*.
5. Canadian Hockey Association registration statistics for the 1994–95 season: 19,050. The CHA estimated registration would total well over 20,000 for the 1995–96 season.
6. Ontario Women's Hockey Association registration statistics for the 1995–96 season, 17 January 1996. (Figure given to Megan Williams by president Fran Rider.)
7. Justine Blainey, interview with Megan Williams, 10 April 1993.
8. Gwen Brodsky, "Justine Blainey and the Ontario Hockey Association: An Overview," CAAWS Newsletter, 1987, 17.

9. Sport Canada contributions from 1987–88 to 1994–95.

10. Canadian Hockey Association, Special Insert, *Coach Level Participant's Manual, A.1.0 Female Hockey*, 1995, 3.

11. Don Morrow and Mary Keyes, *A Concise History of Sport in Canada* (Toronto: Oxford University Press, 1989), 233.

12. Nancy Theberge, interview with Megan Williams, 15 June 1995.

13. Ellie Kirzner, "Powerplay," *Now* Magazine, 24-30 December 1992.

14. Helen Lenskyj, "Women, Sport and Physical Activity: Selected Research Themes." Canada Heritage, Sport Canada, 1994.

15. Helen Lenskyj, interview with Megan Williams, 10 May 1993.

16. Fran Rider, interview with Megan Williams, 1 June 1995.

17. Fran Rider, interview with Megan Williams, 5 April 1995.

18. Phyllis Berck addressing a meeting of female sports organizers at the St. Lawrence Community Hall in Toronto, 30 May 1995.

19. Pam McConnell, Toronto City Hall Neighbourhood's Committee Meeting, 5 April, 1995.

20. Pam McConnell, interview with Megan Williams, 26 September 1995.

21. John R. Gardner, *Toronto Star*, 14 September 1995.

22. Ibid.

23. John R. Gardner, interview with Megan Williams, 26 October 1995.

24. Ibid.

25. Fran Rider, interview with Megan Williams, 20 January 1996.

26. Paige Brodie, interview with Megan Williams, 31 January 1996.

27. Chris Cardy, interview with Megan Williams, 2 June 1995.

28. Ibid.

29. Roger Czerneda, interview with Megan Williams, 5 June 1995.

30. Cliff Turner, director of Parks and Recreation for the City of Orillia, in a letter to Julie and Roger Czerneda, 20 March 1995.

31. Roger Czerneda, interview with Megan Williams, 5 June 1995.

32. Sandy Johnson, interview with Megan Williams, 21 June 1995.

33. Fran Rider, interview with Megan Williams, 20 January 1996.

34. Janis Lawrence-Harper, "The Herstory of the CAAWS," (CAAWS, November 1991), 15.

35. Marion Lay, interview with Megan Williams and Elizabeth Etue, 29 March 1995.

36. Ibid.

37. Sue Scherer, interview with Megan Williams, 24 May 1995.

38. Dale Kryzanowski, interview with Megan Williams, 23 June 1995.

39. Pat Jackson, interview with Megan Williams, 16 June 1995.

40. "The Final Report on Enrolment 1992/1993" (Office of Statistics, Records and Convocation, University of Toronto, 1993).

41. Hilary Korn, interview with Megan Williams, 12 June 1995.

42. Karen Hughes, interview with Megan Williams, 1 June 1995.

43. Paul Carson, interview with Megan Williams, 25 May 1995.

44. Julie Healy, interview with Megan Williams, 15 November 1995.

45. Kathryn M. Reid, "Playing Fair: A Guide to Title IX in High School and College Sports," 2nd ed. (Women's Sport Foundation, 1994), 4.

46. R. Acosta and L. Carpenter, "As the Years Go By: Coaching Opportunities in the 1990s," *JOPERD*, 63, no. 3 (1992): 36–41.

47. Ann Hall et al., "The Gender Structure of National Sports Organizations," Sport Canada Occasional Paper 2:1, 1990.

48. Sue Inglis, "Board-Staff Relations in Amateur Sport" (Report prepared for the Ministry of Culture, Tourism and Recreation, Province of Ontario, December 1994), 24.

49. Penny Werthner, interview with Megan Williams, 27 June 1995.

50. Ibid.

51. Marilyn Wickenheiser, interview with Megan Williams, 19 March 1995.

52. Shirley Cameron, interview with Megan Williams, 13 May 1995.

53. Ibid.

54. Helen Lenskyj, *Out of Bounds: Women, Sport and Sexuality* (Toronto: Women's Press, 1986), 57.

55. Peter Gzowski, *The Game of Our Lives*, (Toronto: McClelland and Stewart, 1981), 191.

**CHAPTER 7**

1. Antonia Zerbisias, "Manon! Manon! Manon!" *Toronto Star*, 1 December, 1991.

2. Bruce Kidd, *The Struggle for Canadian Sport* (Toronto: University of Toronto Press, 1996), 218–19.

3. Ibid., 257.

4. Ibid., 223.

5. Ibid., 260.

6. Lou Clancy in "Fighting for the CAAWS," Don Sellar, *Toronto Star*, 31 January 1995.

7. David Perkins, interview with Megan Williams, 25 March 1996.

8. Sheila Robertson, interview with Megan Williams, 15 April 1996.

9. Mary Ormsby, "Survey Ignores Realities of Sports — and News," *Toronto Star*, 22 January 1995.

10. Ibid.

11. Wendy Long, interview with Megan Williams, 11 July 1995.

12. Alison Griffiths, *Undercurrents*, CBC-TV, 9 January 1996.

13. "Finding New Sports Readers," Truth & Rumours, *Globe and Mail*, 15 December 1995.

14. David Langford, *On Your Mark*, Episode 13, Women's Television Network, Spring 1995.

15. David Perkins, interview with Megan Williams, 25 March 1996.

16. Jane O'Hara, interview with Megan Williams, 22 March 1996.

17. Ormsby, "Survey Ignores ...."

18. Ibid.

19. *Hockey Night in Canada* statistics, Truth & Rumours, *Globe and Mail*, 3 February 1996.

20. Ormsby, "Survey Ignores ...."

21. David Perkins, interview with Megan Williams, 25 March 1996.

22. Jane O'Hara, interview with Megan Williams, 22 March 1996.

23. "Lack of Media Attention Angers Female Athletes," *Action*, CAAWS Newsletter, Summer 1995.

24. Wayne Moriarty, CAAWS news release, 8 February 1994.

25. Steve Dryden, interview with Megan Williams, 15 July 1995.

26. Ibid.

27. Bruce Kidd, *The Struggle for Canadian Sport*, 97.

28. Jane O'Hara, interview with Megan Williams, 22 March 1996.

29. Mary Ormsby, interview with Megan Williams, 22 March 1996.

30. Mary Ormsby, interview with Megan Williams and Elizabeth Etue, *By All Means*, CIUT Radio, Toronto, 8 January 1993.

31. Mary Ormsby, interview with Megan Williams, 22 March 1996.

32. Marg McGregor, *On Your Mark*, Episode 13, Women's Television Network, Spring 1995.

33. Wendy Long, fax to Megan Williams, 6 May 1996.

34. Ibid.

35. Diana Davis Duerkop, "Only Ourselves to Blame," *Action* (Spring 1995), 4.

36. Mary Jollimore, "Gender Equity in Canadian Hockey May Be Impractical," *Globe and Mail*, 25 February 1996.

37. Steve Dryden, interview with Megan Williams, 15 July 1995.

38. David Perkins, interview with Megan Williams, 25 March 1996.

39. Bruce Kidd, "Missing: Women from Sports Hall of Fame," *Action*, Fall 1994.

40. *Gender Portrayal in English Television Coverage of the Games*, Research conducted for Sport Canada, 1994, Canadian Heritage, Sport Canada.

41. Margaret MacNeill, "Networks: Producing Olympic Ice Hockey for a National Television Audience," *Sociology of Sport Journal* (forthcoming issue).

42. Ibid.

43. Statistics Canada, "Television Viewing," 1993.

44. Norm Carrotte, interview with Megan Williams, 16 April 1996.

45. Research & Forecasts, "Miller Lite Report on American Attitudes toward Sports" (Milwaukee: Miller Brewing Company, 1983), 19.

46. Rick Brace, interview with Megan Williams, 21 March 1996.

47. Ibid.

48. Glynis Peters, letter to Rick Brace, May 1992.

49. Rick Brace, interview with Megan Williams, 21 March 1996.

50. Rhonda Taylor, interview with Megan Williams, 26 March 1996.

51. Ron Robison, interview with Megan Williams, 14 July 1995.

52. Ibid.

53. John Dunlop, interview with Megan Williams, 21 March 1996.

54. Norm Carrotte, interview with Megan Williams, 16 April 1996.

55. Doug Philpott, interview with Megan Williams, 20 March 1996.

56. Ibid.

57. Sylvia Klasovec, "The Sexual Politics of Women in Sport: A Survey on 'Lesbophobia,'" *Canadian Women's Studies Journal* 15, no. 4: 63–66.

58. Susan K. Cahn, "Crushes, Competition, and Closets: The Emergence of Homophobia in Women's Physical Education," in *Women, Sport and Culture*, eds. Susan Birrell and Sheryl Cole (Windsor: Human Kinetics, 1994).

59. Helen Lenskyj, interview with Megan Williams, 11 May 1993.

60. Mary Ormsby, "Fired National Volleyball Coach Fighting Back," *Toronto Star*, 22 August 1992.

61. Shirley Cameron, interview with Megan Williams, 17 March 1995.

62. Heather Ginzel, interview with Megan Willams, 17 June 1995.

63. Susanna Levin, "Who Gets Big Money from Sponsors and Why," *Women's Sports and Fitness,* April 1992, 62.

64. By 1996, according to Corel WTA Tour, the governing body of women's professional tennis, Navratilova had won fifty-six Grand Slam titles, Steffi Graf had won nineteen, Monica Seles had won nine and Jennifer Capriati had not won any and Gabriela Sabatini had won once. Doug Clery, interview with Megan Williams, 30 April 1996. The players' agents would not release information on sponsorship of the players.

65. Mariah Burton Nelson, *The Stronger Women Get, the More Men Love Football* (New York: Harcourt Brace and Co. 1994), 219.

66. Lynn Hacket, interview with Megan Williams, 9 November 1995.

67. Melody Davidson, interview with Megan Williams, 22 February 1996.

68. Brian Pronger, *The Arena of Masculinity: Sports, Homosexuality, and the Meaning of Sex* (Toronto: University of Toronto Press, 1990), 2.

69. Marg McGregor, *On Your Mark*, Episode 13, Women's Television Network, Spring 1995.

70. Glynis Peters, fax to Elizabeth Etue, April 1996.

71. Gary Shelton, "Women's Ice Hockey Play in a League of Their Own," *St. Petersburg Times*, 1 August 1991.

72. Glynis Peters, interview with Megan Williams and Elizabeth Etue, 8 January 1993.

73. Sue Scherer, interview with Megan Williams, 24 February 1992.

74. Mary Ormsby, "Hockey Needs Rhéaume at Top" *Toronto Star*, 4 April 1992.

75. Mary Ormsby, "Rhéaume Little More Than a Puck Pawn," *Toronto Star*, April 4, 1993.

76. Rosie DiManno, "All Dressed Up and Nowhere to Goalie," *Toronto Star*, 19 September 1992.

77. Tony Davis, "The Puck Stops Here," *Winnipeg Free Press*, 15 May 1994.

78. Manon Rhéaume with Chantal Gilbert, *Manon: Alone In Front of the Net* (Toronto: HarperCollins, 1993), 106.

79. Brian Preston, "Shots on Goal," *Saturday Night*, February 1995.

80. Michael Farber, "Rhéaume's Message Is Unsettling — Success Is Measured on Male Terms," *Vancouver Sun*, 25 September 1992.

81. Mary Jollimore, "All Rhéaume Wanted Was a Chance to Play," *Globe and Mail*, 28 September 1992.

82. Rhéaume, *Manon: Alone In Front of the Net*, 50.

83. Ibid., 54.

84. Nancy Theberge, "Playing with the Boys: Manon Rhéaume, Women's Hockey and the Struggle for Legitimacy," *Canadian Women Studies Journal*, 15, no. 4 (Fall 1995): 40.

85. Liz Shea, "Should Women Play Hockey; Yes," *Newsday*, 6 February 1994.

86. Angela James, interview with Megan Williams, 19 July 1995.

87. Cathy Phillips, interview with Megan Williams, 21 July 1995.

88. Shirley Cameron, interview with Megan Williams, 17 March 1995.

## CHAPTER 8

1. Andreas Lauer, treasurer of the German Hockey Federation, letter to Fran Rider, 13 April 1987.

2. Angela James, interview with Elizabeth Etue, 13 June 1994.

3. Angela James, interview with Elizabeth Etue, 15 May 1995.

4. Donna Barato, interview with Elizabeth Etue, 24 March 1995.

5. Angela James, interview with Elizabeth Etue, 13 June 1994.

6. Barbara Stewart, *She Shoots, She Scores* (Toronto: Doubleday, 1993), 67.

7. Alison Gordon, "Superstar Athlete Has No Future: Best Woman Hockey Player Is Stymied By Her Sex," *Toronto Star*, 13 January 1985.

8. Lois Kalchman, *Toronto Star*, 27 April 1987.

9. Glynis Peters, interview with Elizabeth Etue and Megan Williams, 4 January 1993.

10. Lois Kalchman, interview with Elizabeth Etue and Megan Williams, 17 March 1992.

11. James Davidson, "Women's Hockey Intent on Escaping Obscurity," *Globe and Mail*, 26 March 1990.

12. Bruce Garrioch, "Team Canada," *Ottawa Sun*, March 1990.

13. Lois Kalchman, "Pink, White and Blue for Women's Hockey Outfits," *Toronto Star*, 16 March 1990.

14. Earl McRae, "Team Canada: Stereotype or High Fashion?" *Ottawa Citizen*, 16 March 1990.

15. Jane O'Hara, "Sorry Girls, Pink Stinks," *Ottawa Sun*, 18 March 1990.

16. Wayne Scanlan, "Breaking The Ice," *Ottawa Citizen*, 22 March 1990.

17. Mary Ormsby, "Canada Savours Golden Moment," *Toronto Star*, 26 March 1990.

18. CAHA Media Guide, 10 April 1992.

19. Rick Polutnik, interview with Elizabeth Etue, 12 January 1992.

20. Fran Rider, interview with Elizabeth Etue, 17 July 1992.

21. *Ice Times*, Hockey Development Centre for Ontario, March 1994.

22. Randy Phillips, "Women's Hockey Is Thriving," *Montreal Gazette*, 10 April 1994.

23. Randy Phillips, "Canadian Women Make Hockey History," *Montreal Gazette*, 18 April 1994.

24. Shannon Miller, interview with Elizabeth Etue, 6 December 1995.

25. Shannon Miller, interview with Elizabeth Etue, 16 April 1996.

26. CHA press release, 8 November 1995.

27. Shannon Miller, interview with Elizabeth Etue, 16 April 1996.

28. Steve Keating, "National Hockey Team Picks its Spots," *Globe and Mail*, 8 November 1994.

29. Mary Jollimore, "Gender Equity in Canadian Hockey May Be Impractical," *Globe and Mail*, 26 February 1996.

30. Mary Ormsby, "Gold Rush Begins," *Canadian Hockey Magazine*, 1995–96 edition.

31. Canadian Hockey Association Budget 1994–95.

32. John MacKinnon, "Female Worlds Prove a Point," *Ottawa Citizen*, 25 March 1990.

33. CAAWS news release, 31 January 1995.

34. Shannon Miller, interview with Elizabeth Etue, 6 December 1995.

35. Gwen Smith, CBC Radio, *Inside Track*, 23 May 1995.

36. Jennifer Neil, interview with Elizabeth Etue, 13 May 1995.

# · NOTES ·

## CHAPTER 9

1. Gord Renwick, interview with Elizabeth Etue, 6 September 1995.
2. Jan-Äke Edvinsson, interview with Elizabeth Etue, 22 January 1995.
3. Brian McFarlane, *Proud Past, Bright Future: One Hundred Years of Canadian Women's Hockey* (Toronto: Stoddart, 1994), 162.
4. Gord Renwick, interview with Elizabeth Etue, 25 October 1994.
5. Kris Pleimann, letter and statistics from USA Hockey, Inc., 9 October 1995.
6. Lynn Olson, interview with Elizabeth Etue, 26 April 1996.
7. Cammi Granato, interview with Elizabeth Etue, 18 March 1995.
8. Harry Blauett and Carol M. Blumerg, "Providence Star Got Her Start vs Antagonistic Brothers," *USA Today*, 8 January 1993.
9. Karyn Bye, interview with Elizabeth Etue, 5 April 1995.
10. USA Hockey, Inc., Kris Pliemann fax to Elizabeth Etue, 14 March 1996.
11. Kathleen Sharp, "Foul Play," *Ms Magazine*, September/October 1993.
12. Lynn Olson, interview with Elizabeth Etue, 21 June 1995.
13. Ibid.
14. Julie Healy, interview with Elizabeth Etue, 10 March 1994.
15. Val Belmonte, interview with Elizabeth Etue, San Jose, California, 5 April 1995.
16. Ibid.
17. Kim Urich, interview with Elizabeth Etue, 13 April 1994.
18. Barbara Müller, interview with Elizabeth Etue, 25 September 1995.
19. Shannon Miller, interview with Elizabeth Etue 10 April 1996.
20. Jack Grover, interview with Elizabeth Etue, 21 June 1995.
21. Ibid.
22. Rick Polutnik, interview with Elizabeth Etue, 5 April 1995.
23. Ibid.

## CHAPTER 10

1. Manon Rhéaume, interview with Elizabeth Etue and Megan Williams, 19 October 1995.
2. Andria Hunter's Web site: http://www.cs.utoronto.ca/~andria/
3. France St. Louis, interview with Megan Williams, 3 December 1995.
4. Therese Brisson, interview with Megan Williams, 15 January 1996.
5. Shannon Miller, interview with Megan Williams, 11 February 1996.

# BIBLIOGRAPHY

Acosta R. and L. Carpenter. "As the Years Go By: Coaching Opportunities in the 1990s" in *JOPERD*, 63, no. 3 (1992): 36–41.

Cahn, Susan K. *Coming on Strong: Gender and Sexuality in Twentieth-Century Women's Sport*. Cambridge, MA: Harvard University Press, 1994.

Cahn, Susan K. "Crushes, Competition, and Closets: The Emergence of Homophobia in Women's Physical Education." In *Women, Sport and Culture.*, ed. Susan Birrell and Sheryl Cole. Windsor: Human Kinetics, 1994.

Corbet, Rachel and Hilary Finlay. *An Introduction to the Law, Sport and Gender Equity in Canada*. Gloucester, Ont: Canadian Association for the Advancement of Women and Sport and Physical Activity, March 1994.

Dryden, Ken and Roy MacGregor. *Home Game: Hockey and Life in Canada*. Toronto: McClelland and Stewart, 1989.

*Gender Portrayal in English Television Coverage of the Games*, Research conducted for Sport Canada, 1994, Canadian Heritage, Sport Canada.

Gruneau, Richard and David Whitson. *Hockey Night in Canada: Sport, Identity and Cultural Politics*. Toronto: Garamond Press, 1993.

Gurney, Helen. *A Century to Remember 1893–1993: The Story of Women's Sports at the University of Toronto*. Toronto: University of Toronto Women's T-Holders' Association, 1994.

Gzowski, Peter. *The Game of Our Lives*. Toronto: McClelland and Stewart, 1981.

Hall, Ann, D. Cullen and Trevor Sack. "The Gender Structure of National Sports Organizations." Sport Canada Occasional Paper 2, no. 1 (1990).

Hall, Ann et al. *Sport in Canadian Society*. Toronto: McClelland and Stewart, 1991.

Inglis, Sue. "Board-Staff Relations in Amateur Sport." Report to the Ministry of Culture, Tourism and Recreation, Province of Ontario, December 1994.

Kidd, Bruce. *The Struggle for Canadian Sport*. Toronto: University of Toronto Press, 1996.

Lawrence-Harper, Janis. *The Herstory of the CAAWS*. Gloucester: Canadian Association for the Advancement of Women and Sport and Physical Activity, November 1991.

# - BIBLIOGRAPHY -

Lenskyj, Helen. *Out of Bounds: Women, Sport and Sexuality.* Toronto: Women's Press, 1986.

MacNeill, Margaret. "Networks: Producing Olympic Ice Hockey for a National Television Audience." *Sociology of Sport Journal* (forthcoming).

McFarlane, Brian. *Proud Past, Bright Future: One Hundred Years of Canadian Women's Hockey.* Toronto: Stoddart Publishing, 1994.

McPherson, B. D., and L. Davidson. *Minor Hockey in Ontario.* Toronto: Ministry of Culture and Recreation, 1980.

Messner, Michael A. and Donald F. Sabo. *Sex, Violence and Power in Sports.* Freedom, CA: The Crossing Press, 1994.

Morrow, Don et al. *A Concise History of Sport in Canada.* Toronto: Oxford University Press, 1989.

Nelson, Mariah Burton. *The Stronger Women Get, the More Men Love Football.* New York: Harcourt Brace, 1994.

Pronger, Brian. *The Arena of Masculinity: Sports, Homosexuality, and the Meaning of Sex.* Toronto: University of Toronto Press, 1992.

Research & Forecasts, Inc. "Miller Lite Report on American Attitudes Toward Sports." Milwaukee: Miller Brewing Company, 1983.

Reid, Kathyrn M. Playing Fair: *A Guide to Title IX in High School and College Sports.*, 2nd ed. East Meadow, New York: Women's Sport Foundation, 1994.

Rhéaume, Manon with Chantal Gilbert. *Manon: Alone In Front of the Net.* Toronto: HarperCollins, 1993.

Stevens, Julie. "Development of Women's Hockey: An Explanation of Structure and Change within the Canadian Hockey System." Master's thesis, Queen's University, May 1992.

Stewart, Barbara. *She Shoots ... She Scores! A Complete Guide to Women's Hockey.* Toronto: Doubleday, 1993.

Theberge, Nancy. "Gender, Sport, and the Construction of Community: A Case Study From Women's Ice Hockey." *Sociology of Sport Journal,* 12, (1995): 389–402.

Theberge, Nancy. "Playing with the Boys: Manon Rhéaume, Women's Hockey and the Struggle for Legitimacy." *Canadian Women Studies Journal,* 15, no. 4 (Fall 1995): 37–41.

Varpalotai, Aniko. "Girls' Sports and Role Models: Implications for Education." *CAPHER Journal,* Winter 1991.

Zeman, Brenda. *Eighty-eight Years of Puck-Chasing in Saskatchewan.* Regina: The Saskatchewan Sports Hall of Fame, 1983.

# WOMEN'S SPORTS & HOCKEY ASSOCIATIONS

## NATIONAL ORGANIZATIONS

*Canadian Association for the Advancement of Women and Sport and Physical Activity* (CAAWS)
1600 James Naismith Drive
Gloucester, ON K1B 5N4
Tel: (613) 748–5793   Fax: (613) 748–5775
E-mail: wmnsport@magi.com

*Canadian Association for Health, Physical Education, Recreation, and Dance* (CAHPERD)
809–1600 James Naismith Drive
Gloucester, ON K1B 5N4
Tel: (613) 748–5622   Fax: (613) 748–5737
E-mail: cahperd@activeliving.ca

*Canadian Hockey Association*
Olympic Saddledome
Calgary, AB T2P 2K8
Tel: (403) 777–3636   Fax: (403) 777–3635
E-mail: hockey@rtm.cdnsport.ca

*Canadian Interuniversity Athletic Union*
1600 James Naismith Drive
Gloucester, ON K1B 5N4
Tel: (613) 748–5619   Fax: (613) 748–5764

*Olympic Oval High Performance Female Hockey Program*
2500 University Drive NW
Calgary, AB T2N 1N4
Tel: (403) 220–7954   Fax: (403) 284–4815
E-mail: lwood@acs.ucalgary.ca

## PROVINCIAL ORGANIZATIONS

### BRITISH COLUMBIA

*Promotion Plus*
305–1367 West Broadway,
Vancouver, BC V6H 4A9
Tel: (604) 737–3075   Fax: (604) 738–7175
E-mail: promoplus@mindlink.bc.ca

### ALBERTA

*In Motion Network*
c/o Margaret Schwartz
409–11010 142 St. NW
Edmonton, AB T8N 2R1
(403)  454-4745

### SASKATCHEWAN

*52% Solution*
Faculty of Physical Activity Studies
University of Regina
Regina, SK S4S 0A2
Tel: (306) 585–4842   Fax: (306) 585–4854

### ONTARIO

*F.A.M.E.* (Female Athletes Motivating Excellence)
Ontario Sport and Recreation Centre,
201–1185 Eglinton Ave., E.,
North York, ON M3C 3C6
Tel: (416) 426–7183   Fax: (416) 426–7353

*Ontario Women's Hockey Association*
#30–1100 Central Parkway West,
Mississauga, ON L5C 4E5
Tel: (905) 275–8866
Fax: (905) 275–2001

*Ontario Women's Interuniversity Athletic Association*
1185 Eglinton Ave. E.
Don Mills, ON M3C 3C7
Tel: (416) 426–7047   Fax: (416) 426–7386

### NEW BRUNSWICK

*Alliance des femmes actives*
c/o Institut de Leadership
Université de Moncton
Moncton, NB E1A 3E9
Tel: (506) 858–4350   Fax: (506) 858–4058

## UNITED STATES

*Women's Ice Hockey Fund*
21 Seavey Road
Danville, NH 03819
Tel: (603) 382–1537
E-mail: julia.ashmun@wang.com

*Women's Sport Foundation*
(United States)
Marjorie Snyder,
Eisenhower Park,
East Meadow, NY 11554
Tel: (516) 542–4700  Fax: (516) 542–4716
Infoline: 1-800-227-3988

*USA Hockey Inc.*
4965 No. 30th Street
Colorado Springs, CO 80919
Tel: (719) 599–5500  Fax: (719) 599–5899

## INTERNATIONAL ORGANIZATIONS

*International Association of Physical
Education and Sport for Girls and Women*
(IAPESGW)
Editorial Office,
11 Wright St., Middle Park,
Victoria 3206, Australia
In Canada: Dr Sandra Kirby
University of Winnipeg
515 Portage Ave.,
Winnipeg, MB R3B 2B9

*International Ice Hockey Federation*
Todistrasse 23
CH–8002 Zurich, Switzerland
Tel: 41-1-281-1430  Fax: 41-1-281-1433

*International Working Group* (IWG)
Anita White
Sports Council
16 Upper Woburn Place,
London, England WC1HOQP
Tel: 44-71-388-1277
Fax: 44-7-383-5740
In Canada: Sue Neill,
Place du Centre,
200 Promenade du Portage,
Hull, PQ K1A 0X6
Tel: (819) 956–8023  Fax: (819) 956–8058

*Women's Sport Foundation*
(United Kingdom)
Wesley House
4 Wild Court London, England
WC2B 5AU
Tel: 071 831-7863

*WomenSport International* (WSI)
Libby Darlison, Executive Vice President
Box 227, Lawson 2783
New South Wales, Australia
Tel: 61 47 87 69 05  Fax: 61 47 87 69 06
E-mail: wsidarli@opennet.net.au

*Electronic Women-in-Hockey Mailing List*
E-mail: women-in-hockey-request@plaidworks.com

# INDEX

*Page numbers in italic indicate an illustration.*

# CREDITS

# ABOUT THE AUTHORS

Owner of a marketing company in Toronto which specializes in women's sports, ELIZABETH ETUE is also a radio journalist. She has written for *Hockey News* and *Canadian Woman's Studies*. During her twenty-year career in book publishing she has lived in Vancouver, Whitehorse and Ottawa.

An award winning writer, MEGAN K. WILLIAMS received a Pulitzer Fellowship from the Columbia School of Journalism. The author of numerous articles and works of fiction, her education and writing career have taken her to Montreal, Italy and New York. She now lives in Toronto with her partner and two children.